I AM A FILIPINO

NICOLE PONSECA
& MIGUEL TRINIDAD

I AM A FILIPINO

AND THIS IS HOW WE COOK

With Rachel Wharton

Foreword by Jose Antonio Vargas
Photographs by Justin Walker

ARTISAN | NEW YORK

To the life and legacy of Anthony Bourdain

Library of Congress Cataloging-in-Publication Data

Names: Ponseca, Nicole, author. |
    Trinidad, Miguel, author.
Title: I am a Filipino / Nicole Ponseca and
    Miguel Trinidad ; foreword by Jose Antonio Vargas.
Description: New York : Artisan, a division of
    Workman Publishing Co., Inc., [2018] |
    Includes index.
Identifiers: LCCN 2018014210 | ISBN 9781579657673
    (hardcover : alk. paper)
Subjects: LCSH: Cooking, Philippine. |
    LCGFT: Cookbooks.
Classification: LCC TX724.5.P5 P66 2018 |
    DDC 641.59599—dc23
LC record available at
    https://lccn.loc.gov/2018014210

Art direction by Michelle Ishay-Cohen
Design by Toni Tajima
Map by Josh Cochran

Artisan books are available at special discounts when purchased in bulk for premiums and sales promotions as well as for fund-raising or educational use. Special editions or book excerpts also can be created to specification. For details, contact the Special Sales Director at the address below, or send an e-mail to specialmarkets@workman.com.

For speaking engagements, contact speakersbureau@workman.com.

Published by Artisan
A division of Workman Publishing Co., Inc.
225 Varick Street
New York, NY 10014-4381
artisanbooks.com

Artisan is a registered trademark of
Workman Publishing Co., Inc.

Published simultaneously in Canada by
Thomas Allen & Son, Limited

Printed in China

First printing, October 2018

10 9 8 7 6 5 4 3 2 1

I am a Filipino—inheritor of a glorious past, hostage to the uncertain future. As such I must prove equal to a two-fold task—the task of meeting my responsibility to the past, and the task of performing my obligation to the future.

—"I Am a Filipino,"
Ｇeneral Carlos P. Romulo, 1941

CONTENTS

JOSE ANTONIO VARGAS

Foreword

In March 2018, the *New York Times*, America's newspaper of record, declared, as if by decree: "Filipino Food Finds a Place in the American Mainstream."

Three years prior, in April 2015, the *Washington Post* had proclaimed: "At long last, Filipino food arrives."

You cannot discuss Filipino food and its arrival in the American mainstream without mentioning Nicole Ponseca, the owner of Maharlika, Jeepney, and Tita Baby's, all operating within New York City's highly competitive restaurant world, and chef Miguel Trinidad. Together, they celebrate and centralize Filipino culture like no other restaurateur and entrepreneur.

Filipino food is the original fusion food, an idiosyncratic mélange of cultures and tastes, from Malay and Arab to Chinese, Spanish, and American. All that mixing makes Filipino food wholly original, much like the Filipino people, who are scattered all over the world, a diaspora numbering in the millions, almost four million of whom are in the United States. We are our food, with a special kind of pride that permeates the preparation and presentation of every delicacy. Nicole embodies that Filipino pride, which seeps through every page and every recipe in this book.

I met Nicole on New Year's Eve 2011. Like all Filipino professionals in New York City, I had heard about Maharlika. There was a joke going around that when you met someone Filipino, or someone who knew someone who was Filipino, the first question you asked them was "Have you been to Maharlika?" To kick off 2012, I wanted to introduce my friend Jehmu Greene, an African American woman from Texas and the former president of Rock the Vote and the Women's Media Center, to Filipino food, which she hadn't tried before. I figured it was time to see if Maharlika lived up to all the hype.

Upon entering the restaurant, walking past a chalkboard featuring the "Tagalog Word of the Day," I was struck immediately by the crowd. There were some Filipinos, but there were more non-Filipinos. Up to that point, I'd never seen non-Filipinos eat at a Filipino restaurant without a Filipino friend serving as the culinary translator, explaining what *bagoong* is (a paste of salted seafood) and the necessity of *suka* (vinegar). The bigger shock, however, was the menu, filled with all the dishes I grew up eating in the Philippines. *Dinuguan* was listed as dinuguan, not as "chocolate meat" or some other whitewashed name to make it more palatable and accessible to Americans. It was as if my culture—

and food strikes at the very heart of every culture—were being exposed, not out of shame but out of love. Unabashed, unapologetic, fearless love.

When I realized that the woman with the big, warm smile who was busy serving tables was one of the owners, I couldn't help but pepper her with questions.

"Why did you open this restaurant?" I asked.

This is what Nicole replied to me, and to anyone who's ever asked that question: "I wanted to change the conversation about Filipino food."

Nicole has more than changed the conversation about Filipino food. Part cultural ambassador, part epicurean anthropologist, part pioneering entrepreneur, she has led the Filipino food movement, which, over time, has touched every corner and every nook of what makes up Filipino culture. Instead of merely criticizing and deconstructing how Filipino food was being framed—and who was doing the framing—Nicole and Miguel got to work, constructing an idea from scratch and executing a different vision. What's more, they've done all of this in a food industry where very few people of color thrive, in the process leading a seismic shift in how the global Filipino community thinks about food, identity, entrepreneurship, and what it means to claim ourselves. We all, Filipinos and non-Filipinos alike, are the beneficiaries of what they've built.

Maraming salamat talaga, Nicole and Miguel. Thank you very much.

Jose Antonio Vargas, the founder and CEO of Define American, is a Pulitzer Prize–winning journalist and the author of *Dear America: Notes of an Undocumented Citizen.*

Why Not Filipino Food?

This is not just a cookbook. It's a manifesto.

For most of my lifetime, Filipino food was overlooked or treated as an afterthought. Sure, there were a handful of eateries for families like mine—immigrants who wanted a taste of home and the convenience of having someone else cook. These little enclaves were mostly mom-and-pop-type places that housed a small grocery and a steam table perpetually filled with Filipino staples. The people who worked there greeted you like family, and it was common to call them "Uncle" or "Auntie."

Every now and then, you'd find a few non-Filipinos who were either related to someone Filipino by marriage or knew to make the trip to a strip mall in the suburbs for a taste of Filipino food.

Somehow, the complex beauty of what Filipinos actually cooked at home or ate in the Little Manilas always remained hidden—stuck in the shadows of our kitchen cupboards, wedged between Mama Sita's flavor packets, bottles of *patis* (fish sauce), and cans of Spam. Meanwhile, the foods of our Asian sisters—Thailand, Vietnam, Korea, Malaysia, and India—were becoming mainstream and getting a lot of attention.

Why not Filipino food? It's not because we don't have the numbers. With more than 3.5 million Filipinos living in the United States, we are its second-largest population of Asian Americans after the Chinese. In many American cities—like San Diego, where I grew up—Filipinos are by far the largest immigrant group. We are part of the fabric of many cities that rely on our Filipino nurses, migrant workers, military servicemen and -women, professionals, and Overseas Filipino Workers (OFWs).

And it's not because what Filipinos eat isn't universally delicious. Our *pansit*—noodle dishes—can take the form of everything from a vegetable sauté to a decadent seafood bisque. Our barbecue skewers marinated in sugarcane vinegar, which renders the meat sweet and juicy, are popular potluck fare. The list of iconic Filipino must-eats includes the fresh seafood dish dressed in coconut milk,

ginger, and bird's-eye chiles called *kinilaw*; sweet, yeasty rolls called *pandesal*; the subtly sweet and savory rice flour and salted egg cake called *bibingka*; the crispy fried pork hock called *pata*; sour soups called *sinigang*; the Chinese-Filipino braised pork belly called *humba*; and a full roster of spicy, savory, and sour condiments that are the hallmark of a properly stocked larder—and much, much more.

Perhaps one reason Filipino food has long been overlooked by others is because of the history. The indigenous people of our Southeast Asian country—in reality an archipelago of more than 7,000 islands, 18 regions, and 81 provinces in the Pacific Ocean, which are classified into three distinct island groups: Luzon, Visayas, and Mindanao—have been influenced and colonized over and over again in what has been described as the "Malay Matrix." The influences range from China and India (through trade), Arabia (through trade and Islamization), and Spain and America (through colonization). Not to mention the brief and grisly stints by the Japanese and British, whose influences on the cuisine are more of a footnote. Filipino food changed right along with that turbulent history. How all these interlopers affected the islands is colonialism, and its consequences reverberate even today. Perhaps one effect of colonialism was that it convinced Filipinos that our food didn't measure up on its own.

How could this impact me, an American kid in San Diego, almost eighty years after Spain left the Philippines and fifty years after the United States did? When I was growing up, our food was literally a joke. Howard Stern notably made fun of Filipinos because of what we ate, and

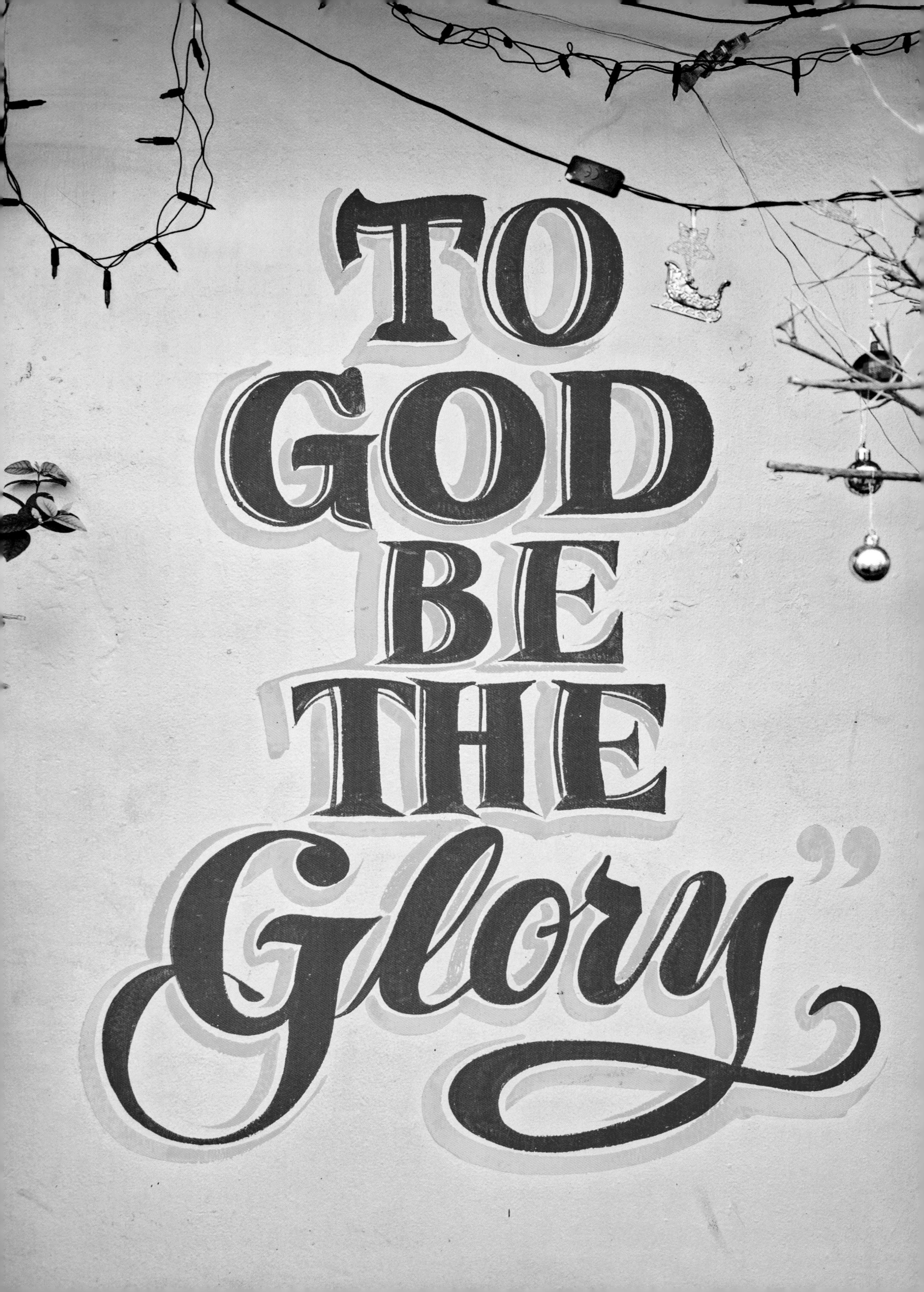
TO
GOD
BE
THE
Glory"

Fear Factor had to bribe contestants to eat our *balut* and *dinuguan*. The message was clear: I should be ashamed of our food. But I *liked* the food—the balut, a duck embryo still in the shell, served as is; and the dinuguan, a rich, deeply flavored pork blood stew. While other cultures openly called their blood recipes *morcilla* or blood cake, I was told to call dinuguan "chocolate stew," disguising its key ingredient.

It wasn't always bad. When someone finds out I am a Filipino, a common response is, "I love adobo." And no wonder. Who can resist the addictively sour, salty, garlicky classic adobo, which seemed to be the friendly bridge for many to connect with Filipinos? But when this happens, I want to tell people there's so much more to Filipino food than adobo. And not only that, there's even more to adobo than one might expect. Because depending on the region, the province, the city, or even the cook, the dish changes due to the Philippines' own ocean-to-farm-to-table foodways.

From the most northern tip of the archipelago to the most southern, the nuance of flavors varies from province to province: bitterness in the north, sweetness in the west/center, and heat and spice in the south. But just when you think you understand and can classify Filipino food and its regional differences, another door opens to another matrix of influences and techniques. Despite these many influences from outside cultures, what I've found in Filipino people and Filipino food is a resilient adaptability that consistently evolved and changed with the times. Over time, I've become less interested in why Filipino food wasn't popular and more interested in finding out "What is Filipino food?" and "How does food become

Filipino?" The latter question is the heart of this book.

I want people to taste the pungent, unctuous, *real* Filipino flavors—confidently funky (with cameos from *bagoong*—fermented seafood pastes—and patis), highly acidic (thanks to sugarcane vinegar and calamansi fruit), and coyly sweet (with the addition of *ube*, coconut milk, and earthy muscovado sugar).

Which brings us to our Filipino food manifesto: it's our goal to help change the conversation about the foods I grew up on, so that no one ever has to feel embarrassed about Filipino food and its customs like I was. We want to reframe the thinking so that people can consider Filipino food modern, authentic, and relevant. By highlighting details like its choice ingredients, unique flavors, and distinct techniques, we want to give Filipino food a seat at the culinary table. Let Filipino food be universally regarded as one of the world's classic cuisines.

From Manhattan to Manila

When I moved to Manhattan in 1998, the only Filipino restaurants I could find were steam table joints called *turo-turo* (turo means "point," so it's a point-point joint).

These were efficient eateries where you'd hardly see anybody other than Filipinos dining. Typically, you point at what you want behind a glass-protected steam table and the staff gives you a hefty combo plate of rice, two or three *ulam* (entrées), and some broth for about $8. The food is good and uncomplicated. And the staff might be pleasant, but there's very little in terms of service and decor. There were a few elegant high-end restaurants in Manhattan with Filipino owners or influences. But I longed for a place more boisterous and lively that felt like home.

At that time, Food Network was popular and Emeril Lagasse was hamming and bamming all over the place. People were increasingly becoming aware of world cuisine, and chefs were the new rock stars. Early food bloggers were trailblazing their way to Flushing or Woodside. Dining out became a competitive sport, and we kept score with our Zagat guides. Suddenly, it wasn't enough to be well-read— you had to be well-fed, too.

Simultaneously, there was a tall, lanky, Ramones-loving chef traveling to the far corners of the world. Anthony Bourdain and his TV show were giving audiences a taste of flavors that had previously been inaccessible. Food knowledge was becoming the new social currency. Inspired by their dining experiences, people were visiting places like Vietnam and Japan.

I was working for an ad agency, and I had an expense account that allowed me to take my clients to all the best restaurants of the time. Thai and Malaysian foods were just becoming popular—people were adventurous about trying pad thai and spicy curries. My clients asked to try Filipino food like the kind I grew up eating at home. But where was I going to take them? I was supposed to wine and dine our clients, and a turo-turo—despite the delicious food—wouldn't do. On weekends or on business trips, I would travel to Seattle, San Francisco, Los Angeles, San Diego, or New Jersey hoping to find the kind of restaurant I envisioned, and there was nothing in those cities, either.

My parents taught me to be proud of being a Filipino. Like many first-generation Filipino Americans (aka Fil-Ams), my dad came to America by enlisting in the U.S. military, and my mom was a nurse. My drive and work ethic come from my mom, but my love of Filipino food comes from my dad. I think both of them unwittingly set the foundation for me to be a restaurant owner.

My dad was a navy man and was often away from home, deployed overseas cooking on a ship. When he was home, he taught me to cook. He showed me how to make rice using your fingertips to measure the water and how to slow-cook oxtails to coax out the best flavors. He introduced me to *suki*, the concept of being a regular at his favorite shops for baguettes, fish, vegetables, and meats. His cooking tips—gleaned from years of working in kitchens—resulted in dishes that were different from anyone else's. Friends and family always complimented his food. Being in the kitchen with my father was a form of escapism for me, and it brought me closer to my heritage. But I never intended to be a restaurateur, and working in a restaurant wasn't exactly what my parents had in mind when I went to college. I had to do right by them, which meant building a solid career with benefits, a 401(k), and low risk. If you'd asked me in college or high school what I wanted to be, I'd tell you I was going to be the next Donny Deutsch.

He inspired me to become laser-focused while studying advertising; I was learning how to build brands and a connection to consumers. But I had a big problem with advertising and pop culture—I hardly ever saw Filipinos represented. I could count three: Dante Basco, Lou Diamond Phillips, and Nia Peeples. I felt uplifted whenever I saw someone who looked remotely like me in the media. I was hungry for it. *Starving.*

With $75 in my pocket, I moved to New York City, determined to be a great ad exec. When I finally got a job working for one of the top advertising agencies in the world, I should have felt exuberant. Instead, I felt alone. I had taken for granted the Filipino community I had had back home in San Diego. In New York City, you're an itty-bitty fish in a sea of people from all over the world. I'd hear questions like "Are you Thai?" or "Where are you *really* from? China?" or

"Wait, I thought you were Mexican?" I was both exoticized and dismissed at the same time. I was learning about advertising and the power of representation in the media—and realizing I had none.

The void of Filipino-ness was glaring at me, practically taunting.

Here I was in arguably one of the best culinary cities in the world, and I couldn't think of one Filipino restaurant that fed my cravings and upheld a competitive New York sensibility. Once again, I was confronting a question that kept gnawing at me: *Why not Filipino food?*

I began picturing a modern Filipino restaurant that was accessible but didn't sacrifice identity. I envisioned a front-of-house staff that could tell guests about Filipino food with intelligence and eloquence—what bagoong is and why it is used, for example—the same way a sommelier could describe a Sauvignon Blanc from a specific region, or a server could speak with authority on Tuscany. I wanted to blur the lines between generations, play old-school hip-hop and serve new-school Filipino food. It would be a place that was delicious and fun. It had to be fun.

So I thought, *If nobody else is doing it, maybe I should.*

A Tale of Two Restaurants

It took me more than a decade to open a restaurant, because I wanted to pay my dues.

Up until then, I had worked at only one restaurant in my life—as a hostess in San Francisco while I was in college—and I quit after one day.

As I did for my advertising clients, I made myself a creative brief and took this project on as if I had been hired to do it. My client was Filipino food. I studied the demographics and psychographics of diners and the Filipino diaspora, and I wrote up business plans. I did competitive research and collected any book or article I could find that focused on Filipino food, which wasn't easy because back then, so few people wrote about it.

For more than a decade, to learn the business, I was an advertising exec by day and a hostess-server-busser-dishwasher-bartender-manager in New York City's restaurants by night. I hosted at the Soho Grand and Tribeca Grand, and was a manager and server at Colors, the restaurant created by surviving employees of the Windows on the World restaurant at the World Trade Center. I learned so much working for restaurant owner Estella Quinoñes of Restaurant EQ in the West Village and for the management team led by Peter Crippen at the Mermaid Inn.

By 2007, I was working nights and weekends as a catchall front-of-house staff member at a French-Creole restaurant in Soho. I was trying to find a Filipino chef to help me open my first restaurant, Maharlika Filipino Moderno—*maharlika* means "royalty" in Tagalog; some define it as "warrior class." I was going to be the restaurant owner, and I needed a chef to help bring my dream into reality.

I scoured newspaper articles and the few blogs dedicated to restaurant musings to find somebody—*anybody*—to join me on the journey. I'd take a bus to New Jersey if I found out there was a Filipino chef cooking. I'd eavesdrop on conversations, hoping to find clues about where to find a chef. But no Filipino chef at that time wanted to take the risk. The thinking then was, *Who's going to pay New York prices for the food Filipinos cook at home?* or, more to the point, *Who are you?*

Sulking at a table during pre-service at the French-Creole restaurant, I realized I was ten years into this dream and nothing was materializing. I didn't know if this idea was going to take off, because without a chef, I couldn't move forward. Miguel Trinidad was the chef of the restaurant at the time, and seeing the distressed look on my face, he asked what was wrong. When I told him, he said, "I'll give it a shot."

I didn't know if it would work; Miguel is Dominican, not Filipino, and he wasn't well-versed in the food. But he is a headstrong guy from New York City's Lower East Side and has confidence for days—plus, he's an excellent chef and a good leader. So I jumped at the opportunity. After years of plotting, the band was coming together. We had Miguel on food, and this really cool Hunter S. Thompson–type character from Manila named Enzo Lim on cocktails. I'd take the lead.

We had to fast-track Miguel's education on Filipino food. Luckily, the similarities in Latino and Filipino cuisine are strong. Still, our education was steadfast; we cooked every weekend for two full years before we served any paying customers. We would have dinners at my small apartment in Williamsburg, where I would invite strangers to experience and critique the food. I remember meeting a guy named Ray in Queens. He was Filipino and I invited him to dinner. That was the requirement; if you were Filipino, you were in. Slowly, we built a group of supporters.

We worked through every single dish we wanted to serve—the traditional dishes that I had grown up with and had come to love, and new ones that were influenced by our teachers. We traveled to the Philippines, where our education felt like family reunions when we met with professional chefs and astute home cooks from faraway provinces. I think at the time, people found us to be an unlikely and unusual duo—the Dominican and the Filipina curious about Filipino food when no one else really was.

The provincial dishes were heartfelt, with aging *kusineros* (cooks) holding on to recipes as the last remaining vestiges of their past. I still can taste the slow-cooked broth with a deliciously startling spike of fresh red onions in Isabela; the vibrant hue of an orange empanada with a runny yolk in Batac; the heat in Bicolano cuisine; the nutty sweetness of burnt coconut found

in the Autonomous Region of Muslim Mindanao (ARMM); the ocean salt in Cavite's *pansit pusit*; the ginger notes of Cebu and Iloilo and so much more.

Because we couldn't find any investors or a space we could afford, we started Maharlika as a pop-up restaurant before there was even a word for it (people then called it a "limited engagement"). We were doing Filipino brunches at a French restaurant in the East Village that normally wasn't open on weekend mornings. The first two days there was nobody there; by the third weekend, a line had formed around the block— in the dead of January!

Meanwhile, we bounced around in some other temporary spaces. We served barbecue and *siopao* out of a shipping container in downtown Brooklyn and had another brunch pop-up in Williamsburg. We were hustling hard, barely sleeping. Miguel pulled multiple overnights in a row to prep the food. We longed for our own place. One day a guy overheard us talking and said, "I have a restaurant that's empty if you want to take a look at it." It was in New York City's East Village. We went to see the place on a Friday. By Sunday we had the keys. A week later we opened Maharlika.

Ligaya Mishan, a *New York Times* food critic, wrote a flattering review of Miguel's cooking—she is Filipino American, too, which made it extra-special—and that's what really blew things up for us. Shortly after, Maharlika was winning awards and accolades, and was acknowledged as a must-go-to restaurant by *Condé Nast Traveler* (among a select group of such restaurants in New York City). After we'd been open just seven months, somebody asked us to take on a struggling restaurant in a space down the street, so we took that over, too, and made Jeepney, a gastropub with food and decor that are rambunctious and bold. While Maharlika serves classic dishes in a bistro atmosphere, Jeepney reigns with creative riffs like chori burgers made with Filipino sausage called *longanisa*, *halo-halo*, and tiki cocktails.

Our first months at Jeepney were rough. We spent every cent of our $80,000 start-up fund to build out the restaurant. We opened right before Hurricane Sandy ravaged New York City and wiped out the power grid, which left us unable to pay rent for months. We had zero operating capital, which meant no backup funds. I had to think of a plan fast, and memories of my dad eating with his hands flooded me. *Kamayan* is a Filipino way of eating at home without utensils; it's simple and there's nothing particularly special about it. I remember being embarrassed about my dad eating with his hands when my American friends came over. But now I wanted to embrace the custom and turn it into something to be proud of. We started serving large-format kamayan dinners as a last-ditch effort to jump-start the business. We reimagined kamayan as a table-length feast with no plates or silverware, just a spread of aromatic, flame-kissed banana leaves laid out with a pile of perfect white rice mounded high with juicy longanisa sausages; head-on jumbo shrimp cooked in *adobo*; a whole fried fish topped with vinegar-pickled peppers called *escabeche*;

plus fresh cucumber salad dressed in sugarcane vinegar and patis. The dinners soon sold out, the spots reserved months in advance, and we were on our way.

The Filipino Food Movement

When we first opened Jeepney and Maharlika, we primarily served Filipinos and Filipino Americans. And I could feel what my guests felt: pride.

It was no small thing to be in a restaurant that was unabashedly Filipino. It was our party, and everyone was invited. Now when I look around the restaurants, I get a little gobsmacked seeing people from all walks of life coming to try Filipino food. When I was growing up, seeing a non-Filipino in a Filipino restaurant meant the person was likely married into the family. Now all kinds of people come just for the food. I also love that the restaurants have become places to have a first date or celebrate a special occasion; you can bring your coworkers or your mom and dad. But it always comes down to the food. And it's a joy to have people from all over the world dine on our style of cooking the flavors of the Philippines.

Running a restaurant is filled with pressure. Miguel and I receive a lot of feedback and we appreciate it—even when the reviews are mixed. Some guests don't like the way we serve our dishes or are surprised that a non-

Filipino is cooking Filipino food. Others say that their mom's adobo is better than Miguel's. And how could it not be? Who else can cook like your mother?!

But in the years that our restaurants have been open, the conversation has changed. Before, the barometer of success for an ethnic restaurant was how much the food resembled your mother's cooking. Now it has broadened. For me, I want to know how much a restaurant can push the envelope and remain devoted to flavor. So it's with great pride that I see Filipino food happening all over the world. Kamayan, *kare kare*, and kinilaw are on menus cooked by Filipino and non-Filipino chefs alike. We see the Filipino food movement in New York City, but in other cities, too—New Orleans, London, Los Angeles, Chicago, and Washington, D.C., all have groundbreaking modern Filipino restaurants.

Out of the shadows, Filipino food is finally enjoying its time in the sun. And diners and chefs are going deeper—researching their roots, making things from scratch, redefining what we previously accepted as culinary truths. There is a desire to know who we are, in the context of the global interest in our cooking: regional specialties, the ingredients themselves, the history and culture behind our food, the country itself—especially because Filipino cuisine is as rich and diverse as the more than 175 languages and dialects spoken in the Philippines. It finally feels like a Filipino food renaissance.

I Am a Filipino, and This Is How We Cook

The Filipino food I grew up on helped inform me as to who I am. I am a Filipino—a "Latino Asian" born in America with dark brown skin and almond eyes.

My childhood home served tightly rolled fried *lumpia* and divine peanut butter stews like kare kare. And rice. Lots and lots of rice. I am part Caviteño and part Ilocano, and not only did my parents have different recipes and dishes, they also spoke different languages. My parents' mother tongues were different, denoting their respective provinces in the Philippines and also their penchant for the salty/bitter versus the sweet/savory. They shared their love for me and shared other languages like Tagalog and English. They shared a penchant for *ampalaya* (bitter melon) and karaoke. And American love songs. Lots and lots of love songs.

Together, Miguel and I, along with our team, built the restaurants and this cookbook as our way of writing a love song to Filipino food. We have spent the past years learning, reading, and especially traveling to all corners of the Philippines, cooking, eating, talking, and learning as much about the country's food as we could. Many of these felt like once-in-a-lifetime trips, and I feel profoundly lucky: never in a million years would I have guessed that I could travel extensively in my parents' homeland and finally understand all the stories they told me when I was a kid.

These recipes are a distillation of our travels and a reflection of the many chefs who taught us along the way. We hope they influence your travels or your grocery cart. Most of all, we hope they further inspire you to create, experiment with, and hone your own version of Filipino food.

KARE KARE

My all-time, forever-and-ever-amen favorite Filipino dish is *kare kare*. I was three years old when my dad first fed it to me—with a healthy dollop of *bagoong*—and to my mother's disbelief, I wanted more. My dad's response was, "Of course. She's Filipino."

We cook the vegetables and meat separately for a better texture, and slow-cook the oxtails first with aromatics and wine. You must serve kare kare with rice and bagoong to balance out the sweet, rich flavors in the dish. Ideally, you should have a little bit of bagoong in every bite. **SERVES 4 TO 6**

5 pounds (2.3 kg) oxtails, cut into 2-inch (5 cm) pieces

Kosher salt and freshly ground black pepper

7 tablespoons vegetable oil, plus more as needed

2 red onions, cut into large dice

2 celery stalks, cut into large dice

1 carrot, cut into large dice

½ bunch fresh thyme

4 cups (1 L) red wine (about 1¼ bottles), like a Cabernet Sauvignon

1 cup (240 ml) Chinese Shaoxing cooking wine or sherry (see Notes, page 152)

4 to 6 cups (1 to 1.4 L) stock, preferably beef

1 pound (455 g) Chinese long beans or green beans (see Notes)

1 garlic clove, minced

1 pound Japanese eggplant, thickly sliced

1 pound baby bok choy

2 cups (480 ml) natural creamy peanut butter

¼ cup (60 ml) soy sauce

Sugar

½ cup (120 ml) Achuete Oil (page 58)

4 to 6 cups (800 g to 1.2 kg) cooked white rice (see page 40)

Bagoong (see Key Ingredients, page 35)

Notes: The goal of the long cooking here is to make the meat very tender, though it looks best when you serve the oxtails whole—meaning don't cook them so long that the meat totally falls off the bone. If you can't find Chinese long beans—they're exactly what they sound like: long green beans grown in Asia—use green or yellow snap beans.

Preheat the oven to 375°F (190°C).

Season the oxtails well with salt and pepper.

In a Dutch oven or large, heavy-bottomed oven-safe pot, heat 3 tablespoons of the vegetable oil over medium to medium-high heat. Brown the oxtails on all sides, then transfer them to a plate. (You may need to do this in batches to avoid crowding the pan.)

Remove all but a tablespoon or so of the fat from the pot and reduce the heat to medium. Add the onions, celery, and carrot

and cook until they are soft and aromatic, 3 to 6 minutes.

Stir in the thyme, letting it just soften, then add the red wine and stir with a wooden spoon or spatula, scraping up any browned bits from the bottom of the pot.

Return the oxtails to the pot and add the Shaoxing wine and enough stock to cover the meat. Cover the pot, transfer it to the oven, and cook for 2½ to 3 hours, or until the meat is fork-tender but not falling off the bone (see Notes).

While the oxtails cook, bring a large pot of salted water to a boil and fill a large bowl with ice and water. When the water boils, add the long beans and cook for 1 minute, or just until they turn bright green. Immediately plunge them into the ice water and stir until all the beans feel cold to the touch. Drain and set aside.

In a large skillet, heat 2 tablespoons of the vegetable oil over medium heat. Add the garlic and cook, stirring often, just until it begins to soften, about 2 minutes. Add the eggplant and cook, stirring occasionally, until it is soft, about 10 minutes, then transfer the eggplant and garlic to a bowl and set aside. Wipe the skillet clean and heat 2 tablespoons more oil over medium heat. Add the bok choy and a pinch of salt and cook until bright green and tender yet firm, then set it aside on a separate plate.

When the oxtails are tender, remove the meat from the liquid in the pot and set it aside on a plate. Strain the braising liquid and discard the solids, then return the liquid to the pot and simmer over medium-high heat until it has reduced by half.

Reduce the heat to low, add the peanut butter and soy sauce, and stir until the peanut butter is incorporated and the sauce begins to thicken, 2 to 3 minutes. Taste and add sugar, if desired, then stir in the achuete oil.

Return the meat to the pot and cook until it is heated through, a minute or two.

Serve hot, with the vegetables, rice, and bagoong on the side.

Filipino Food 101

We have spent hours—days, weeks, months—thinking about what makes Filipino food Filipino in order to define the cuisine, or *kusinero*. This book encourages you to cook from scratch and to think of Filipino food as a classic cuisine with its own set of techniques, flavor profiles, influences, and culinary customs.

People have said Filipino food is a cuisine of occupation, because so many waves of people from elsewhere inserted their culture into ours, often by force. We were a Spanish colony for three hundred years, and one under dear ol' Uncle Sam for almost forty more, and even Japan invaded during World War II. The Chinese came centuries ago as traders and businessmen, and Indians, Arabs, South Asians, and other nomadic Pacific Islanders came even earlier. The Philippines also has many families with Mexican roots, as the Spanish fleets brought settlers from Mexico, another Spanish colony. These factors are important to keep in mind when you think about the Filipino culinary family tree, and personally, I love knowing how Filipinos have influenced the world and how the world has influenced us. (In fact, Filipinos were among the first Asian people to settle in the New World.)

But there is much more to Filipino food than colonialism, exploration, and occupation, and the food starts not with these cultures but with our Malayan ancestors and all that was on the islands from the beginning. This includes ingredients, ways of cooking, cultures, and tribes that did and still do change from province to province, island to island. To paraphrase José Rizal, a nineteenth-century Filipino national hero who helped the Philippines finally break from Spanish rule, "You must know where you're from in order to get where you're going."

Though it is growing, there is not a large body of historical work about the original traditions of Filipino cooking, which at the beginning was called not "Filipino" but "Visayan" or "Luzon" or by the name of whatever island or group of islands you lived on, which then functioned as independent states. And there are not many truly indigenous people who still keep to the traditional ways left in the Philippines. But we've read nearly everything we can and have traveled to more remote areas of the Philippines where older customs are more or less intact, and that has further sharpened my thoughts.

The Regions of the Philippines

The food of the Philippines varies widely by region—there are officially eighteen regions, grouped together by commonalities in climate, terrain, culture, and ethnicity. Each region has its own specialties and nuances, with shifts in flavor, subtle swaps in the proteins or vegetables, or sometimes just a change in a dish's name depending on the location. (You can find remarkably similar dishes with different names in different regions and cooks who wax poetic on the drastic change one ingredient can make.) For example, there is a strong use of fresh vegetables in Ilocos Norte, where farmland is fertile and people have long been encouraged to farm backyard gardens. The Bicol region is known for its use of chiles and therefore hot and spicy food, while the neighboring Visayas boast incredible seafood and crustaceans. And in the islands to the south, in the Zamboanga Peninsula or Northern Mindanao, you see influences from Mexico, Indonesia, and the Middle East.

PACIFIC OCEAN

What follows is our approach to cataloging the basics of Filipino cooking. At first we created this organization just for ourselves, but we've come to realize that the information is extremely useful in understanding not just the uniquely layered Filipino cuisine but also the recipes in this cookbook, which is roughly organized into main sections with chapters that focus on foods with intrinsic Filipino flavors and techniques; other chapters that focus on the recipes that reflect our influences from elsewhere; and two chapters about our daily culinary customs. Some of the complex recipes include numbered step-by-step how-to photographs that you'll see referenced within the method with accompanying parenthetical numbers.

The Mother Sauces and the Holy Trinity

Calling these Filipino flavors "sauces" is a bit of a stretch—technically they are more like flavor profiles. But I like to borrow the term *mother sauce* from the French because I believe that, like a béchamel or velouté, these five profiles are the building blocks of Filipino cuisine and the foundation of the recipes in this book. The flavors are built on the ingredients Filipinos traditionally had available as a tropical island country: Miles and miles of shoreline give us ample seafood; coconut and palm trees grow with abandon; we have copious fresh fruits that are used when sour and green or ripe and sweet; and lush fields of rice grow using terracing

techniques developed in the Philippines before being sent out into the world.

SOUR

Maasim is Tagalog for "sour." There are some who like foods so spicy it leads to sweat, shakes, and gasps for air, but I've met countless Filipinos with a preference for a sourness so intense it provokes salivation and lip-smacking. Sourness is a cuisine-defining flavor profile. Sour is the gateway to Filipino food, and it sets the cuisine apart.

Filipinos cook with tart fruits like unripe guava and papaya, using tamarind pods and leaves, and squeezing tart calamansi citrus fruit into nearly everything—are there other cuisines that rely on such a variety of vinegars and souring agents? Vinegars are made from palm, pineapple, sugarcane, rice, coconut, and countless other fruits—which are plentiful all over the Philippines—and then those vinegars are infused with chiles and garlic and all manner of aromatics and herbs. In fact, adobo, the stew that is the best-known dish in the Philippines, can be broadly defined as anything cooked in vinegar. We make ceviches, or *kinilaw*, with a variety of proteins, and vegetables are "cooked" with vinegar; we also have many versions of *sinigang*, a Filipino sour soup (see pages 82–89) made using almost every possible combination of sour fruits and citrus, from unripe watermelon to a precious little tree fruit called *bilimbi* (tree cucumber).

There is some kind of sour element in every Filipino meal, if not directly in a dish, then applied in the form of a marinade or the condiment called *sawsawan* (see page 34), which, generally, is not meant to be a last-minute splash or dash, but to work deeply with the food and marry the flavors.

COCONUT

Coconut palms were everything to the Philippines at one point in time: They provided food, drink, and cooking oil. Husks were burned for fuel; the leaves were dried and used to make hats and furniture and to build housing. The sap was used to make vinegar; the meat was eaten young and soft or firm and chunked or shredded and toasted, especially in the far southern islands in the province of Mindanao—or, of course, pressed into the milk and cream that flavor the majority of sweet Filipino dishes. Coconut milk, or *gata*, also forms the basis of a sauce known as *ginataan*—basically, anything cooked in gata— that is applied to pork, chicken, crabs, whole fish, vegetables, and even sweet things like tapioca pearls or little dumplings of glutinous rice. Ginataan is ubiquitous throughout the Philippines—while flavorings and seasonings and ingredients may change from dish to dish, ginataan is one of the linchpins of the cuisine.

FUNK

In many traditional dishes, the umami kick is not from meat but from the funk of fermentation. First, you have *patis*, which is the Filipino version of fish sauce, a salty, funky liquid made from fermenting seafood in salt. It is largely used instead of table salt; thus, nearly every dish has a little bit of funk.

And perhaps even more important is the thick seafood paste called *bagoong*. This ingredient—which has several variations (see Key Ingredients, page 35)—is a defining one in Filipino food. Add bagoong to a simple vegetable broth, and you have sustenance; add it to a coconut milk sauce, and you have instant complexity. Take the dish called *pinakbet*, the ratatouille of the Philippines. It's a simple vegetable dish of eggplant, summer squash, squash blossoms, pumpkin, and Southeast Asian long beans simmered with tomatoes, ginger, onion, bay leaf, and bagoong, in which the bagoong provides the real flavor. And a dollop of the paste is what takes the sweet, rich sauce of kare kare from any ordinary oxtail stew into a dish that is uniquely Filipino.

It's important to note that Filipino food does not get funky, complex flavors from seafood alone. There are several other traditional fermentation techniques used in the cooking. *Suka*—Filipino vinegar— is fermented from palm, coconut, or cane sugar. Many sausages or cured meats get a sour tang from natural fermentation techniques (just like the process for making salami). Salted eggs (see page 41)—used liberally in salads, sauces, and baked goods—get a bold tang from being cured in salt. Pickled green mango and pickled mustard greens—or *burong mangga* and *burong mustasa*—are nearly always placed on a Filipino table to eat as condiments or companions to a meal. (As you may have guessed, *burong* means "pickle" or "ferment.") And there is also fermented rice (page 32), which is sautéed with garlic and tomato and often served as an umami-packed dip with crisp cold fresh greens and fried fish.

TOMATO

Three hundred years of Spanish rule made its mark on Filipino food, and today there are nearly half a dozen iconic Filipino dishes rooted in a tomato-based sauce, often enhanced with garlic and onion. While they are obviously Spanish in origin, the addition of seasonings like patis gives them an unmistakable Filipino flavor. Like all Filipino foods, they vary slightly from region to region and kitchen to kitchen, but they include things like menudo, a rich, deeply flavored stew made with meat like beef or lamb shank, tomato, chicken livers, carrots, potato, and the obviously Spanish addition of olives. *Kaldereta* can be similar, though it's often slightly sweet or tangy and includes sweet green peas, also not an ingredient originally grown in the Philippines. And there's *lengua estafada*—tongue with tomato sauce—and chicken *guisantes*, or chicken stewed with fish sauce, tomatoes, and sweet bell peppers.

THE HOLY TRINITY

In French cooking, the holy trinity is the mirepoix, a diced mix of onion, celery, and carrot that is sautéed in fat until it is soft and sweet and then used as the base for all kinds of soups, stews, and sauces. The Spanish have their *sofrito* of onions, garlic, and tomato, and the Cajuns use onions, celery, and bell peppers. There are likely many other holy trinities in the cuisines of other cultures. For Filipinos, our holy trinity is browned garlic, Spanish onion, and ginger (notes most prevalent in Visayan cooking). Alternatively, instead of or in addition to ginger, our trinity might include some kind of umami in the form of pork belly (the Philippine diet leans on pork, and we even have a native black pig, *baboy damo*), canned liver paste (see page 39), or bagoong.

Culinary Techniques

Here are an introduction to and translation of a few key Filipino cooking methods to better understand the cuisine.

KINILAW

Kinilaw means to cook in "liquid fire"—aka citrus or vinegar, as with ceviche—and its importance as a technique in Filipino cooking can't be overstated. If adobo is the national dish, kinilaw is likely its origin. The food writer Doreen Fernandez, a culinary hero in the Philippines, documented Filipino food long before it was cool. Her first book was *Kinilaw*, and in it she notes that kinilaw is the oldest known cooking technique in the Philippines. It is the basis for the Filipino food preferences of sour, salty, bitter, funky, and sweet. Though kinilaw is typically made with a fish—usually tuna—cooked or cured in citrus or vinegars, its use is much broader. Kinilaw can also be made with vegetables, and it is sometimes employed with meat or shellfish, always pickled or quickly cooked, then joined by fruit (calamansi, pineapple, pomelo) or coconut milk and a fish sauce.

We believe that the first real Filipino dish was kinilaw, created thousands of years ago, long before kitchens existed. Today you'll see this type of dish listed on menus as either "kinilaw" or "*kilawen*," depending on where you are or who is making it. The difference could just be one of language, maybe a slightly different noun originally used in Visayan, the language from the central islands, or Tagalog, from Luzon and the north. Some might say one is for raw meat cooked in vinegar and the other for seafood. Fernandez wrote that she believed kinilaw was originally anything raw "cooked" in citrus juice or vinegar—meats like beef tartar or thin slices of caribou, any kind of seafood, or vegetables and fruits. Kilawen, on the other hand, meant starting with something cooked, like grilled meats, and tossing them in vinegar.

If kinilaw/kilawen is at the root of our cuisine and the source of our penchant for a sour flavor profile, it grew into *paksiw*—a protein cooked simply with vinegar, like the one on page 70—and then adobo, which is essentially a paksiw with the addition of flavorings like soy sauce from the Chinese and bay leaf and peppercorn from the

Spanish. These are links on the chain of Filipino food history.

NILAGA

Nilaga means "to boil," but it is also the name of a simple boiled beef soup that is the basis of a range of special dishes found across the country, like the *bulalo* on page 96.

INIHAW

Inihaw means "grilled." Grilling most certainly started by necessity. Before there were stoves or ovens, there was live fire. Filipino grilling is at its best when done the original way, over dried coconut husks or other natural charcoal or kindling, which imparts an amazing flavor. Seafood might be charred whole and blasted with citrus, while meats are basted with sour-sweet glaze and served on skewers cooked right over the flames (see the chicken barbecue on page 258), but this charred flavor is applied in other ways, too: the eggplant on page 127, the *sinuglaw* on page 67, the amazing grilled fish soup on page 99, even the sweet coconut rice cake called *bibingka* on page 282, are traditionally cooked over charcoal.

STEAMING

Traditionally, Filipino kitchens did not have an oven, and as a result we still steam many of our cakes and other sweets, like those on page 275, often tidily wrapped in aromatic banana leaves, which also impart a uniquely Filipino flavor.

BURRO

Burro means "fermented" or "pickled." Fermentation, essentially controlled spoilage, is one of the oldest cooking techniques in the Philippines, used as a way to preserve food before the advent of refrigeration. Today the word *burro* can apply to traditional fermented pickles, where duck eggs (see page 41) or vegetables are fermented in salt, but also to modern vinegar-brined pickles.

BURONG ISDA

Fermented Fish

Burong isda—cooked rice fermented with layers of salted raw fish—is a specialty from the region of Pampanga. When placed in an airtight container, the rice and fish break down into a chunky paste that gets sautéed into a guisado of ginger, onions, and tomato that becomes a rich, thick, aromatic savory porridge almost like *arroz caldo* (page 184). You can serve it alone or as a side with boiled vegetables or fried fish. Try it wrapped into crisp, crunchy fresh mustard greens with a wedge of fried *hito*, or catfish. **MAKES THREE 1-PINT JARS**

FOR THE FERMENTED FISH

6 cups (1.2 kg) freshly cooked white rice (see page 40)

1½ pounds (680 g) skinless red snapper fillets

¼ cup (45 g) kosher salt

FOR THE GUISADO

3 tablespoons vegetable oil

¼ cup (30 g) minced red onion

3 tablespoons minced garlic

3 tablespoons minced fresh ginger

¼ cup (45 g) diced tomato

1 tablespoon fish sauce

1 teaspoon soy sauce

½ teaspoon white sugarcane vinegar (see Key Ingredients, page 42)

Note: This recipe requires glass canning jars (see Note, page 120, for sterilizing instructions) and 7 to 10 days of fermentation time.

Let the cooked rice cool completely.

Wash and thoroughly dry the snapper fillets, then cut them into small strips. Put the fish strips in a large bowl or a large pot and rub at least half the salt over the fish pieces, making sure you cover all sides of every piece.

Tightly pack the fish-and-rice mixture into three sterilized 1-pint mason jars (be sure they're dry), pushing down to make sure there are no air pockets in the jars, but leaving at least 1 inch (2.5 cm) of empty space between the mixture and the top of each jar.

Cover the mouths of the jars with cheesecloth secured with a rubber band. Place the jars in a cool, dark place to ferment for 7 to 10 days, or until the smell is sour when the jar is opened. (You can let the mixture ferment for up to 3 weeks; the flavor and sourness will grow more intense.)

Once the fish mixture has finished fermenting, refrigerate the jars. You will have about 3 pints (1.5 L); it will keep in the refrigerator for up to several weeks, though it will grow more tart and intensely flavored over time. (If any liquid appears in the jar, drain it off before cooking with the fermented fish.)

MAKE THE GUISADO: In a large saucepan, heat the vegetable oil over medium heat. Add the onion, garlic, and ginger and cook, stirring often, until the onion is translucent and the garlic is lightly browned, about 5 minutes. Add the tomato and cook just until it begins to release some liquid, about 2 minutes.

Add 3 cups (750 g) of the fermented fish and 2 cups (½ L) water and stir until fully combined. Bring the mixture to a boil over medium-high heat, then reduce the heat to maintain a simmer. Cook for at least 15 minutes, or until most of the liquid

has evaporated and the mixture has the consistency of thick porridge.

Stir in the fish sauce, soy sauce, and vinegar, and serve.

PRITO

You can preserve food by removing water, which is what you do when you deep-fry, or *prito* in Tagalog. Many Filipino fried snack foods—the pork belly on page 261, the fried bananas on page 252, the vegetable and shrimp fritters called *ukoy* (see page 249), and our famous *lumpia* (see pages 152 and 154)—are traditionally served not hot, but at room temperature, from a counter or a street cart.

SMOKING/DRYING

Like fermentation, smoking and drying are ancient ways of preserving food, dating back long before the era of refrigeration. Filipinos have their own traditional version of beef jerky or even charcuterie (often made by a combination of fermentation and smoking or air-drying) made with wild boar, venison, or carabao, Filipino water buffalo. The smoked fish called *tinapa* is often eaten for breakfast with eggs or tossed into a simple fried rice or *pansit*. All manner and size of fish are also salted and left to dry cure in the sun, and meats are dried as well.

The latter were eventually also flavored with black pepper and sugar, which begat our modern-day *tapa* (dried meat cured in a mixture of black pepper, sugar, garlic, soy sauce, and calamansi juice or vinegar). Today many kinds of fresh or cured *longanisa* (sausages) are the great-grandchildren of those techniques, which are an underappreciated aspect of Filipino cookery. Take the northern specialty called *kiniing*, made from the leaner meat of our indigenous wild black pigs. The meat is soaked in water steeped with guava leaves, which both flavors the meat and keeps away the insects, then smoked over pinewood, hung to dry over the stove, and stored in woven bamboo baskets; it's an artisanal and innovative form of charcuterie. If that is not advanced artisanal charcuterie making, I don't know what is.

SAWSAWAN

Filipino food is always served with condiments within easy reach, even at a street vendor where you stand and eat. These condiments let diners customize the flavor of the meal in the form of a self-mixed dipping sauce, which is generally known as *sawsawan*. The most common of these are vinegars (plain, and sometimes those flavored with chile and garlic or herbs, like the *pinakurat* recipe that follows); fish sauce (*patis*); soy sauce; a bowl of limes, lemons, or the native calamansi fruit, cut and squeezed to order; and whole fresh hot and mild chiles. Occasionally, you'll find chopped tomatoes, sliced onions, and *bagoong*, too.

Diners get individual bowls and use their spoons or forks to mash chiles with vinegar as they see fit, or stir together patis and calamansi, or make whatever sawsawan they prefer. No Filipino dish is seasoned perfectly until it is on the table in front of you and you add the salt, sour, heat, and even umami flavors that make it perfect to you.

PINAKURAT

Spiced Vinegar

You can store this all-purpose sweet-and-spicy vinegar in clean mason jars, but it is easier to keep it in repurposed glass bottles. Note that this recipe can be adjusted as you like—try using different chiles or other spices like bay leaf. **MAKES 3 CUPS (720 ML)**

10 garlic cloves, peeled and sliced

¼ cup (35 g) dried fruit, such as raisins, cherries, or mangos (optional)

5 whole bird's-eye chiles (see Key Ingredients, page 37)

1 (3-inch/7.5 cm) knob fresh ginger, scrubbed and minced

1 tablespoon whole black peppercorns

3 to 4 cups (720 ml to 1 L) white sugarcane vinegar (see Key Ingredients, page 42)

¼ cup (60 ml) fish sauce

Put the garlic, dried fruit, chiles, ginger, and peppercorns in a clean glass jar or

bottle and cover with the vinegar and fish sauce. Loosely cover or cap the jar and let sit at room temperature in a dark place for 48 hours.

Transfer the jar to the refrigerator. The pinakurat will keep indefinitely, and the flavors will continue to develop over time.

Key Ingredients

Here you'll find the most common Filipino ingredients used in Filipino recipes, along with suggestions for substitutions, where possible. For suggestions on where to find the ingredients outside of your local Filipino food shop (if you're lucky enough to have one), see page 342.

ACHUETE

Achuete (*ash-u-WET-ay*) is the Tagalog word for the seeds of annatto trees, which other Spanish-speaking countries often call achiote. Annatto adds a mild flavor, and it's primarily used for its appealingly rich orange-red color. You can probably find both annatto seeds and powder in stores; we use the seeds, and we usually incorporate them into recipes in the form of achuete butter (page 197) or achuete oil (page 58), both of which you can make in bulk to keep on hand to use as you need.

BAGOONG

Bagoong (*bah-GOONG*) is a salty, funky paste made from fermented seafood. Microscopic little shrimp called krill, anchovies, or small fish like scad—essentially whatever is plentiful—are washed, dried in the sun, then piled into

big, beautiful clay urns with sea salt and left to ferment for weeks or months. The liquid gold that rises to the top is *patis* (see page 29), while the thick sediment below is the bagoong. This both preserves the seafood and provides instant layers of flavor when little else is available.

There are many regional types of bagoong, and you can find several kinds for sale in the States: *bagoong isda* is bagoong made with mixed fish; *bagoong balayan* is made with anchovies; and *bagoong alamang* is made with shrimp or krill. The bagoong we actually use most often is *bagoong guisado*. This is a less funky, sweeter, more complex-flavored version also known as *ginisang bagoong*, essentially "stir-fried fish paste" (*ginisang* means "stir-fry"; *guisado* means "sautéed"). Bagoong guisado is bagoong alamang fried with a little oil and other spices and is far less funky. I look for the brands that add garlic to this mix, such as Kamayan, but it is fairly easy to make your own from the following recipe. If you can find only one variety, by all means use it; just add it to taste. (And if you do not see a specific type of bagoong called for in a recipe, improvising and experimenting is okay.) Note that fermented fish pastes are used in other Southeast Asian countries as well, and you could substitute one of those in a pinch, though they are made in slightly different ways with slightly different ingredients and thus have different flavors.

BAGOONG GUISADO

Sautéed Fish Paste

Bagoong guisado—essentially fermented shrimp paste fried with oil, aromatics, and other spices—is easily found in stores that carry Filipino products, but when we can, we make it ourselves. The homemade version is so much better and doesn't include the food coloring found in the store-bought kind. This version is laced with garlic and tomato and is less pungent than raw *bagoong*. **MAKES ½ CUP (120 ML)**

> **2 tablespoons vegetable oil**
>
> **2 tablespoons minced garlic**
>
> **3 tablespoons minced red onion**
>
> **¼ cup (45 g) chopped tomato**
>
> **3 tablespoons bagoong alamang (see Key Ingredients, page 35)**

In a small skillet, heat the vegetable oil over medium heat. Add the garlic and cook, stirring occasionally and being careful not to let it burn, until it begins to brown, 3 to 5 minutes.

Add the onion and cook just until it turns translucent, about 3 minutes. Add the tomato and cook until it is soft and begins to break down, about 5 minutes.

Add the bagoong and cook, stirring often, until the liquid has evaporated, 4 to 6 minutes. Let cool completely. Store in an airtight container in the refrigerator for several weeks.

BANANA LEAVES

The thick, waxy leaves of the banana plant are used to wrap many foods for steaming, acting as both a vessel and a secret ingredient: a tropical flavor and aroma unattainable from any other source. In many cases, to use them you must first heat them to make them more pliable, either by gently and quickly passing them over a flame—such as the burner of a gas stove—or by dunking them in boiling water for a second or two. Outside of the tropics—or California or Florida—it is almost impossible to find fresh banana leaves, but you can find frozen packages in specialty markets or online, and they work just as well. The key to maintaining their quality and flexibility is to defrost them slowly in the refrigerator overnight.

CALAMANSI

Tiny green calamansi, or calamondin, tangy tart cousins of lemon or lime, are used as a squeezed-on seasoning or flavoring for cakes, ice cream, and drinks. An ancient cross between a mandarin and a kumquat, calamansi tastes a little like a key lime, meaning it's both tart and floral. Though it is rare to find fresh calamansi in the United States, the juice is sold bottled and, better still, frozen in small packets, which is what we prefer to use. You can also substitute lime juice or lemon juice, though the flavors won't be exact. Often, we use a blend of both packaged calamansi and a little fresh lemon or lime for maximum flavor, if fresh calamansi is scarce.

CHILES

In our recipes we use two main types of chile, *sili* in Tagalog, but always fresh rather than dried. For real heat, we use small, skinny, very spicy bird's-eye chiles, sometimes called finger chiles or, in Tagalog, *siling labuyo*—a fresh cayenne pepper would work here as well, or really any small, very hot chile. You may find them green or ripening into red—either is fine to use. The other type of chiles are known as long green chiles, or *siling mahaba*, though they also turn red when ripe. These are larger and have more flesh, less heat, and a vegetal, aromatic flavor. You could use any larger, not-so-hot chile like an Anaheim or New Mexican chile, a milder serrano, or a small jalapeño. Just be mindful of how much heat the chile you are using has and adjust the recipe (or the amount of chile you are using) to your own tastes.

COCONUT

Coconut's versatility is put to work in all forms. Some, like coconut meat, water, and milk—*gata* in Tagalog—and thicker, richer coconut cream are easy to find in the United States: just look for good-quality brands that are pure coconut and nothing else. (And if you live in a part of the world where you can get fresh coconut milk and cream, all the better.) We also use young coconut flesh, which is called *buko* in Tagalog. Young coconut meat is just that—the soft, tender, silky meat of a not-quite-mature coconut. There is usually a thinner layer of it than the mature meat, which is thick and hard, the stuff you usually see sold shredded, grated, chunked, or flaked. (Mature coconut meat, by the way, is called *niyog*.) You will most often find buko strips canned in syrup—a common brand is Aroy-D. Last but not least, we also use *macapuno*, which is also known as coconut "sport." Macapuno hails from a mutant coconut from a specific tree varietal. It's soft and chewy and jellylike, as if it were unfinished. It is like a mutant coconut from a specific varietal of tree. It's also sold canned and used in desserts.

FISH SAUCE

Fish sauce is a salty, funky, fishy yellow-brown liquid seasoning made from long-fermented seafood and salt and is used throughout Southeast Asia. Our version is called *patis* (pah-TEECE), which was traditionally a by-product of the bagoong fermentation process (see page 35). It is often used instead of table salt or mixed with vinegar or calamansi juice and used as a dipping sauce; thus, nearly every Filipino dish has a little bit of its funk. Also note that patis is added right at the end, meaning that Filipino dishes may often taste underseasoned during the cooking process. Many recipes in this book use a little of both patis and salt—either way, a key takeaway is to taste and adjust as you see fit before you serve the dish. Flavors vary by maker, and you can really substitute any fish sauce from any country you may have on hand in these recipes, though a Filipino brand like Silver Swan or Datu Puti will obviously give you a little more traditional Filipino flavor.

GREEN FRUITS (PAPAYA, GUAVA, JACKFRUIT, AND MANGO)

Filipinos often cook with "green"—aka firm, sour, unripe—fruits. Green fruits (which are still green, hence their name) maintain their crunch and texture when cooked and provide the tartness and sourness Filipinos crave. Green mangoes, for example, are served on the street with bagoong and chile, and a common snack or side is *burong mangga*, green mango pickled with sugar and salt. Green mangoes are fairly easy to find in the United States, considering that many supermarket mangoes are not yet close to ripe—just look for the firmest, greenest ones. But green papayas—which look a little like a crumpled football—and unripe or green guava are harder to find: your best bets are markets that serve the Caribbean, Indian, or Asian shoppers familiar with these fruits. If you can't find green fruit at all, in a pinch, a tart, crisp green apple could be a stand-in for most of the recipes where we call for unripe green fruit. We also cook with green jackfruit; you might occasionally find these giant, spiky green fruits in the shops mentioned above,

but jackfruit is also available canned and prepped—as in peeled, cored, and so on—and that is what we use most often in our recipes.

BURONG MANGGA

Pickled Green Mango

Pickled green (unripe) mango is ubiquitous on Filipino tables, and is eaten as both a snack and a condiment. **MAKES ABOUT 2 CUPS (480 ML)**

> ½ cup (120 ml) white sugarcane vinegar (see Key Ingredients, page 42)
>
> ¼ cup (50 g) sugar
>
> 2 tablespoons kosher salt
>
> 1 green (unripe) mango (see Key Ingredients, left), pitted, peeled, and cut into 1-inch-long (2.5 cm) sticks

---

Note: This recipe requires a 16-ounce (475 ml) glass canning jar (see page 120 for sterilizing instructions) and 4 to 6 days of curing time.

In a medium saucepan, combine the vinegar, sugar, salt, and 2 cups (480 ml) water and bring to a boil. Turn off the heat and let the mixture cool. This is your brining liquid.

Put the mango slices in a clean, dry 16-ounce (475 ml) mason jar and pour in the brining liquid; if needed, add water so the slices are fully submerged.

Cover the jar and refrigerate for at least 4 days before serving. This will keep in the refrigerator for up to several weeks, though the mango will continue to soften over time.

LIVER PASTE

Many recipes call for a smidgen of canned liver paste, which is also called liver spread or liver pâté. I like to say it's the "dirty dust" that adds an additional umami flavor to many dishes. Two brands we prefer are Sell's and Argentina. If you can't find it, an Eastern European-style liverwurst spread will also work, or you could even use cooked chicken livers.

LONGANISA

Most sausages are known as *longanisa* (*LONG-gah-NEES-ah*), a word borrowed from the thin, long Spanish pork sausages called *longaniza*, which no doubt influenced the product in the Philippines during Spanish occupation. Like all things in the Philippines, we've long since made them our own, starting with the spelling of the word. There are many variations made around the country with various ingredients—not just pork, but also chicken, beef, fish, and so on—many of them with hyperregional seasonings, some fresh, and some lightly smoked. There are essentially two main types: One is called *longanisa hamonado*, or *jamon* for short (as in the Spanish word for ham). These have a sweet taste like that of a baked ham, hence the name. The other style is heavily garlicky, aka *de recado*, or spiced. In this book we call for two kinds: hamonado and Vigan longanisa, a garlicky, spicy pork sausage with a little sourness from sugarcane vinegar. ("Vigan" sausage

is not a typo—it is named after the city of Vigan in western Luzon.) It's got a very specific flavor, but you can substitute any garlicky fresh—meaning not smoked or cured—pork sausage. We also provide a recipe using Lucban longanisa, a garlicky sausage from the region of Quezon. You'll find Filipino sausages sold frozen in most Asian supermarkets and from the online vendors mentioned in the resources on page 342, but if you live in a region with a large Filipino population, you might even be able to find fresh links. If you can't find Filipino longanisa, look for another pork sausage made with paprika and add a pinch of sugar when you add the meat.

PANSIT

Pansit (*PAHN-sit*) is both an ingredient and a style of dish adapted over the years from the Chinese. The word basically means "noodles," and the countless regional dishes made with them, traditionally dry or lightly sauced stir-fries, though many fantastic soups (like the *pansit Isabela* on page 169) include them, too. Many pansit dishes are named after the type of noodle—for example, *pansit canton* is named after the canton noodle, a thick Chinese wheat noodle, like the kind used for lo mein; *pansit miki guisado* is made with thick egg noodles called *miki*; while *pansit bihon* is named after the bihon noodle, a thin translucent rice stick you have to soak before sautéing. (If you mix noodles, you could call it *pansit canton-bihon*.) Another famous pansit is *luglug*, which has hard-boiled eggs and a thick achuete-shrimp sauce, almost like a bisque. Any Chinese or Asian supermarket (and possibly even a well-stocked grocery store) will have something close to these kinds of noodles, as they are Chinese in origin, and specific recipes in the Noodles and Dumplings chapter (which starts on page 147) will also have suggestions on substitutions.

RICE

Rice is more than an ingredient: it is a part of life in the Philippines, and is served with every meal, even many soups. In fact, it's believed Filipinos were the first, two thousand years ago, to figure out how to plant and grow rice in terraces carved into mountainsides, a technique we then shared with the rest of Asia. In this book we use fragrant long-grain jasmine and short-grain glutinous or "sticky" rices, both readily available in supermarkets. Jasmine rice is what you serve with a meal, and sticky rice is what we use (often in tandem with coconut milk) to make a whole range of sweets like the *suman* on page 275. In the recipes, when we say rice, we usually mean white rice. Today in the Philippines, you may see white rice replaced with grains that are healthier— like quinoa or brown rice.

WHITE RICE

Many Filipinos use a rice cooker to make rice, but you can do it on the stovetop. You can scale the recipe up or down as needed. The key is to always use three parts water to two parts rice. **MAKES 4 CUPS (800 G)**

> 2 cups (370 g) uncooked jasmine rice
>
> 2 tablespoons vegetable oil
>
> 1 tablespoon kosher salt

WASH THE RICE: Place the rice in a large saucepan and add water to cover. Vigorously stir the rice around with your hands and then pour off the water. Working over the sink, cover the rice with water one more time and carefully pour off as much water as you can.

To the saucepan with the rice, add 3 cups (600 ml) water, the vegetable oil, and the salt. Stir everything together once or twice so the rice grains are just coated with the oil.

Bring the water to a boil over high heat, then reduce the heat slightly to maintain a strong simmer. Cook, stirring frequently so the rice doesn't stick to the bottom, until most of the liquid has been absorbed and you see a few air holes forming in the rice—like the bubbles you see when you reduce sugar water or make risotto. Cover the pot, reduce the heat to very low—as low as it can possibly go—and let cook for 20 minutes, or until the rice is cooked through.

Fluff the rice and serve hot.

SALTED EGGS

Salted eggs, or *itlog na maalat* (*it-log nah MAH-ah-laht*), generally refers to whole, shell-on duck eggs (though you can find salted chicken eggs, too) cured in a salt solution until they are pickled and shelf-stable. They are salty and a little funky and have a unique soft-but-dry texture. Salted eggs can be made in a variety of ways, though salt is always involved: you can soak them in brine, bury them in a mixture of mud and salt, or roll them in vodka and salt and wrap them in plastic wrap. Salted duck eggs are most likely Chinese in origin, and are eaten in other parts of Asia. You can usually find them in the egg section of Asian supermarkets in egg cartons, with each egg individually wrapped. If you can't find salted eggs or don't have time to make them, just substitute hard-boiled duck or chicken eggs.

ITLOG NA MAALAT

Salt-Brined Duck Eggs with Star Anise, Cinnamon, and Szechuan Peppercorns

Most Filipino salted eggs are simply brined in plain salt, which you can do here as well—just leave out the spices. But for a little more flavor, add the spices to get something like a cross between a salted egg and a Chinese-five-spice egg. **MAKES 12**

6 cups (1.1 kg) kosher salt

½ cup (20 g) star anise pods (optional)

2 tablespoons Sichuan peppercorns (optional)

2 cinnamon sticks (optional)

12 duck or large chicken eggs, well washed

Note: The eggs need to cure for 21 days, but you can boil and taste one after 14 days to see if it's salty and flavorful enough for your taste—if it is, drain the eggs and hard-boil them as directed in the recipe.

Bring 12 cups (3 L) water to a boil in a stockpot. Turn off the heat and stir in the salt and, if using, the star anise, peppercorns, and cinnamon sticks; stir until the salt dissolves. Let the liquid cool to room temperature.

Place the eggs in a large glass jar or other nonreactive container. Cover with the brine and spices, making sure the eggs are submerged in the liquid. Cover the jar or container tightly and let the eggs sit at room temperature for 21 days (see Note).

Drain the eggs and place them in a saucepan. Cover with cold water and bring the water to a boil. Turn off the heat, cover the pot, and let the eggs sit for 12 minutes.

Drain the eggs and let them cool completely, then refrigerate in an airtight container. If the shells have no cracks, the eggs will keep in the refrigerator for up to 1 month. (If the shells *do* have cracks, use the eggs right away.)

SOY SAUCE

Filipino soy sauce is usually thicker-bodied and very salty. Soy sauces—we call soy sauce *toyò*—vary widely by country and brand: some are saltier, some are thicker, some have additives, some are made in a lab rather than naturally brewed as per tradition, and all of that subtly changes their flavor. Just as with fish sauce, you can use any soy sauce you have on hand for Filipino recipes, but a Filipino brand like Silver Swan—which is what we used to test these recipes—is going to taste just like home, if home is in the Philippines. No matter what you choose, it is always wise to taste as you go.

SUCKLING PIGS

This is what we use when making *lechon* indoors. These weigh between 10 and 24 pounds (4.5 and 11 kg), but 20 pounds (9 kg) is about the largest that will fit in a regular home oven, and those on the smaller side are also easier to refrigerate and to cook so that the skin gets nice and crispy. You can order suckling pigs from most butchers or online sources like McReynoldsFarms.com.

VINEGAR

There are many kinds of vinegar, but the most common come from sugarcane. The vast majority of the recipes in this book call for sweet "white" sugarcane vinegar known as *sukang maasim*. (We press sugarcane for three main products: sugar, vinegar, and the moonshine called *lambanog*.) If you can't source it via the resources on page 342, reasonable substitutes are champagne vinegar, white wine vinegar, apple cider vinegar, or rice vinegar, all of which have ample sweetness. It also has about 4.5 percent acidity, as compared to 5 percent for regular distilled white vinegar.

There is also a native vinegar made from molasses left over from pressing and refining sugarcane to make sugar. This is called *sukang iloco*, and it has a rustic, raw sweetness and dark brown color. I also recommend you try spiced vinegars loaded with garlic, herbs, and chiles if you see them, or make your own from the recipe on page 34, and also seek out *sukang tuba*, which is made from the sap of a coconut palm. In the Philippines it's often homemade and has a sharp, funky, alcoholic undertone, as if it has only halfway finished the fermentation process from alcohol to vinegar. It's intense at first, then quickly becomes addictive.

ADOBO AND KINILAW

COOKING WITH VINEGAR

THE HIGH ACIDITY FROM VINEGAR IS what links all Filipino food. The acid in vinegar cooks fish or meat, as in *kinilaw*. It may be one of the oldest techniques in the cuisine. The art of cooking meat in vinegar is also a form of preservation and the key technique in making adobo. Traditional Filipino *kusineras*, or cooks, never worried about spoilage; they likely knew that even in sweltering high temperatures, a covered *kaldero* (pot) of adobo can sit on the table without refrigeration, because the vinegar in the dish protects the meat from bacteria, and inside that pot, fat from the meat, spices, and vinegar simultaneously cure, flavor, and protect.

Many people think of adobo as a stewed chicken or pork dish with soy sauce, white vinegar, black peppercorns, bay leaf, and garlic, but there are endless variations on what is essentially the national dish of the Philippines. Adobo is not just a dish but also a technique—roughly to cook something in vinegar with spices. In the Filipino culinary lexicon, one eats adobo (the noun), and one cooks in the manner of adobo (the verb). When you start to explore different regions of the country or visit different families, you see the soy sauce replaced with achuete oil for the red adobo (page 57), or fresh turmeric root for the yellow adobo (page 60), or you might see the addition of coconut milk, or cinnamon and cloves. Adobos can also be dry or wet, or they can be salty or sweetish, and they can be made with pork, chicken, lamb, fish, shrimp, or even vegetables. In other words, adobo is as varied as the people of the Philippines.

The Spanish and Mexican influence on Filipino food (see page 217) makes its debut with adobo: Mexico has a stewed meat dish called *adobado*, and the Spanish have their own dish called *adobo*, both based on the Spanish word *adobar*, meaning "to pickle or brine." These mirror the Filipino adobo techniques. But given the Filipino dishes that bear the imprint of sourness and high acidity—including kinilaw (page 68), *sinigang* (the sour soups on pages 82–87), and *paksiw* (the sour stew on page 70)—there should be no doubt that this famous dish is all Pinoy.

ADOBO 101

Many Filipino home cooks are protective of their adobo recipe and reluctant to share details. Sometimes the exact method of making the family adobo may be known only to one cook, who might be so secretive that even his or her own relatives don't know how to reproduce it. For the rest of us, the following guidelines are a good start to mastering the national dish.

DRY VS. WET

There are roughly two types of adobos, though the borders between them blur with the cook. One is a dry adobo, which some chefs assert is the traditional method of making adobo: you marinate the meat in the vinegar, seasoning it overnight, then cook it slowly until the liquid all but evaporates, so that eventually the meat is frying in its own fat, tender and supple inside but crispy on the outside and swathed in a fragrant, infused oil. For a wet adobo, the liquid does not evaporate, or more liquid is added at the end of the cooking process. The result is more like a stew, with a sauce that turns into a gravy perfect for eating over rice.

The two kinds of adobos once each had their own name: Dry adobos were *adobo*, but wet adobos were *adobado*, which means something like "the little sibling of adobo" and is perhaps a nod to the Mexican stewed meat of the same name. Though you occasionally see adobado on menus, today the term is a little outdated. Try adobo wet or dry—or somewhere in between—as you prefer.

LOW AND WIDE

For this and many other Filipino stews, adobo is made in a pan called a rondeau or a braiser. Rondeaus are wide but low-sided—the ideal shape for cooking proteins in liquid that you want to reduce slowly, which is exactly what you do with most adobos. Home cooks don't always have a rondeau (though if you make a lot of adobos, it's a wise investment), so a good substitute is a Dutch oven, which is what we call for in all these recipes. You can also use a regular stockpot, though the taller sides mean liquids take longer to reduce.

LET IT BROWN

It's important in most basic adobos, unless it says otherwise, to let the garlic slightly brown. That nutty, toasted flavor is important to Filipino cooking, and if you only soften the garlic, it won't taste quite the same. The best approach is to watch your pot carefully, stirring almost continuously, and when the garlic gets brown, add the next ingredient or lower the heat so that the garlic doesn't move beyond brown to burnt. If it burns, clean out your pan and start again.

SUBSTITUTIONS WELCOME

Think of the recipes on the following pages as a template: you can make any of the adobos in this chapter with any protein you like—beef, tofu, shrimp, pork, or chicken—or even with hearty tubers or vegetables.

PATIENCE = FLAVOR

Adobo is best enjoyed after it's been allowed to sit, preferably overnight, so the flavors can develop. If you're short on time and don't have the luxury (or patience) to wait, sometimes even a few minutes of rest are all you need for the ingredients to emulsify, unify, and intensify. If time permits, cook your adobo the day before serving it. Good things come to those who wait.

WARNING

When you add the vinegar, stand back. It sends up an acidic plume that you don't want to inhale.

PERFECTLY SOUR: TASTE AND TASTE AGAIN

If you taste the sauce right after you add the liquids, it'll be too tart. Over time, the sauce mellows into something slightly sour yet balanced: that's adobo. It's important to taste your adobo sauce near the end of the cooking process to make sure it has the right sourness, adding a little more vinegar if necessary. The level of sourness is up to you, but generally speaking, a proper adobo should give you a tang in the back of your throat but shouldn't be so sour that it is overpowering.

ADOBONG MANOK AT BABOY

Classic Adobo

THE CLASSIC ADOBO most commonly known in homes and in restaurants throughout the Philippines and in America, *adobong manok at baboy*, has a silky, fatty, sour sauce. The ingredients for this dish—soy sauce, vinegar, black peppercorns, bay leaves, garlic, chicken (*manok*), and pork (*baboy*)—are easy to find in any grocery store. Despite the simplicity of the ingredients, you'd be surprised at how different the dish can taste from cook to cook, based on shifts in cooking time or a predilection for sour or salty. Some people add coconut milk; some cooks add a bit of sweetness in the form of sugar, honey, ripe fruit, or even preserves to round out the adobo's sharp acidity and saltiness. Think of it like you do music: the notes are familiar, but the arrangement is what makes it unique. This is a "dry" adobo, which is less saucy. Try this method at least once, then adjust the proportions to your own preferences. Serve it with rice and crunchy cucumber relish. **SERVES 4 TO 6**

1 cup (240 ml) white sugarcane vinegar (see Key Ingredients, page 42)

1 cup (240 ml) soy sauce

10 garlic cloves, minced

2 teaspoons whole black peppercorns

3 tablespoons fruit preserves, jam, or jelly, such as blueberry or fig

3 bay leaves

2 bone-in, skin-on chicken thighs

2 bone-in, skin-on chicken legs

1 pound (455 g) fresh pork belly, cut into 1-inch (2.5 cm) cubes

2 tablespoons vegetable oil

4 to 6 cups (800 g to 1.2 kg) cooked white rice (see page 40), for serving

Cucumber-Tomato Relish (see page 123; optional)

Notes: This recipe requires long marinating, preferably overnight.

You could make this dish without the pork belly; just double the amount of chicken pieces.

In a large ziplock bag or nonreactive container, stir together the vinegar, soy sauce, garlic, peppercorns, fruit preserves, and bay leaves until the preserves are thoroughly combined. Add the chicken and pork belly, seal the bag or container, and marinate in the refrigerator for at least 6 hours, or preferably overnight.

Transfer the chicken, pork, and marinade to a large Dutch oven or heavy-bottomed pot with 4 cups (1 L) water and bring the liquid to a boil over high heat. Immediately reduce the heat to medium and simmer for 30 minutes, or

> recipe continues →

ADOBONG MANOK AT BABOY

Classic Adobo

continued →

until the chicken is cooked through. Turn off the heat and transfer the meat to a bowl.

In a Dutch oven or heavy-bottomed deep-sided pot, heat the vegetable oil over medium heat. Remove the pork belly pieces from the cooking liquid (do not discard the liquid) and add them to the pot. (Be careful, as the oil may spatter.) Cook, stirring frequently, until the pork belly is brown on all sides and crispy, about 7 minutes.

Add the chicken pieces to the pan and cook, flipping them occasionally, until they are browned, about 5 minutes.

Add ½ cup (120 ml) of the cooking liquid to the pan and cook until all the liquid has evaporated and the only thing left in the bottom of the pan is the fat from the chicken and pork, about 10 minutes.

Serve hot, with plenty of white rice and relish, if using, making sure to pour a little bit of fat from the bottom of the pan over each serving of rice.

You'll see that many of the adobos on the following pages are named *adobong*. In Tagalog, *ng* loosely translates to "of," and is often joined together with the word it follows, similar to a contraction in English. So adobo is a dish, but *adobong manok at baboy* means "adobo with chicken and pork." Sometimes the "–ng" is dropped altogether, meaning you see both "adobong" and "adobo" on menus.

Vinegar, or *suka*, plays an integral role in Filipino cooking. We stew and slow-cook with it for the adobos and other recipes in this chapter. But we also monitor the acidity of a dish while it's cooking, splashing on more vinegar to taste and seasoning our food with vinegar at the table. Some Filipino chefs obsess over the minutiae of vinegars and look at them the same way some people look at wine: what terrain they are from, the quality of the fruit that goes into them, and how they are stored and aged, which traditionally is in big stone urns in a shady spot outside the kitchen, though most are made in a large-scale, commercial way today.

ADOBONG PUTI

White Adobo with Duck

PUTI MEANS "WHITE," and basic white adobo is usually one made without soy sauce, which gives it a lighter color and flavor, making it a close cousin to *paksiw* (page 70). The recipe is inspired by our friend Nyle, whose family is from the Visayan region of Samar. But there's a similar version that comes from the southern region of Mindanao, whose distinct cuisine is described in more detail on page 189. This recipe is one of the few in the Philippines to use ingredients like clove, cinnamon, and star anise. Duck is a fatty, deeply flavored meat, and its richness is delicious slow-cooked with vinegar and these aromatic spices. **SERVES 4 TO 6**

¼ cup (60 ml) vegetable oil

6 bone-in, skin-on duck legs

10 garlic cloves, smashed with the side of a knife

15 whole black peppercorns

2 cinnamon sticks

3 star anise pods

5 whole cloves

5 bay leaves

1 cup (240 ml) white sugarcane vinegar (see Key Ingredients, page 42)

2 cups (480 ml) chicken stock (see page 179)

4 to 6 cups (800 g to 1.2 kg) cooked white rice (see page 40), for serving

In a Dutch oven or heavy-bottomed deep-sided pot, heat the vegetable oil over medium-high heat. Add the duck legs and cook until browned on all sides, about 10 minutes. Transfer them to a plate and set aside.

Reduce the heat to medium and add the garlic to the pot. Cook, stirring continuously, until the garlic turns golden brown, 3 to 5 minutes. Be careful not to let it burn.

Add the peppercorns, cinnamon, star anise, cloves, bay leaves, vinegar, and stock, then return the duck legs to the pot. Bring the liquid to a low boil, then immediately reduce the heat so that the duck cooks at a simmer. Simmer for 30 to 45 minutes, until the duck legs are fork-tender, then increase the heat to medium-high. Let the liquid bubble away and reduce; when the liquid has fully reduced and the duck legs start to fry in their own fat, turn off the heat.

Serve hot, with plenty of rice.

ADOBONG PULA ACHUETE

Red Adobo with Lamb Shanks and Annatto

THIS RED ADOBO IS AN ILONGO dish—specifically from the Hiligaynon people, one of the many ethnic groups in the central Philippines. This adobo uses amber-red achuete oil instead of soy sauce, giving the dish a vibrant red hue and an earthy bitterness. *Achuete* is the Filipino word for annatto seeds (see Key Ingredients, page 35). Though lamb isn't common in Filipino cooking, lamb shanks are outstanding slowly cooked in this rich red sauce fortified with a spoonful of miso and some liver paste. **SERVES 4**

3 tablespoons vegetable oil

2 bone-in lamb shanks, about 1½ pounds (680 g) each

Kosher salt and freshly ground black pepper

1 cup (240 ml) coconut vinegar (see Key Ingredients, page 42)

1 cup (240 ml) Achuete Oil (recipe follows)

3 to 4 tablespoons fish sauce

5 garlic cloves, smashed with the side of a knife

2 tablespoons red miso paste

⅓ cup (80 ml) liver paste or liverwurst spread (see Key Ingredients, page 39)

1 small white onion, thinly sliced

10 whole black peppercorns

5 bay leaves

4 cups (800 g) cooked white rice (see page 40), for serving

Preheat the oven to 350°F (175°C).

In a large skillet, heat the vegetable oil over medium-high heat. Season the shanks on all sides with salt and pepper and cook until browned on all sides, about 6 minutes per side. Set the shanks aside on a large plate.

In a Dutch oven or roasting pan, whisk together the vinegar, achuete oil, 2 tablespoons of the fish sauce, and the garlic. Whisk in the miso and liver pastes until they are completely incorporated.

Add the onion, peppercorns, and bay leaves. Add the browned lamb shanks to the pan, pressing them under the liquid. Add water as needed to submerge the meat and onion.

> recipe continues →

continued →

Cover the pan tightly with a lid or several layers of aluminum foil and bake for 2½ hours, or until the shanks are fork-tender.

Transfer the shanks to a large plate, then place the Dutch oven over medium-high heat and cook until the liquid has reduced and is thick enough to coat the back of a spoon, about 10 minutes.

Stir in 1 tablespoon of the fish sauce and taste; add more until the taste is to your liking. Return the shanks to the sauce to heat them through, if necessary.

For the best flavor, refrigerate the adobo for a few hours before serving, then reheat it and serve it in deep bowls, with rice.

ACHUETE OIL

Like garlic oil (see page 183), you can use achuete oil to add luster and flavor when finishing a dish. Or you can drizzle it on anything you like—eggs, rice, grilled meats, tomato sauce–based dishes like *kaldereta* (page 226) or *afritada* (page 224)—or use it to add a slightly nutty undertone to stews. This recipe is easy to scale up or down as you like. **MAKES 1 CUP (240 ML)**

¼ cup (70 g) annatto seeds
(see Key Ingredients, page 35)

1 cup (240 ml) vegetable oil

Heat a skillet over medium-high heat. When it is smoking hot, add the annatto seeds and toast them, stirring frequently, until they just begin to smoke and pop. This should take only a minute or so.

Add the vegetable oil and simmer, stirring frequently, until the oil takes on the deep red color of the seeds—again, this takes only a minute or two.

Remove the pan from the heat and let the oil cool. Strain the oil through a fine-mesh sieve set over a mason jar and discard the seeds. Store the oil in the tightly sealed mason jar for up to 1 month.

With the exception of certain regions like Mindanao (see page 189), duck is not a common ingredient in the Philippines. That's possibly because ducks are typically consumed as *balut*, a famous Southeast Asian snack for which fertilized eggs (usually duck eggs) are hard-boiled while the developing bird inside is in its embryo stage.

ADOBONG MANOK DILAW

Yellow Adobo with Chicken

THE FRESH TURMERIC IN THIS DISH adds not just an earthy, slightly bitter flavor but also a sunny yellow hue. Turmeric root is really a rhizome, and looks similar to ginger (a relative) when fresh. You can find it dried or ground, but if you use either of those in this adobo, the results will be too bitter; you really need to use fresh. Turmeric's popularity—as an ingredient in health foods and juices thanks to its anti-inflammatory properties—means it is a lot easier to find fresh in the produce section of specialty supermarkets, or you can order it online (see Resources, page 342). Like most adobos, this dish benefits from resting for a few hours or overnight so that the flavors intensify. **SERVES 4**

3 tablespoons vegetable oil

2 pounds (910 g) bone-in, skin-on chicken legs or thighs

1 small white onion, diced

5 garlic cloves, minced

3 finger-size knobs fresh turmeric root, peeled and minced

2 cups (480 ml) chicken stock (see page 179)

1 cup (240 ml) coconut vinegar (see Key Ingredients, page 42)

1 cup (75 g) white button mushrooms, cleaned and quartered

Kosher salt and freshly ground pepper

4 cups (800 g) cooked white rice (see page 40), for serving

In a Dutch oven, heat the vegetable oil over medium-high heat. Add the chicken pieces—it's best if they don't overlap. Cook, stirring occasionally, until the chicken pieces are lightly browned on all sides. Transfer the chicken pieces to a plate and set aside.

Reduce the heat to medium. Add the onion and garlic and cook, stirring occasionally, until the garlic is just beginning to brown and the onion is soft and translucent, about 7 minutes.

Add the turmeric and cook, stirring occasionally, until it just starts to soften, about 3 minutes.

Return the chicken to the pan. Add the stock and vinegar, then cover the pan tightly and simmer for 30 minutes. Remove the cover, increase the heat to medium-high, add the mushrooms, and simmer until the liquid has reduced by half, 10 to 15 minutes. Season to taste with salt and pepper and serve with rice.

ADOBONG PUSIT
Adobo with Squid

ADOBOS MADE WITH SEAFOOD are the easiest and quickest to make, because the seafood cooks so fast. The trick to making this dish—also known as *ginisang pusit*—which is essentially stewed squid, is in how you clean the squid. Remove the plastic-like filament from the body, but keep everything else, including the guts and delicate ink sacs, intact. These provide a silky, creamy texture as they render into the simmering liquid, and they bump up the umami factor; the squid ink complements the vinegar and soy sauce and is an important ingredient in the recipe. A little butter is added to the sauce to help boost this adobo's velvety texture, along with a spike of oregano, which grows wild in the Philippines. Oregano is an ingredient common in Mexican and Spanish cooking, but not so common in Pinoy recipes, so this adobo pays homage to our Mexican culinary ancestry. Reheating squid doesn't result in great textures, so unlike other adobos, allow this to rest only a short time for the flavors to meld and deepen before digging in. **SERVES 4 TO 6**

Note: Uncleaned squid is not easy to find in American markets, but you can sometimes hit pay dirt. Visit a real fishmonger—those at farmers' markets or those who buy direct from fishermen are best—and ask if they have fresh, uncleaned squid, or if they can set some aside for you for a future visit. If you can't find it, use regular cleaned squid and buy a little squid ink to supplement the sauce (most fish markets sell squid ink in small packets).

1 pound (455 g) whole medium squid, uncleaned (see Note)

3 tablespoons vegetable oil

1 cup (110 g) chopped white onion

2 tablespoons minced fresh ginger

Kosher salt

5 garlic cloves, smashed with the side of a knife

1 cup (145 g) diced cherry or Roma (plum) tomatoes

1 teaspoon dried oregano

2 bay leaves

1 bird's-eye chile (see Key Ingredients, page 37)

½ cup (120 ml) white sugarcane vinegar (see Key Ingredients, page 42)

½ teaspoon freshly ground black pepper

¼ cup (60 ml) soy sauce

1 teaspoon muscovado or brown sugar

3 tablespoons cold unsalted butter, cut into pieces

Fish sauce

4 to 6 cups (800 g to 1.2 kg) cooked white rice (see page 40), for serving

Place the squid in a large bowl and wash it well under cool running water. Drain off all the water. Working right in the bowl, use a pair of clean kitchen scissors to separate the heads from the bodies. Use your hands to remove the beak from the head—just pull it out—and the plastic-like filament in the body. Cut the bodies into 1-inch-thick (2.5 cm) rings, being sure to keep all the ink, guts, and so on in the bowl. Set the bowl aside.

In a medium saucepan, heat the vegetable oil over medium heat. Add the onion and then the ginger and a pinch of salt and cook, stirring frequently, for 1 minute.

Add the garlic, tomatoes, oregano, bay leaves, chile, a pinch of salt, and ¼ cup (60 ml) water. Cook over medium heat until everything is very soft and broken down, 12 to 15 minutes. Add a generous sprinkle of water as needed to keep the mixture from drying out and browning or sticking to the bottom of the pan.

Once everything is soft, add the vinegar and ¼ cup (60 ml) water and raise the heat to medium-high. Once the mixture is bubbling, cook, stirring continuously, for about 2 minutes.

Add the squid bodies, tentacles, guts, and ink, a pinch of salt, the pepper, and the soy sauce and cook just until the squid is tender—the tentacles will curl and the rings will become opaque—which can happen in as little as 2 to 3 minutes. Use a slotted spoon to transfer the squid to a large bowl.

Add the sugar and stir. Simmer the sauce over medium-high heat until it has reduced slightly and begun to thicken, 5 to 7 minutes. Add the butter, stirring continuously until it is incorporated into the sauce.

Turn off the heat and return the squid to the pan, stirring so it is covered with the sauce. Season with fish sauce to taste. Let sit for 15 to 20 minutes to allow the flavors to meld.

Serve with rice.

SINUGLAW

Cured Tuna with Grilled Pork

SINUGLAW IS A COMBINATION OF FISH ceviche—in this case, tuna—plus *inihaw na liempo*, or grilled pork belly. The two are eaten together for a wonderful dish that pairs smoky, fatty meat with the clean, tart flavors of vinegar-cured fish. They're dressed with a mix of coconut milk, ginger, red onion, chiles, and tomato. In the Philippines, you often eat *kinilaw* made from fresh catch right at the beach, but it tastes better after it rests for at least ten minutes. You can even let it sit in the refrigerator for a few hours to cure to your liking; the texture of the fish will firm up over time. **SERVES 4 TO 6**

½ pound (225 g) sushi-grade tuna, cut into large dice

½ cup (120 ml) white sugarcane vinegar (see Key Ingredients, page 42) or white vinegar

Kosher salt and freshly ground black pepper

½ cup (120 ml) coconut milk

2 tablespoons minced fresh ginger

2 tablespoons minced red onion

1 tablespoon minced long green chile (see Key Ingredients, page 37), seeded, if desired

1 tablespoon fish sauce

½ pound (225 g) grilled pork belly (page 260), sliced

1 cup (118 ml) peeled, seeded, diced cucumber

1 avocado, peeled and diced

¼ cup (10 g) picked fresh cilantro leaves, for garnish

¼ cup (35 g) quartered cherry tomatoes, for garnish

1 tablespoon orange or lime zest, or a mix of the two, for garnish

In a nonreactive bowl, toss the tuna with the vinegar and a pinch each of salt and pepper. Let it sit, tossing it from time to time, for at least 10 minutes, or let it rest in the refrigerator for 2 to 3 hours.

While the fish sits, in a small bowl, stir together the coconut milk, ginger, onion, chile, and fish sauce, then transfer the mixture to a serving platter or shallow bowl. Taste the tuna and season with salt and pepper as desired, then use a slotted spoon to transfer it to the serving platter.

Top the tuna with the pork, cucumber, avocado, cilantro, tomatoes, and zest. Toss the sinuglaw together and serve right away.

KINILAW NA HIPON
Cured Shrimp

SO SIMPLE: FRESH, RAW TIGER SHRIMP are tossed with ginger, chiles, shallots, sugarcane vinegar, calamansi juice, and a bit of mashed salted egg for creaminess. Gently cooked in vinegar, the thin slices of shrimp take on the texture of a raw oyster, though you could let them "cook" a little longer if you prefer them a bit firmer. **SERVES 4**

1 pound raw tiger shrimp, peeled and deveined

¾ cup (180 ml) white sugarcane vinegar (see Key Ingredients, page 42)

2 tablespoons minced shallot

2 tablespoons minced fresh ginger

¼ cup (59 ml) peeled, seeded, diced cucumber

½ teaspoon thinly sliced bird's-eye chile (see Key Ingredients, page 37), plus more to taste

2 tablespoons diced salted egg (see Key Ingredients, page 41)

1 teaspoon fish sauce, plus more to taste

1 teaspoon calamansi juice (see Key Ingredients, page 37), plus more to taste

2 pinches of ground white pepper

2 tablespoons torn fresh cilantro leaves

Cut the shrimp in half lengthwise (along the spine, so you end up with two long, thin pieces) and then into 1-inch (2.5 cm) pieces. Put the shrimp in a large nonreactive bowl and cover with the vinegar, making sure all the pieces are covered. Let sit at room temperature for 20 minutes.

Meanwhile, in a small bowl, toss together the shallot, ginger, cucumber, chile, and half the salted egg.

Scoop out the shrimp with a slotted spoon, leaving the liquid in the bowl, and set them aside in a separate medium bowl. Add the remaining salted egg to the liquid left in the bowl and blend it in with the back of a spoon or a fork until it forms a rough emulsion.

Return the shrimp and any liquid it has released back to the bowl, add the shallot-ginger mixture, and toss. Add the fish sauce, calamansi juice, and white pepper and toss everything together well with two large spoons or clean hands. Let the mixture sit for 10 minutes more, then taste, adding more fish sauce, calamansi juice, and/or chiles as desired.

Garnish with cilantro and serve immediately. (You can let this sit for another hour or so and it will still taste good, but the shrimp will continue to cook in the vinegar and the cilantro will darken.)

KILAWEN NA BAKA

Pickled Beef with Chiles

KILAWEN IS A COUSIN OF *KINILAW*—USUALLY the term is used for meats, raw or cooked, that have been cured in seasoned vinegar. Though this is traditionally made with goat skin, we use a mix of thinly sliced cooked beef tripe, which provides a little of the same chewy texture, and grilled, very tender slices of lean steak, whose smoky char is fantastic when lightly pickled with garlic, ginger, and onion. Like steak tartare, this is best when the meat is well tenderized and served cold. **SERVES 4 TO 6**

Kosher salt

½ pound (225 g) honeycomb tripe, cleaned (see Notes)

¼ cup (60 ml) white sugarcane vinegar (see Key Ingredients, page 42)

3 tablespoons fish sauce

2 tablespoons minced red onion

2 tablespoons minced fresh ginger

1 tablespoon minced garlic

1 tablespoon sugar

1 tablespoon vegetable oil

½ pound (225 g) ⅛-inch-thick (3 mm) lean beef steaks, pounded thin (see Notes)

3 bird's-eye chiles (see Key Ingredients, page 37), thinly sliced (optional)

1 tablespoon thinly sliced fresh cilantro leaves (optional)

Notes: This dish requires several hours of prep time.

Honeycomb beef tripe, or the frilly lining of a cow's stomach, is available at most butcher shops and even many supermarkets. There are three kinds of beef tripe, taken from different parts of the stomach; be sure to get honeycomb (not blanket or leaf), and to rinse it well with cool running water before using.

For the steaks, any lean cut of beef will do, such as eye of round, top sirloin, top round, bottom round, or sirloin tip. You can ask a butcher to slice the meat into thin steaks, or freeze it for an hour at home to make it easier to cut. Once the meat is sliced, pound it with a mallet or meat tenderizer into thin pieces.

Bring a large pot of salted water to a boil over high heat. Add the cleaned tripe, reduce the heat slightly to maintain a simmer, and cook for 1½ hours, or until the tripe is soft and can be easily cut with a fork. Drain the tripe, rinse it well, and let it cool completely, then cut it into thin strips.

While the tripe cools, in a large nonreactive bowl, combine the vinegar, fish sauce, onion, ginger, garlic, and sugar. Mix well. Add the tripe to the bowl and stir until everything is well mixed. Set aside at room temperature.

Heat a cast-iron skillet or grill pan over high heat. When the pan is hot, add the vegetable oil and the steak, making sure not to crowd the pan. (You may need to cook the steak in batches.) Cook the steak pieces for 2 minutes on each side, then transfer to a cutting board to cool. (You could also cook these on a gas or charcoal grill; just make sure the grill grates are well oiled so the meat doesn't stick.)

When the steak is cool, cut it into 1-inch (2.5 cm) strips and add it to the bowl with the tripe. Toss until everything is coated with the vinegar.

Refrigerate the kilawen for 1 hour, then stir in the chiles and cilantro, if desired, and serve immediately.

PAKSIW NA ISDA
Stewed Fish and Vegetables

PAKSIW is a relative of both adobo and *kinilaw* and is another method of cooking meats and fish in vinegar. Like its cousins, it is very sour and also practical—it's designed both to flavor foods and to preserve them. Paksiw—also called *inun-unun* in some regions—is generally prepared two different ways, depending on whether you're cooking meat or fish. A seafood paksiw may include *siling mahaba* (long pepper), ginger, and bitter melon (see Note). When made with meat, paksiw is usually sweeter, thanks to the addition of sugar. This fish paksiw is rich with the oily, earthy flavor of eel, but king mackerel is easy to find and an excellent substitute. The combination of sour and bitter flavors with the fatty fish is delicious, and a great way to imagine how generations of Filipinos have enjoyed the fruits of the sea and land. **SERVES 4 TO 6**

Note: Bitter melon is an oblong, bumpy green gourd that thrives in humid climates and is used throughout India and Asia; it is usually available in any Indian or Chinese market. If possible, look for smaller melons and one of the Indian varieties—they're less bitter. Scoop out the inside flesh and seeds before using the melon. If you can't find bitter melon, you could use a firm summer squash, such as yellow squash or zucchini.

2 cups (480 ml) fish stock (see page 95)

1 small white onion, quartered

1 tablespoon fish sauce

6 garlic cloves, smashed with the side of a knife

1 thumb-size knob fresh ginger, smashed with the side of a knife

1 long green chile (see Key Ingredients, page 37)

½ cup (120 ml) white sugarcane vinegar (see Key Ingredients, page 42)

1 cup (115 g) seeded bitter melon (see Note), cut into sticks (¼ inch/6 mm thick and 2½ inches/ 6 cm long)

1 cup (115 g) daikon radish sticks (¼ inch/6 mm thick and 2½ inches/ 6 cm long)

2 pounds (910 g) king mackerel or freshwater eel fillets

1 cup (20 g) loosely packed fresh baby spinach

1 thinly sliced scallion, for garnish

4 to 6 cups (800 g to 1.2 kg) cooked white rice (see page 40), for serving

In a large saucepan, combine the stock, onion, fish sauce, garlic, ginger, chile, and vinegar and bring the mixture to a boil. Reduce the heat to medium so the liquid cooks at a simmer.

Add the bitter melon and radish and simmer for about 6 minutes, then add the mackerel fillets. Cook until the fish is cooked through and the vegetables are tender, about 4 minutes more. Stir in the spinach and turn off the heat once it starts to wilt.

Serve the paksiw in bowls, garnished with a sprinkle of scallion, over rice.

DINUGUAN

Blood Stew

THE WORD *DINUGUAN* comes from the root word *dugo*, meaning "blood," which, when cooked, becomes a thick, dark brown (almost black) liquid. Dinuguan is a uniquely creamy, decadent, rich, pungent, tangy, and sour stew, thanks in part to the beef blood that also gives it that chocolaty color. We learned this tip from Glenda Barretto, chef/owner of Via Mare restaurant in the Philippines. This slow-cooked stew is not an adobo, but vinegar is key to its flavor and construction; it helps keep the blood from clotting as it cooks, making for a luscious and creamy sauce. Versions of this dish may use innards, but we prefer meaty pork shoulder. Serve dinuguan with the soft steamed rice flour cakes called *puto*. **SERVES 4 TO 6**

½ pound (225 g) skinless pork belly, cut into 2-inch (5 cm) chunks

½ pound (225 g) boneless pork shoulder, cut into 2-inch (5 cm) chunks

Kosher salt and freshly ground black pepper

White sugarcane vinegar (see Key Ingredients, page 42)

3 tablespoons vegetable oil

1 medium red onion, diced

2 tablespoons minced fresh ginger

2 tablespoons minced garlic

1 cup (240 ml) pork stock (see page 107) or chicken stock (see page 179) (see Notes)

2 long red chiles (see Key Ingredients, page 37)

½ cup (120 ml) beef blood (see Notes)

Fish sauce

Puto (page 277), or 4 to 6 cups (800 g to 1.2 kg) cooked white rice (see page 40), for serving

Notes: This dish is even better if you marinate the pork overnight in the refrigerator.

If you have access to pork stock, use it; otherwise, chicken stock is fine, preferably if it's homemade.

To find a source for fresh, organic beef blood, it's best to ask a butcher. It's also often sold in tubs in the freezer section of Asian supermarkets.

In a large bowl, toss the pork belly and shoulder with salt and pepper and enough vinegar to lightly coat the meat. Cover and marinate in the refrigerator for at least 1 hour or preferably overnight.

Remove the pork chunks with a slotted spoon and set them aside, making sure to save any liquid collected at the bottom of the bowl.

In a Dutch oven, heat the vegetable oil over medium heat. Add the onion, ginger, and garlic and cook, stirring occasionally, until the garlic is just beginning to brown and the onion is soft and translucent, about 4 minutes.

Add the pork chunks to the pot and cook, stirring occasionally, until they just begin to brown, 5 to 7 minutes. Be careful not to let the onion, ginger, and garlic burn.

> recipe continues →

DINUGUAN

Blood Stew

continued →

Add the reserved pork juices, the stock, ½ cup (120 ml) vinegar, the chiles, and water as needed to fully cover the pork. Bring the liquid to a boil, then reduce the heat until it is cooking at a low simmer. Cover the pot and cook until the meat is fork-tender. (This should take 35 to 40 minutes, but check it after 20 minutes.)

When the pork is tender, stir in the blood and let it just cook through—it will thicken and darken in color—3 to 5 minutes. Taste and add fish sauce and vinegar to your liking.

Ladle into bowls and serve with puto or white rice.

Dinuguan is called different names in different regions, reflecting subtle shifts in how it is made. I don't know another dish in the Philippines with as many specific place-related names. They include *dinardaraan* in Ilocos Norte, *tid-tad* in Pampanga, *dugo-dugo* in Cebu, *sinugaok* in Batangas, *rugodugo* in Waray, *tinumis* in Nueva Ecija, *mollo* in Ilocos, and *champayna* or *sampayna* in Mindanao.

BISTEK TAGALOG
Filipino Steak and Onions

Note: You want the piece of steak to have some fat, so the best choice is not the most expensive high-end butcher shop offering with little veins of intramuscular fat. Instead, you want a slightly cheaper grocery store cut with mottled marbling, which results in little knobs of crispy fat throughout the meat. (Though you should trim off any large pieces of fat if the steak has them; you can cook the onions in that, if you want even more flavor.) It also helps to start with thinner steaks before you tenderize the meat; if it is a thick steak, you can begin by cutting it horizontally into two thinner steaks, or have your butcher do this for you.

LIKE *DINUGUAN* (page 71), *bistek tagalog* is not technically an adobo, but it is a dish in which meat is cooked with an acid—citrus juice here, rather than vinegar. It's our version of the steak and onions—*bistek encebollado*—served in many Spanish-speaking countries, and one trick, other than citrus juice, is flavoring the marinade and the cooking oil with the onions. When you add them to the skillet for just a few minutes in the first step, it's to get their good, sweet flavor into the oil. It's also one of the most approachable recipes you'll find: the ingredients to make this dish are available in your local grocery store; it's the technique that makes this a classic home-style Filipino dish. Our recipe is inspired by Glenda Barretto's cookbook *Flavors of the Philippines*, and each of the steps to preparing the dish is important to create the ideal texture and level of *asim*, or sourness. Note that this dish is meant to be served over white rice, which tames some of its saltiness and sourness, but you can also soften the flavors a bit by cooking the sauce for less time at the end or adding a little liquid. Either way, finish the dish with a squeeze of fresh lemon juice. **SERVES 4**

1 (1-pound/455 g) rib-eye steak (see Note)

5 garlic cloves, smashed with the side of a knife

¼ cup (60 ml) calamansi juice (see Key Ingredients, page 37) or fresh lemon juice

¼ cup (60 ml) soy sauce

2 teaspoons muscovado or brown sugar

2 (½-inch-thick/1.5 cm) slices white onion, rings separated

3 tablespoons vegetable oil, plus more as needed

1 tablespoon cold unsalted butter

2 lemons, cut into wedges, for serving

4 cups (800 g) cooked white rice (see page 40), for serving

Rub the steak with 2 of the garlic cloves. Using a meat tenderizer or the bottom of a clean heavy skillet, pound the steak until it is about ¼ inch (6 mm) thick, like a cutlet. Cut or tear the steak into roughly 3-inch-wide (7.5 cm) pieces, about the size of the palm of your hand.

In a nonreactive bowl or container, stir together the calamansi juice, soy sauce, 1 teaspoon of the sugar, the remaining garlic cloves, and ¼ cup (60 ml) water until the sugar has dissolved. Add the steak and the onion and mix well. Let the mixture sit at room temperature for 30 minutes. (It can sit for up to 3 hours in the refrigerator, but after that, the texture of the beef begins to change.)

In a large skillet, heat 2 tablespoons of the vegetable oil over medium-high heat. When the oil starts to smoke, add the onion rings and cook until they just soften, about 2 minutes, making sure they do not brown. Use tongs or a slotted spoon to set them aside on a plate.

Remove the steak from the marinade with tongs or a slotted spoon and set aside in a separate bowl, reserving the marinade.

In the same pan, heat the remaining 1 tablespoon oil until it is very hot. Add a few pieces of the steak in a single layer, using a slotted spoon or tongs to shake off as much clinging marinade as you can. Cook the steak for 3 to 4 minutes per side, until it is well browned in spots—the meat will release some liquid, which will start to evaporate, then the meat will get crispy around the edges. Transfer the meat to a platter with tongs or a slotted spoon, and repeat until all of the steak is cooked, adding just a little oil to the skillet each time. The bottom of the pan may get brown and crusty—that's okay. The meat will also be cooked through; that's the consistency you're looking for.

Return the onion rings to the skillet and cook for 2 to 3 minutes, until warm, then lay them on top of the steak. Add the marinade to the pan and stir, scraping up any browned bits from the bottom of the pan. Whisk in the butter and the remaining 1 teaspoon sugar and let the sauce reduce slightly and become a little less sour.

Pour the sauce over the platter of steak and serve immediately, with lemon wedges and rice.

SOUPS

A TASTE OF HOME

SOUPS PLAY MANY ROLES at the Filipino table. Called *sabaw* in Tagalog—the word means both "soup" and "broth"—they run the gamut from simple consommés meant to serve as a palate cleanser during a large meal to thick and hearty stews to complex flavored soups. Historically, most ordinary Filipino homes had only one heat source—originally an open fire—which meant that to *nilaga*, or boil, everything together in one pot was an efficient way to make a meal. Over the years, souring agents have been added to that pot, or fermented seafood paste and grilled fish (see page 99), or the coconut water in the delicate soup called *binakol* (page 90), taking simple boiled meat and vegetables to the next level: a taste of home.

Sinigang is one of the most beloved Filipino soups. Along with adobos, *kinilaw*s (our version of ceviche), and tableside vinegars, it is a go-to for the high-acid notes that are distinctive of Philippine cuisine. It's sometimes said to be the Filipino version of the Thai soup *tom yum*, though I think that's a disservice to both dishes. While tom yum is delicately sour, sometimes with a bit of condensed milk that curbs the sharp edges of the acid, sinigang is never subtle. It is deliberately and reliably sour: it's a dish that almost screams "take it or leave it." In the Philippines, sinigang is made with locally grown ingredients to sour the soup and round out the bowl. The ingredients vary depending on the area of the country, which is why we offer three different versions in this chapter (pages 82, 85, and 86).

Bulalo (page 96) is another soup that is important to understand to truly appreciate Filipino cuisine. While sinigang is sour, bulalo is at the other end of the spectrum, mild and accommodating in contrast. The beef bone broth with vegetables is lightly seasoned with black pepper and fish sauce and eaten all over the country, though the name of the dish and the vegetables used tend to change from region to region.

When you visit a Filipino *karinderia*, or cafeteria, a quick, takeout restaurant with a steam table and simmering pots, you can order a combo meal from an array of choices that are quickly piled on your plate as you point to what you want. These restaurants are often called *turo-turos*, or "point-point" spots, affordable places for families or jeepney drivers to enjoy a quick, no-fuss meal. Most customers typically order rice and a couple of *ulams*, or main dishes, and fried items like *lumpia* and *ukoy*. You can also ask for a cup of broth from a soup pot to *pampainit ng sikmura*, or "heat your stomach." Eating this can be a cheap meal when you're short on cash: just pour a little broth over your rice, and you have a meal. These broths are typically something like a simple *sinigang* or *bulalo*.

SINIGANG NA BABOY

Sour Soup with Pork Belly, Taro, and Water Spinach

SINIGANG IS AN UNAPOLOGETICALLY SOUR SOUP, and you should think of it as a base: You can add anything to it, and you can use many things to make it sour. That includes citrus, vinegar, tamarind, unripe pineapple or guava, tart fruits like Granny Smith apples, or a combination of any of the above. You can also make it as sour as you want: some like their sinigangs milder, while others prefer a full-on pucker that hits the back of your throat. This version is a craveable combination of pork belly and water spinach, an Asian green with crunchy hollow stems and diamond-shaped leaves that become soft and silky when cooked. This *sinigang na baboy* uses a blend of tamarind, tomatoes, and green or unripe guava fruits as the souring agents. Tamarind gives the soup an earthy, rich flavor, the guava lends fruitiness, and the tomatoes supply sweetness. You can also add a whole fresh banana pepper to the pot for a little heat. Try serving a cup of the plain tart broth from this or another sinigang as an accompaniment to a rich stew. **SERVES 4 TO 6**

Notes: Taro root is a brown-skinned tuber found at Asian, Caribbean, and Indian markets and, these days, at many mainstream supermarkets.

Filipinos call hollow-leaved water spinach *kangkong*—it's usually found in the produce section of Chinese or Asian markets, and sold in bunches like regular spinach. You can substitute any spinach you can find.

3 green (unripe) guavas
(see Key Ingredients, page 38),
cut into small dice

½ pound (225 g) dried
tamarind pods

2 tablespoons vegetable oil

1 small onion, quartered

⅓ cup (35 g) fresh ginger, peeled
and cut into matchsticks

4 garlic cloves, minced

1½ pounds (680 g) skinless
pork belly, cubed

1 whole banana pepper (optional)

1 pound (455 g) taro root
(see Notes), peeled and cubed

2 medium tomatoes, chopped

2 tablespoons fish sauce,
plus more as needed

¼ pound (115 g) fresh water spinach
(see Notes)

Bring 6 cups (1.4 L) water to a boil in a large saucepan over high heat. Add the guavas and tamarind pods and cook for 10 minutes, or until they are soft enough to mash. Strain the guava-tamarind mixture through a fine-mesh sieve into a bowl, discarding the pulp and seeds. Set the liquid aside.

In a large soup pot, heat the vegetable oil over medium heat. Add the onion, ginger, and garlic and cook for 3 minutes, or until just beginning to soften, being careful not to let them burn.

Add the pork and cook, stirring occasionally so that all sides cook, for about 4 minutes, or until the pork is just beginning to brown.

Add 6 cups (1½ L) water, half the guava-tamarind liquid, and the banana pepper (if using) and bring to a boil. Use a large spoon to skim off any impurities from the surface of the liquid, reduce the heat to low, and simmer for 40 minutes. Add the taro and cook until it is tender and you can easily pierce it with a fork, about 20 minutes more.

Add the tomatoes and fish sauce. Taste. At this point, the soup should be tart, but not salty or too sour. Add more guava-tamarind liquid and fish sauce, if desired.

Turn off the heat and add the water spinach. Let the soup sit on the stove for 5 minutes more, or until the leaves have wilted. Stir and serve immediately.

SINIGANG NA ISDA

Sour Soup with Fish Heads

OUR FAVORITE SEAFOOD *SINIGANG* relies on the South Asian vegetable called *kamias*, also known as *bilimbi* or "tree cucumber"—it looks like a cucumber and has a similar crunchy texture but grows on trees found in backyards all over the Philippines. This recipe calls for fish heads, which are an homage to the "Alaskeros," Filipinos who migrated to Alaska and worked in salmon canneries dating back to the late 1800s. It also includes miso, borrowed from the Japanese, who also migrated to Alaska—and oversaw a deadly occupation of the Philippines in the 1940s. The miso in this recipe is a rare occurrence of Japanese fusion in Filipino cooking, one likely born out of sharing among the cannery workers. The soup should have a sourness followed by a gentle undercurrent of nuttiness from the miso; it's thickened by the collagen in the fish heads. **SERVES 4 TO 6**

2 tablespoons vegetable oil

1 white onion, halved and thinly sliced

¼ cup (35 g) minced garlic

6 cups (1.4 L) fish stock
(see page 95)

8 ounces (225 g) packaged kamias
(see Notes), drained

¼ cup (60 ml) miso paste

2 tablespoons minced fresh ginger

2 bird's-eye chiles (see Key
Ingredients, page 37), minced

1 large tomato, quartered

1 (1½-pound/680 g) salmon head
(see Notes)

White sugarcane vinegar
(see Key Ingredients, page 42)

In a stockpot, heat the vegetable oil over medium heat. Add the onion and garlic and cook, stirring occasionally, until soft and translucent, about 4 minutes. Do not let them brown.

Add the stock, kamias, miso, ginger, chiles, and tomato and raise the heat to medium-high. Add the salmon head and simmer for 30 minutes, or until it is cooked through and the meat easily flakes with a fork.

Taste the broth and adjust the sourness with a little vinegar to taste: it should be tart and bright. Serve hot in deep bowls, giving each bowl a piece of the salmon head.

Notes: Unless you live in a tropical climate, you likely won't find fresh kamias, but they're available in most Filipino markets, usually frozen in plastic packages. You can also substitute any other souring ingredient you like from the sinigangs on the following pages, or use any citrus, vinegar, or tart fruit you have on hand to create your own.

If possible, have your fishmonger split the head in half lengthwise—so each side has an eye—so it's easier to serve pieces of the head in each bowl. If you prefer, you can substitute fish steaks.

SINIGANG NA HIPON

Sour Shrimp Soup

THIS *SINIGANG*, like many that use unripe fruit as the souring agent, is brightly flavored and a little floral tasting, making the broth a perfect match for shrimp. It uses an interesting souring agent: the fruit and core of unripe pineapple. The pineapple is less popular in the Philippines than many other fruits because most are exported for sale. And recipes cooked with green pineapple have become virtually extinct because of the exportation. Another unique aspect of this sinigang is the addition of rice-washing water, which is exactly what it sounds like: the water left over from washing rice before you cook it. It's used here so all the starch from the rice can lend body to the soup. Use whole, unpeeled, head-on shrimp in this soup; it gives it a richer flavor. You will have to peel the shrimp as you eat them, but think of it as a way to slow down a bit, adding to your enjoyment of this wonderful and unique version of sinigang. **SERVES 4 TO 6**

Notes: You will need cheesecloth and butcher's twine for this recipe.

For the green pineapple, use the firmest, least-ripe fruit you can find.

Don't overcook the shrimp; it will turn tough and rubbery. Alternatively, you can prepare the broth a few hours in advance, then reheat it and add the shrimp just before serving.

2 cups (300 g) uncooked jasmine rice (see headnote)

1 green (unripe) pineapple (see Notes), peeled

2 medium white onions, diced

2 medium underripe or green tomatoes, diced

Juice of 1 lemon (optional)

⅓ cup (80 ml) white sugarcane vinegar (see Key Ingredients, page 42)

¼ cup (60 ml) fish sauce, plus more if needed

1 pound (455 g) Chinese long or green beans, cut into 1-inch (2.5 cm) pieces

1 teaspoon freshly ground black pepper

1 pound (455 g) raw medium head-on shrimp, peeled (heads left on) and deveined

Put the rice in a bowl. Cover the rice with 8 cups (2 L) water and use your clean fingers to massage the rice grains in the water, rubbing them between your fingers for a second or two until you have washed all the grains. Reserve the rice-washing water. You can prepare the rice as per the instructions on page 40 to serve with the soup or save it for another use.

Core the pineapple with a sharp knife, coarsely chop the core, and wrap it in cheesecloth. Tie the cheesecloth tightly shut with butcher's twine. Cube the rest of the pineapple and set both aside.

In a large pot, combine the rice-washing water, onions, tomatoes, pineapple core in cheesecloth, and cubed pineapple. Bring to a boil over high heat, then reduce the heat until the mixture is at a simmer. Cook for 45 minutes, then taste the soup for sourness.

If it's not sour enough for your liking, whisk in the lemon juice (if using), the vinegar, and the fish sauce. Add the beans and simmer for 5 minutes more, or until the beans are almost fully tender.

Discard the pineapple core in the cheesecloth and season the broth with the pepper.

Add the shrimp and cook for 5 to 6 minutes, until the shrimp are pink and have started to curl up.

Taste the soup and add more lemon juice or fish sauce, if desired.

Serve immediately, with rice, if desired.

In the province of Bicol, there is a version of sinigang made with calamansi juice called *cocido*, and if you have calamansi juice on hand—fresh or frozen—you can add a little of it to any of the sinigang recipes for a special sweet-tartness. Note that cocido is also the name used for a version of *bulalo* or *nilaga* (page 96) made with additional vegetables and a tomato-eggplant sauce on the side.

BINAKOL

Chicken Soup with Coconut Water

THE USES FOR COCONUT GO FAR beyond the usual suspects of desserts with toasted coconut flakes or coconut milk. This soup is made with both coconut water and strands of young coconut meat instead of noodles, both of which add a slightly sweet backbone and depth to the light broth. Be sure to use a light chicken stock or even just water for the base—a roasted stock would be too rich. Use good-quality coconut water, and if you have access to water from a fresh coconut, by all means, use it. **SERVES 4 TO 6**

Note: Pepper leaves— the not-hot leaves from the hot pepper or chile plant—are used in many Filipino soups, and they're sold frozen in most Asian supermarkets. They are small, roundish leaves that dot a clear broth like confetti. To use them, let them defrost slowly in the refrigerator overnight. The next day, pour off any liquid that accumulates (8 ounces/225 g frozen leaves usually equals about ½ cup/90 g thawed). You can also substitute your own pepper leaves or any tender green, like spinach; just blanch or lightly cook the fresh greens first, pour off any liquid, and measure out ½ cup (90 g).

¼ cup (60 ml) vegetable oil

3 lemongrass stalks, thinly sliced

2 thumb-size pieces fresh ginger, peeled and cut into matchsticks

1 medium white onion, diced

5 garlic cloves, smashed with the side of a knife

1 (3- to 4-pound/1.4 to 1.8 kg) whole chicken, cut into serving pieces

6 cups (1.4 L) chicken stock or water

2 cups (480 ml) unsweetened coconut water

1½ cups (120 g) fresh young coconut meat (see Key Ingredients, page 37), drained and cut into thin strips

2 chayote (see Notes, page 130), peeled, seeded, and cut into small dice (optional)

½ cup (90 g) thawed pepper leaves (see Note)

1 small green papaya (see Key Ingredients, page 38), peeled and cut into matchsticks

Fish sauce

Freshly ground black pepper

In a medium saucepan, heat the vegetable oil over medium-low heat. Add the lemongrass, ginger, and onion and cook, stirring occasionally, for 3 minutes, or until they become translucent and aromatic; be careful not to let them brown.

Add the garlic and cook for 1 minute more, or until the garlic has softened—again, be careful not to let it brown.

Add the chicken, stock, and coconut water and bring to a boil. Reduce the heat to low and simmer for 30 to 45 minutes, until the chicken is fork-tender.

Add the coconut meat and the chayote (if using) and simmer for 5 minutes, then add the pepper leaves and almost all the papaya (save a few shreds to garnish each bowl of soup).

Simmer for 5 minutes more, then taste and season with fish sauce and black pepper.

Serve immediately, with the reserved shreds of green papaya on top and more fish sauce on the side.

COCONUT COUNTRY

Coconut palms, once an important natural resource to Filipinos, were sold for profit, yes, but the fruits also provided food, water, and oil; the husks were used for fuel; and the leaves dried and used to make hats, furniture, and housing. In the 1800s, the crop made many people wealthy, and could support plantations the size of small towns. One that still exists is Villa Escudero, a family-owned nineteenth-century coconut plantation turned time machine about two hours south of Manila. The 2,000-acre property in the province of Laguna is now a sprawling resort, with a restaurant serving regional recipes and an important museum of Filipino cultural heritage. The family still runs and operates the plantation, with Don Conrado Escudero at the helm. It purposefully still offers a glimpse into the glorious past of coconut's reign as provider of good fortune and riches for the *haciendero*s, a derivative of the Spanish word *hacienda* that essentially means "the people who owned the land."

SUAM NA TULYA AT MAIS

Corn and Clam Soup

SUAM IS A LIGHT, GINGER-FLAVORED, easy-to-make broth with delicate seafood and vegetables. This version uses Manila clams and corn, whose natural sweetness complements the ginger. If you want to make a heartier version, add a little bit of coconut milk or a few wedges of golden pumpkin to the broth. **SERVES 4 TO 6**

Note: To clean the clams, discard any that are cracked or that are open and don't close when you tap them. Put them in a bowl, cover them with cold water, and soak for at least 20 minutes and up to 1 hour to encourage them to spit out any sand inside their shells. One by one, lift the clams from the sandy water and place them in a colander, then scrub them under cool running water. Use right away.

2 tablespoons vegetable oil

1 medium white onion, quartered

2 thumb-size pieces fresh ginger, peeled and cut into matchsticks

4 cups (1 L) fish stock (recipe follows)

1 pound (455 g) manila clams, soaked and cleaned (see Note)

1 cup (145 g) fresh corn kernels

1 bunch fresh spinach, washed and tough stems removed

Kosher salt and freshly ground black pepper

In a stockpot or large saucepan, heat the vegetable oil over medium heat. Add the onion and ginger and cook, stirring occasionally, until they are soft and translucent, 4 to 6 minutes. Do not let them brown.

Add the stock and bring to a boil. Add the clams and cook for 3 to 5 minutes, then reduce the heat to medium and discard any clams that haven't opened. Add the corn and spinach and cook just until the spinach has wilted.

Taste, season with salt and pepper, and serve immediately.

Years ago, if you drove through farm country in the Philippines, you'd see farms planted with sugarcane and rice, but today you're likely to see corn. Yet this soup (and *bulalo*—see page 96) is one of a few Filipino recipes that actually feature the kernels. Most of the crop is destined for commercial uses like animal feed or by-products like corn syrup, starch, or fuel.

FISH STOCK

For the fish bones, ask your fishmonger for the carcasses left over from filleting fish. You don't want to use heads for this recipe. Fish stock can be frozen for up to 3 months, and this recipe can be scaled up or down as needed. **MAKES ABOUT 12 CUPS (3 L)**

1 teaspoon kosher salt

4 pounds (1.8 kg) fish bones (not heads)

2 cups (480 ml) dry white wine, such as Sauvignon Blanc or Chardonnay

2 yellow or white onions, quartered

2 large carrots, coarsely chopped

2 bird's-eye chiles (see Key Ingredients, page 37)

6 bay leaves

2 tablespoons whole black peppercorns

Stems from 1 bunch cilantro

Fill a stockpot or large saucepan with cold water and add the salt. Soak the fish bones in the salted water for 10 minutes.

Drain off the water, keeping the bones in the pot, and add the wine, onions, carrots, chiles, bay leaves, peppercorns, and cilantro stems. Add 1 gallon (4 L) cold water, or enough to cover the bones, and bring to a boil. Immediately reduce the heat to medium and simmer for 45 minutes.

Strain the stock through a fine-mesh sieve and discard the solids. Store the stock in airtight containers in the refrigerator for up to 1 week or in the freezer for up to 3 months.

BULALO
Bone Marrow Soup

BULALO IS A RUSTIC SOUP with flecks of bone marrow and brawny beef shank bones swimming in a deceptively light but heartily satisfying and deeply flavored broth. The components are remarkably pared down, and the quality of ingredients and subtle technique are what make this dish magnificent. Bulalo is made from flavorful bones (cows are usually grass-fed in the Philippines), plus onions, peppercorns, potatoes, and other vegetables. Time is the most crucial element; slow cooking allows the broth to pull all the flavor from the bones. Bulalo is a specialty in the region of Cavite south of Manila near Taal Lake, whose steep bluffs are surrounded by some of the best land for raising beef cattle. The area is home to many *bulalohan*, little eateries serving bulalo. *Sawsawan* is a must on the table to season the soup to your liking—for this dish, try fish sauce, chopped chiles, and calamansi juice or vinegar. **SERVES 8 TO 10**

When you add corn and cabbage to the soup, as we do, bulalo is sometimes called *nilaga*, which is also the Tagalog term for "boiled." Some people also add bananas or plantains. Another common variation is *kansi*, a blend of bulalo and *sinigang* soured with a tart Filipino fruit called *batwan*.

5 pounds (2.3 kg) beef shanks, preferably grass-fed

Kosher salt and freshly ground black pepper

¼ cup (70 g) whole black peppercorns

½ cup (75 g) whole garlic cloves (about 10), smashed with the side of a knife

4 bay leaves

2 medium white onions, thinly sliced

1 bunch scallions, thinly sliced

2 cups (280 g) coarsely chopped peeled potatoes

¼ pound (115 g) napa cabbage, thickly sliced

1 ear fresh corn, cut crosswise into 1-inch-long (2.5 cm) pieces

Fish sauce

Sawsawan (see page 34), for serving

In a large stockpot, bring 1 gallon (4 L) water to a boil.

Season the beef shanks liberally with salt and pepper. Add them to the boiling water and let the water come back to a boil. Reduce the heat to medium-low so the water simmers. Skim off any impurities from the top.

Add the peppercorns, garlic, bay leaves, and onions and cook the beef shanks for 2½ to 3½ hours, until the marrow is tender. Keep an eye on the pot: Add water as needed to keep the ingredients just covered.

Add the scallions, potatoes, cabbage, and corn and cook for 10 minutes more, or until the potatoes are cooked through. Taste and season with fish sauce.

Serve in deep bowls with sawsawan alongside, making sure each serving has some beef, onions, potato, cabbage, and corn.

LINAGPANG NA ISDA
Grilled Fish Soup

WE WERE INTRODUCED TO THIS SOUP by a Visayan hotel owner and restaurateur named Pepot, who, at fifty, claims he owes his youthful good looks (we guessed he was half his age) to frequent servings of this soup. Maybe it will become your personal fountain of youth, too. Fresh fish is grilled over a blazing-hot fire, then plunged into a broth laced with tomatoes, chiles, ginger, and a little evaporated milk for creaminess and sweetness. The char from the fish flavors the broth, giving it smokiness and substance and underscoring the nuance of technique and innovation in Filipino cooking. **SERVES 4 TO 6**

1 pint (550 g) cherry tomatoes, halved

1 white onion, sliced

2 bird's-eye chiles (see Key Ingredients, page 37)

Vegetable oil

Kosher salt and freshly ground black pepper

1 tablespoon bagoong (fermented seafood paste; see Key Ingredients, page 35)

1½ tablespoons minced fresh ginger

¾ pound (340 g) skin-on red snapper fillet

3 tablespoons evaporated milk

1½ teaspoons fish sauce

Note: If you have access to a wood- or charcoal-fired grill, use it to cook the snapper. The soup will get true smokiness, which takes the dish to the next level.

Heat a cast-iron skillet over high heat.

In a bowl, toss the cherry tomatoes, onion, and chiles in 1 tablespoon vegetable oil. Season with salt and pepper. Place the mixture in the skillet and cook, stirring often, until the vegetables are charred on all sides, 7 to 10 minutes. Set aside.

In the same pan, heat 1 tablespoon vegetable oil over medium-high heat. Add the bagoong and cook, stirring continuously, for 3 minutes. Set aside.

In a large saucepan or stockpot, combine 6 cups (1.4 L) water, 1 teaspoon pepper, the ginger, and the fried bagoong and bring to a boil. Stir in the charred vegetables and reduce the heat to medium-low. Simmer for 20 to 30 minutes, while you cook the fish.

Wipe out the skillet and set it over high heat. Brush the red snapper on both sides with vegetable oil so it doesn't stick while cooking and place it in the hot pan, skin-side up. Sear or grill for 5 minutes, or until it is charred on one side. Flip and cook it skin-side down just until the skin begins to crisp and curl.

Add the charred fish, evaporated milk, and fish sauce to the pot and simmer for 20 minutes more, or until you can taste the smoky fish in the broth.

Taste, season with salt and pepper, and serve right away.

SINAMPALUKANG MANOK
Tamarind Chicken Stew

YOU'LL RETURN TO THIS DISH AGAIN and again, thanks to the memorable combination of tomato, sour-sweet tamarind, and lemongrass slowly simmered together for several hours. It is technically a thicker version of the *sinagang*s on the previous pages, one where the sour comes from tamarind. Both the lemongrass and the onion are thinly sliced rather than minced, adding substance and body to the stew. We first tasted this at the family home of our friend Cocoy, the chef of Villa Escudero (see page 93), who invited us to dinner at his parents' house on former farmland in the northwestern province of Isabela. Some cooks, like Cocoy's father, keep a little more liquid in the bottom of the pot, but in this recipe we cook the stew down until the liquid is a thick, wonderfully fragrant sauce. **SERVES 4 TO 6**

3 tablespoons vegetable oil

½ large white onion, thinly sliced

3 medium tomatoes, cut into eighths

2 pounds (910 g) bone-in, skin-on chicken legs or thighs

2 cups (480 ml) chicken stock (see page 179)

1 cup (240 ml) Tamarind Liquor (recipe follows), plus more if needed

1 large lemongrass stalk, very thinly sliced

2 long green chiles (see Key Ingredients, page 37; optional)

1 tablespoon fish sauce, plus more if needed

4 to 6 cups (800 g to 1.2 kg) cooked white rice (see page 40), for serving

Sawsawan (see page 34), for serving

In a Dutch oven, heat the vegetable oil over medium heat. Add the onion and cook, stirring occasionally, until soft and translucent, about 10 minutes.

Stir in the tomatoes and cook for 10 to 15 minutes, until they are soft and have begun to break down.

Add the chicken pieces, skin-side down—they can overlap a little, if need be—and then add the stock, tamarind liquor, and lemongrass. Raise the heat to medium-high, bring the liquid to a high simmer, and cook for a minute or two.

Add the whole chiles (if using) and stir in the fish sauce. Cover the pan tightly, reduce the heat so the stew is at a low simmer, and cook for 30 minutes. Check the pot from time to time to make sure the stew is still at a low simmer and adjust the heat as necessary.)

After 30 minutes, remove the cover and increase the heat to medium-high to bring the stew to a high simmer. Cook for 10 minutes more, or until the chicken is tender and cooked through.

Taste and season with more fish sauce or tamarind liquor as desired.

Serve hot, with rice and sawsawan.

TAMARIND LIQUOR

Some recipes for this dish call for fresh tamarind leaves, which you can't easily find in the United States. Instead you can make a tamarind liquor using water and the more easily sourced dried seed pods or tamarind paste, both of which are found in Asian, Mexican, Indian, and Caribbean food markets, and occasionally in ordinary grocery stores. Most pastes come in a block with some seeds still inside, though some more expensive jarred versions are seedless. You can use whichever version you find. **MAKES ABOUT 2 CUPS (475 ML)**

**1 pound (455 g) dried tamarind pods,
½ cup (120 ml) tamarind paste with
seeds, or ⅓ cup (80 ml) tamarind
paste without seeds**

In a small pot, cover the tamarind with 2 cups (½ L) water and bring to a boil. Lower the heat and let the tamarind simmer for 5 minutes. Turn off the heat, cover the pot, and let the mixture steep for 1 hour.

Strain the liquid through a fine-mesh sieve into a large bowl. Use a wooden spoon or a spatula to press as much pulp as you can into the bowl. Discard the solids.

Use a fork to mash the pulp into the liquid until it is combined. This is the tamarind liquor. Store in an airtight container in the refrigerator, where it will keep for at least 2 weeks.

MONGGO GUISADO
Stewed Mung Beans

THIS WONDERFUL FILIPINO STEW is made with confetti-size mung beans, or *monggo*. They are soaked first to soften them, then gently stewed with onions and garlic. The flavor of mung beans is unique—vegetal and creamy. Some cooks prefer to season monggo with pork belly; some cooks prefer shrimp; others, like us, use both. To boost the creaminess of the stew, puree half the beans, then add them back to the pot. **SERVES 4 TO 6**

Note: This recipe requires the mung beans to soak overnight, so plan ahead. Sort through the beans, discarding discolored or shriveled beans and any grit or dirt. Rinse the beans under cold running water, then transfer the beans to a bowl, add enough water to cover, and soak overnight in a cool place or in the refrigerator.

2 tablespoons vegetable oil

¼ cup (30 g) diced onion

2 teaspoons minced garlic

1 tablespoon minced fresh ginger

1 cup (135 g) diced pork belly

1 medium ripe tomato, diced

2 cups (390 g) mung beans, soaked overnight (see Note)

¼ pound (115 g) raw medium shrimp, peeled and deveined

Kosher salt and freshly ground black pepper

4 to 6 cups (800 g to 1.2 kg) cooked white rice (see page 40), for serving

½ cup (30 g) thinly sliced scallions, for garnish

Bagoong Bagna Cauda (recipe follows; optional)

In a large saucepan, heat the vegetable oil over medium heat. Add the onion, garlic, and ginger and cook, stirring occasionally, until they are soft and translucent, 4 to 6 minutes. Add the pork belly and tomato and cook, stirring occasionally, until the tomato is soft, 7 to 10 minutes.

Drain the mung beans and add them to the pot with 6 cups (1.4 L) water. Bring the water to a boil, then reduce the heat so everything cooks at a simmer. Cook for 45 to 50 minutes, until the beans are soft and cooked through. You want the beans to thicken into stew but not get totally dry; add a little more water as the beans cook, if needed.

When the mung beans are tender—taste one or two to see—transfer half of them from the pot to a blender or food processor. Puree the beans until smooth (be careful, as they are hot) and return them to the pot.

Add water as needed until the mixture has a thick, stew-like consistency. (If the beans are too wet, cook them over medium-high heat until the liquid reduces a bit.)

> recipe continues →

Add the shrimp and cook just until they turn pink and begin to curl, about 5 minutes. Season with salt and pepper.

Serve hot with rice, and garnish each bowl with scallions and Bagoong Bagna Cauda and roasted vegetables, if desired.

BAGOONG BAGNA CAUDA

Remix the classic mung bean stew by pairing it with a very modern garnish of charred carrots and daikon radish bathed in a Filipino version of the Italian anchovy dip called *bagna cauda*. (It uses *bagoong balayan*, or anchovy bagoong, in addition to anchovies.) It's a Filipino twist on tradition. **MAKES ABOUT 2 CUPS (480 ML)**

2 cups (480 ml) vegetable oil

1 cup (145 g) garlic cloves

1 (2-ounce/56 g) tin anchovy fillets in oil (reserve the oil)

1 tablespoon bagoong balayan (see Key Ingredients, page 35)

1 daikon radish, peeled and cut into batons

1 carrot, peeled cut into batons

In a small saucepan, combine the oil and garlic cloves. Cook over medium heat for 30 minutes, or until the garlic turns light brown.

Use a slotted spoon to transfer the garlic to a food processor; set the oil aside. Add the anchovies, the oil from the anchovy tin, and the bagoong to the food processor and puree until smooth. Set aside. (Both the garlic-infused oil and the pureed garlic mixture will keep in separate airtight containers in the refrigerator for up to 1 week.)

In a medium skillet, heat 1 tablespoon of the reserved garlic oil over medium-high heat. Add the daikon and carrot and cook, stirring often, until lightly browned and tender, 7 to 10 minutes.

Stir in 1 tablespoon of the pureed garlic mixture and toss to coat the vegetables. (The vegetables will keep in a covered container in the refrigerator for 2 to 3 days; gently warm them before eating.) Use the vegetables and the reserved oil as a garnish for Monggo Guisado. Any leftover oil and garlic puree can be eaten on top of toast, crackers, or even hot rice.

AMALIGN
special
PINANGAT
INULUKAN
BICOL EXPRESS
P#09168432

KBL (KADYOS, BABOY, AT LANGKA)

Pigeon Peas, Pork, and Jackfruit Stew

A DISH KNOWN ONLY by its initials is pretty intriguing, and KBL, which stands for *kadyos* (pigeon peas), *baboy* (pork), and *langka* (green or unripe jackfruit), is just that. Pigeon peas are small purplish-black or green legumes, a little like a black-eyed pea, and are a great source of protein, inexpensive, and a delicious way to extend a dish. (They also tend to color the broth of KBL a light gray-purple.) Green or unripe jackfruit is similar in texture and flavor to an artichoke heart, minus the fibrous leaves. **SERVES 4 TO 6**

Notes: Chinese fermented black beans are found in any Asian grocery and can be found online as well (see Resources, page 342).

The bushy plant called *mulunggay* is known in other parts of the world as *moringa*, horseradish tree, or drumstick tree. The leaves are usually sold frozen in most Southeast Asian and Indian supermarkets, often labeled as horseradish leaves. For this dish, you want to use frozen if possible. Let them defrost slowly in the refrigerator overnight and pour off any liquid that accumulates. If using dried leaves, rehydrate them in hot water, then drain. Otherwise, substitute any tender green, like spinach; just blanch or lightly cook the fresh greens, pour off any accumulated liquid, and measure out 1 cup (180 g).

6 cups (1.4 L) pork stock (recipe follows)

2 pounds (910 g) Lechon Kawali (page 261) or fried pork belly, skin removed

1 medium onion, quartered

1 cup (185 g) cooked or canned pigeon peas

2 tablespoons fermented black beans (see Notes)

2 cups (300 g) cubed canned green (unripe) jackfruit (see Key Ingredients, page 38)

1½ tablespoons Tamarind Liquor (see page 101)

Kosher salt and freshly ground black pepper

1 cup (180 g) thawed mulunggay leaves (see Notes)

In a large saucepan, bring the stock to a boil over high heat. Add the lechon kawali and the onion and cook until the meat is tender, about 20 minutes.

Add the pigeon peas and fermented black beans, and cook at a low boil for 10 minutes.

Stir in the jackfruit and tamarind liquor. Season with salt and pepper, cover the pot, and reduce the heat so the liquid is at a simmer. Cook for 15 minutes more, then remove the cover and stir in the mulunggay leaves. Cook for a minute or two, or until the leaves have cooked through. Taste and add more salt and pepper as needed.

Serve hot.

PORK STOCK

This slowly simmered pork stock takes half a day to cook, but the results are rich and flavorful. The recipe can be doubled if you want to keep a stash in your freezer. **MAKES 8 CUPS (1.9 L)**

1 pound (455 g) pork neck bones (see Note)

1 white onion, quartered

1 carrot, quartered

2 celery stalks, cut into thirds

7 whole black peppercorns

Stems from half a bunch cilantro

5 garlic cloves

Note: You can get pork neck bones from a butcher or might be able to find them in some mainstream supermarkets, though you may have to order them in advance.

Put the neck bones, onion, carrot, celery, peppercorns, cilantro stems, and garlic in a large stockpot and fill the pot with 5 quarts (5 L) water. Bring the water to a boil over high heat; use a slotted spoon to skim off and discard any foam and impurities that rise to the top.

Reduce the heat to medium-low and simmer the stock for at least 4 hours and up to 6 hours.

Strain the stock through a fine-mesh sieve, discarding the solids, and store in airtight containers in the refrigerator for up to 1 week or in the freezer for 2 to 3 months.

There are actually two kinds of KBL: The other version is a condiment made of *kamatis* (tomatoes), *bagoong* (fish paste), and *lasuna* (spring onion).

TINOLA

Ginger-Chicken Soup with Pepper Leaves

EVERY HOUSEHOLD has its go-to remedies for when a family member gets sick. In my house, they include Katinko ointment, Vicks VapoRub, and *luya*, or ginger. We eat the ginger in the form of this chicken soup. But with its warm, spicy intensity of ginger, *tinola* is not your run-of-the-mill chicken soup. Stick with fresh ginger to make this dish. It provides relief from nausea or muscle pain, and the pepper leaves, from the hot chile plant, are known for their anti-inflammatory and antiaging properties. Every spoonful of tinola is the best-tasting medicine. **SERVES 4 TO 6**

Note: Use a lighter, not-too-salty chicken stock here (not the rich roasted stock on page 179). You can use your own stock or a store-bought, preferably low-sodium, variety.

2 tablespoons vegetable oil

5 garlic cloves, smashed with the side of a knife

2 (2-inch/5 cm) pieces fresh ginger, peeled and cut into matchsticks

1 small red onion, halved and thinly sliced

8 cups (2 L) chicken stock (see Note)

2 pounds (910 g) skin-on, bone-in chicken legs, wings, or thighs, cut into pieces

1 chayote (see Notes, page 130), peeled, seeded, and cubed

½ cup (90 g) thawed pepper leaves (see Note, page 90)

Fish sauce

In a stockpot, heat the vegetable oil over medium-high heat. Add the garlic, ginger, and onion and cook, stirring often, until they have just started to soften, about 7 minutes.

Add the stock and the chicken and bring to a boil. Reduce the heat to medium and simmer for 45 minutes, or until the chicken starts to fall off the bone.

Add the chayote and cook until it is just tender, about 10 minutes. Add the pepper leaves and cook until heated through, 1 to 2 minutes.

Season with fish sauce to taste and serve hot.

SALADS AND VEGETABLES

OH MY, GULAY

VEGETABLES OFTEN PLAY A SUPPORTING ROLE in home-cooked meals at the Filipino table. Fresh mustard greens, eggplant, okra, and *ampalaya*, or bitter melon, always filled the fridge when I was growing up. We would eat them simply boiled with a bit of *bagoong* for dipping or a dash of *patis*. Vegetables are also always on the table in the form of condiments or side dishes like a tart papaya pickle (page 118) or the classic tomato-onion salad (page 123), meant to accent a meal rather than star in one.

There is a newfound interest in salads made with our tart fruits and crunchy roots, or our deeply flavored vegetable stews built on bitter greens or pumpkin, flavored with some fish or meat. If you visit any Filipino market, you'll see a true rainbow of *gulay*—veggies—including tangles of dark leafy greens, bumpy gourds, and coils of long green beans, not to mention melons, citrus, mango, papaya, and countless other tropical fruits. In other words, we have so much to work with.

Outside of the home, our most famous recipes—and our most popular restaurants—tend to focus on the hearty and the meaty. One reason may be that historically, meat was seen as a sign of wealth and prosperity, so fruits and vegetables took a backseat. Though these meat-free or meat- and seafood-accented dishes aren't necessarily served on their own traditionally, vegetable-driven dishes like the Ilokano clay pot braise called *pinakbet* (page 128); *laing* (page 143), a lush dish of greens slow-cooked with coconut milk, ginger, garlic, and chiles; and charred eggplants whipped until smooth with tomato and scrambled eggs (page 127) make wonderful modern vegetable-centric meals, especially when served with rice.

CONUT & FRESH BUKO   STALL # 1

Though there are modern supermarkets in the Philippines, there's really nothing like an old-school *palengke*, or public market. These sprawling, fantastically chaotic, mainly open-air food meccas are where you go to shop for still-wriggling seafood, artisanal cheeses from carabao milk, meats cut to order, fresh coconut milk, a minimum of twenty different kinds of rice, a rainbow of fresh vegetables, and nearly anything else you need. There are even cafeterias, or *karinderia*s, within these markets, serving up some of the most soul-satisfying meals you'll find in the country.

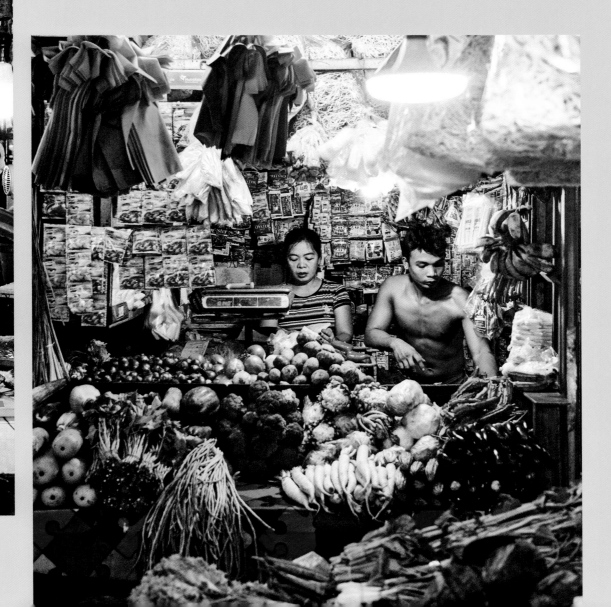

ATSARA
Pickled Vegetables

ATSARA, ALSO KNOWN AS *ATCHARA*, is a combination of shredded green papaya, carrots, bell peppers, and radishes pickled in a sweet and slightly spicy vinegar brine. It's simple to make and easy to store, and it brings a vibrancy to stews, grilled meats, or fried fish. Atsara is versatile enough to add to sandwiches, eat with pork chops, top a burger, or use anywhere else you'd normally have a slaw or a tart and tangy pickle. And if you don't like things spicy, just omit the chile or use less of it. **MAKES ABOUT 1 QUART (1 L)**

FOR THE VEGETABLES

2 cups (340 g) shredded green (unripe) papaya

1 cup (170 g) shredded daikon radish

1 medium red bell pepper, cut into long matchsticks

1 medium green bell pepper, cut into long matchsticks

2 large carrots, peeled and cut into long matchsticks

2 teaspoons kosher salt

FOR THE BRINE

2 cups (480 ml) distilled white vinegar

1½ cups (300 g) sugar

1 tablespoon minced fresh ginger

1 teaspoon kosher salt

1 garlic clove, minced

1 small bird's-eye chile (see Key Ingredients, page 37), minced

¼ cup (35 g) raisins (optional)

Make the vegetables: Spread the papaya, daikon, bell peppers, and carrots out on a baking sheet. Sprinkle them with the salt and let them sit for 1 hour.

Meanwhile, make the brine: In a medium saucepan, bring the vinegar and sugar to a boil, stirring until the sugar has dissolved. Reduce the heat to medium, then add the ginger, salt, garlic, and chile and simmer for 5 minutes.

Put the salted vegetables in cheesecloth or several layers of heavy-duty paper towels and squeeze out as much of the liquid as you can into a bowl or the sink.

Pack the drained vegetables into a 1-quart (1 L) glass canning jar and add the raisins (if using). Pour in the brine, top with the lid, and store in the refrigerator. These are ready to eat immediately, but the flavor and texture will improve after 24 hours in the fridge, and will get even better over time. They will keep in the fridge for several weeks.

BURONG MUSTASA GUISADO

Sautéed Preserved Mustard Greens

THE TART, SLIGHTLY BITTER FERMENTED GREENS called *burong mustasa* are often served alone as a room-temperature appetizer or side dish, especially with grilled or fried fish, and they're even better in a very quick sauté with onion, garlic, and vinegar. The recipe for the pickled greens is nearly as easy, if you follow two important steps. First, use rice-washing water, which has beneficial bacteria that help jump-start fermentation. Second, pay attention to the temperature when you let the greens rest in a cool, dark place during the weeklong fermentation stage. **MAKES ABOUT TWO 1-PINT JARS (475 ML)**

Note: This recipe requires glass canning jars and at least 5 days of fermentation time. To sterilize the jars and lids, use tongs to place them in a pot of boiling water, boil for 10 minutes, then transfer them to a clean wire rack to dry completely.

FOR THE PICKLED GREENS

2 pounds (900 g) mustard greens

3 tablespoons kosher salt

2 to 3 cups (480 to 720 ml) rice-washing water (see page 86)

FOR THE GUISADO

1 tablespoon vegetable oil

2 tablespoons minced red onion

1 tablespoon minced garlic

2 teaspoons fish sauce

2 teaspoons white sugarcane vinegar (see Key Ingredients, page 42)

Kosher salt and freshly ground black pepper

Make the pickled greens: Remove any thick stems from the mustard greens. Wash the leaves in several changes of water, spread them over clean kitchen towels, and let dry completely.

Cut the greens into 3-inch-long (7.5 cm) strips and place them in a large bowl. Sprinkle with the salt and toss with clean hands, squeezing the greens with your hands to crush and bruise the leaves. Let the greens sit while you heat the rice water.

In a medium saucepan, heat the rice-washing water over medium heat, watching the pot, until it is almost at a full boil. Remove the pot from the heat and let the rice water cool until it is still warm, but not hot.

While the rice water cools, drain off any water that has accumulated in the bottom of the bowl of greens. Fill two 1-pint large sterilized jars (see Note) with the greens, making sure not to pack them in too tightly. Cover the leaves

with the warm rice water, leaving ½ to 1 inch (1.5 to 2.5 cm) of space between the leaves and the lid.

Seal the jar and set it aside in a cool, dark place for 5 to 7 days (see box), or until the leaves taste pickled and the rice water is sour. At this point, the pickled greens can be eaten right away or stored in the refrigerator for up to several weeks after opening.

Make the guisado: In a small skillet, heat the vegetable oil over medium heat. Add the onion and garlic and cook, stirring often, until the onion is translucent and the garlic is lightly browned, about 5 minutes.

Add the pickled greens, the fish sauce, and the vinegar and stir until everything is combined. Cook the guisado for another minute or two, then season with salt and pepper and serve.

> The ideal temperature for fermentation is between 50°F and 75°F (11°C and 25°C). Too hot, and the mustasa will spoil before it successfully ferments; too cold, and the fermentation process can take a very long time.

CLASSIC ENSALADA
Salted Egg Salad

A SIMPLE SALAD is eaten at breakfast, lunch, and dinner alongside grilled chicken, adobo, or fried eggs and rice. Our salad is used more like a relish or condiment; it adds texture and seasoning to the main meal. You can serve the salad on a platter with the components separate and still intact, so guests can mix and toss the ingredients together on their plates. **SERVES 6 TO 8**

1 red onion, quartered and thinly sliced

4 salted eggs (see Key Ingredients, page 41), quartered

1 (10-ounce/285 g) container cherry tomatoes, halved

¼ cup (10 g) finely sliced cilantro leaves

3 tablespoons fish sauce, plus more as desired

1 to 2 lemons, quartered

Prepare the salad on a serving platter: Pile the sliced onion on one third of the platter, the eggs in the middle, and the tomatoes on the final third. Sprinkle the cilantro over the tomatoes.

Sprinkle the fish sauce over the top and squeeze over the juice of one of the lemon quarters. Serve the platter with more fish sauce and the remaining lemon quarters on the side. You and your guests can mix, toss, and season the salad with lemon and fish sauce as you like.

Cucumber–Tomato Relish

My father has been making this fast, easy, delicious relish for a long time, and we often serve it alongside an adobo or whole fried fish (and countless other dishes) as a variation on Classic Ensalada. **SERVES 4**

1 cucumber, quartered, seeded, and thinly sliced

1 large tomato, diced, or 1 cup (145 g) cherry tomatoes, halved

½ cup (20 g) fresh cilantro leaves, minced

½ cup (55 g) diced red onion

1 tablespoon fish sauce

Juice of 1 lemon

In a bowl, combine the cucumber, tomato, cilantro, onion, fish sauce, and lemon juice. Serve right away.

PUQUI-PUQUI
Charred Eggplant with Eggs and Tomatoes

THIS SILKY, SMOKY EGGPLANT SPREAD hails from the Ilocos Norte region in Northern Luzon. Eggplants are charred until soft and supple and then blended with tomatoes, onions, and eggs. Though it would be great eaten as a dip with crackers or crudités, in the Philippines, *puqui-puqui* is usually served as a vegetable side dish, sometimes paired with crisp raw bitter greens or grilled shrimp and a bit of the fermented seafood paste called *bagoong isda*. **SERVES 4 TO 6**

3 Asian eggplants

2 tablespoons vegetable oil

¼ cup (30 g) diced red onion

¼ cup (45 g) chopped tomato

1 large egg

Kosher salt and freshly ground black pepper

Bagoong isda (see Key Ingredients, page 35), for serving

Preheat the broiler.

Lay the eggplants in a single layer on a baking sheet and roast, flipping them once or twice, until they are blackened on all sides, about 15 minutes. (If you have a gas stove, you could also do this by holding the eggplants with tongs over a burner on medium-high heat, turning them carefully so they blacken on all sides.)

Place the eggplants in a pot with a lid or in a bowl and cover with plastic wrap. Set aside for at least 10 minutes to steam (this makes the skin easier to peel). Let them cool until you can easily handle them.

Scoop the eggplant flesh out of the skins into a blender or food processor and discard the skins. Puree the flesh until smooth. Transfer it to a small bowl.

In a small skillet, heat the vegetable oil over medium heat. Add the onion and cook, stirring often, until soft and translucent, 5 to 7 minutes. Add the tomato and cook for 3 minutes.

Whisk the egg into the eggplant puree until it is well incorporated. Add it to the skillet and cook, stirring almost continuously, until everything comes together and is cooked through and smooth. Season with salt and pepper and serve with a side of bagoong isda.

In Tagalog, *puqui-puqui* is also a slang word for a female body part.

PINAKBET TAGALOG
Simmered Vegetables with Shrimp Paste

PINAKBET IS AN ICONIC VEGETABLE DISH that was originally cooked in a traditional clay pot called a *palayok* over an open fire. Long beans, eggplant, and okra were simmered together in the pot with a healthy dollop of the fermented seafood paste called *bagoong*. Occasionally the pot would be shaken so that everything mixed together, but the vegetables were left to cook until they shriveled up (*pinakbet* means "shrivel"). We call this version Pinakbet Tagalog because we make it with bright pink *bagoong alamang*, made only with fermented shrimp, rather than *bagoong isda*, which is made from fish and is typical of pinakbet from the Ilocos region. It's funky, bitter, salty, slightly sweet, and uniquely Filipino. **SERVES 4 TO 6**

2 tablespoons vegetable oil

4 garlic cloves, minced

2 small tomatoes, diced

¼ cup (60 ml) bagoong alamang (see Key Ingredients, page 35)

½ pound (225 g) kabocha or acorn squash, peeled, seeded, and cut into 2-inch (5 cm) chunks

1 Asian eggplant, cut into 2-inch (5 cm) chunks

¼ cup (30 g) seeded bitter melon (see Note, page 70), cut into 2-inch (5 cm) half-moons

⅓ cup (30 g) Chinese long beans or green beans, cut into 2-inch (5 cm) pieces

⅓ cup (35 g) whole okra

Kosher salt and freshly ground black pepper

4 to 6 cups (800 g to 1.2 kg) cooked white rice (see page 40; optional)

In a large saucepan, heat the vegetable oil over medium heat. Add the garlic and cook, stirring often, until it is just beginning to brown, about 3 minutes.

Add the tomatoes and cook, stirring occasionally, until they are very soft and falling apart, about 10 minutes.

Stir in the bagoong and reduce the heat to medium-low. Add the vegetables in layers: the squash, the eggplant, the bitter melon, the beans, and then the okra. Cover the pot tightly and cook for about 6 minutes, or until the vegetables are tender.

Mix the vegetables together in the pot and season with salt and pepper.

Serve hot, with rice, if desired.

Ilocos Norte, the region from which pinakbet originates, is Filipino farm country; it's a place where vegetables have long been revered as the main attraction. Thus meat and seafood in this region are used more like a flavoring in dishes rather than a foundation. Some recipes for pinakbet call for *bagnet* or fried pork belly. The *silong* (pictured here) is a traditional rattan *palayak* (clay pot) holder. It's used to remove a hot pot from the cooking fire.

GINISANG SAYOTE

Sautéed Chayote

Notes: Chayote are increasingly found in mainstream grocery stores, and are nearly always available in Mexican, Asian, and Caribbean markets. You can also make this with a blend of chayote and sponge gourd, another South Asian squash also known as loofah, or *patola* in the Philippines; in that case, use 2 chayote, prepped as at right, and 1 medium sponge gourd, peeled and cut into bite-size pieces. It has a slightly bitter flavor that takes this dish to another level.

Tinapa flakes are usually sold in 4-ounce (115 g) packages in Filipino markets, and are also available online (see Resources, page 342). In a pinch, you can substitute Japanese bonito flakes; just crush them up a bit with your fingers.

CHAYOTE IS A PEAR-SHAPED, CELADON GREEN, mild squash with the texture of a honeydew melon and a cooling flavor similar to that of cucumber. It's grown around the world, and in the Philippines it's usually found in soups or in this quick vegetable sauté with onion and garlic. Traditionally *ginisang sayote* is made with ground pork, but we make it a lighter, quicker dish by topping it with just a sprinkle of *tinapa*. Tinapa is smoked fish, usually milkfish, that is sold whole or ground into powdery fish flakes. Serve ginisang sayote alongside whole grilled fish or meats or as a quick vegetable-based meal with a bowl of hot white rice. **SERVES 4 TO 6**

3 tablespoons vegetable oil

3 garlic cloves, minced

1 small white onion, diced

3 chayote, peeled, seeded, and cut into bite-size pieces or a mix of chayote and sponge gourd, cut into bite-size pieces (see Notes)

Kosher salt and freshly ground black pepper

2 tablespoons tinapa or bonito flakes (see Notes)

In a large skillet, heat the vegetable oil over medium heat. Add the garlic and cook, stirring often, until the garlic is just beginning to brown, about 3 minutes.

Add the onion and cook, stirring occasionally, until it begins to soften and turn translucent, about 5 minutes.

Add the chayote and cook, stirring often, until the vegetables are cooked through and tender, 7 to 10 minutes.

Season with salt and pepper and serve hot, sprinkled with the tinapa or bonito flakes.

GINATAANG PUSO NG SAGING

Banana Heart Salad

BANANA BLOSSOMS are the flowers of the banana plant. They require a little bit of work to clean, but it's worth it. Peel away the tough outer layer of magenta-colored petals, and you'll find the banana hearts, as well as many little pale yellow florets that look like baby bananas. The hearts are wonderful sautéed along with the tender parts of the banana florets and a little garlic, onion, vinegar, and coconut milk. You can serve this as a chilled salad or as a hot side dish. **SERVES 4 AS A SIDE**

1 fresh banana blossom
(1 to 2 pounds/455 to 900 g;
see Note)

Juice of 1 lemon

3 tablespoons (60 ml) vegetable oil

3 garlic cloves, smashed with the
side of a knife

1 white onion, diced

1 cup (240 ml) coconut milk

1 to 2 long green chiles, sliced, plus
more to taste (see Key Ingredients,
page 37)

2 teaspoons coconut vinegar,
plus more as needed (see Key
Ingredients, page 42)

Kosher salt and freshly ground
black pepper

Note: Fresh whole banana blossoms are somewhat difficult to source in the United States, though they can often be found in the produce section of Asian markets. If you can't find them, look for the hearts canned in brine (you won't be able to get the florets canned). Use one 18- to 20-ounce (510 or 566 g) can of banana hearts, drained, for this dish.

Clean the fresh banana blossom: Remove and discard the layers of red outer petals, keeping the tender yellow "heart" at the center and any yellow-red florets you find between the petals.

To clean the florets, fill a bowl with water and stir in the lemon juice. For each floret, remove the pinkish outer layer and the long, thin stamen so that only the tender yellow of the plant is left. Place the cleaned florets in the lemon water as you clean them to remove a little bitterness and keep them from oxidizing. (Don't taste them raw, as there will still be some bitterness left in each one; this will dissipate in the cooking process.)

Coarsely chop the banana heart and add it to the lemon water.

In a large skillet, heat the vegetable oil over medium-high heat. Add the garlic and onion and cook until they are soft and translucent, 3 to 5 minutes.

Strain the banana florets and chopped heart; discard the liquid. Add the florets and heart to the skillet and cook, stirring occasionally, for 4 minutes. Add the coconut milk, chiles, and vinegar and cook, stirring occasionally, until the liquid has almost fully reduced, about 7 minutes.

Season with salt, pepper, and more vinegar, as desired. This can be served immediately as a hot side dish, or chilled and served as a cold salad.

TORTANG TALONG

Eggplant Omelet

TORTA IS "OMELET" AND *TALONG* IS "EGGPLANT," but this is more like an egg-battered cutlet eaten for breakfast or lunch. The eggplants are heavily charred before they're battered with egg and panfried, making them smoky and creamy. Sometimes, ground pork or beef is added to the egg, but we often use crab (though that's optional, too).

You can serve *tortang talong* as a vegetable side as part of a bigger meal, or on its own with a bowl of rice alongside and some fish sauce on top. You can also make this dish if you have any leftover grilled eggplant; it would work perfectly. **SERVES 2 TO 4**

Note: Most fishmongers will sell picked cooked crabmeat, but if you have access to fresh crabs, by all means, use their meat.

2 large Asian eggplants
(about ⅓ pound/155 g each)

2 extra-large eggs

Kosher salt and freshly ground
black pepper

3 tablespoons vegetable oil

2 tablespoons picked cooked
crabmeat (see Note; optional)

Fish sauce, for serving

Preheat the broiler.

Lay the eggplants in a single layer on a baking sheet and broil them, flipping once or twice, until they are soft and blackened on all sides, about 15 minutes **(see opposite, photo 1)**. (If you have a gas stove, you can do this by holding the eggplants with tongs over a burner on medium-high heat, turning them so they blacken on all sides.)

Place the softened eggplants in a ziplock bag. Set aside for 10 minutes to steam (this makes the skin easier to peel). Peel the eggplants, discarding the skins, and use a fork to gently flatten the flesh.

Put the eggs in a shallow bowl. Beat well and season with salt and pepper.

In a large skillet, heat the vegetable oil over medium heat. Dip each eggplant in the beaten eggs **(2)**, letting it soak for a second or two so that it is well covered with the egg. Season the egg-dipped eggplant with additional salt and pepper and place it in the skillet **(3)**. Repeat with the other eggplant, making sure there's room between them in the skillet **(4)**. Place 1 tablespoon of the crab (if using) on top of each eggplant, pressing it down with a fork.

When the eggplants are crispy and browned on one side, 4 to 5 minutes, flip them over and cook until browned and crispy on the second side, about 3 minutes more. Transfer the eggplants to a paper towel–lined plate to drain.

Serve hot or at room temperature, with fish sauce.

COOKING THE EGGPLANT

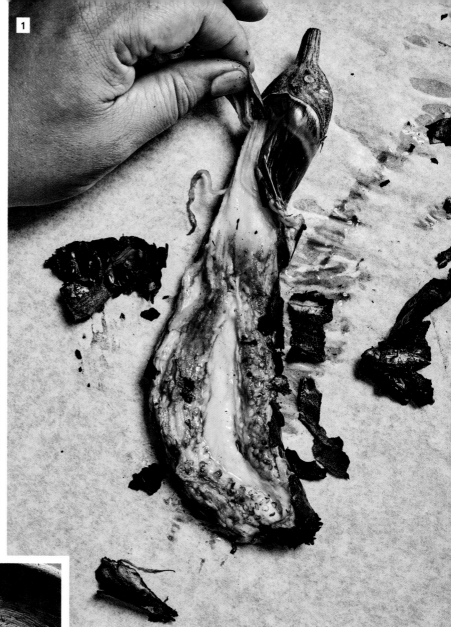

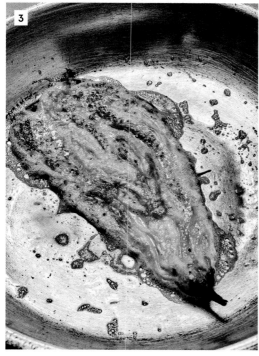

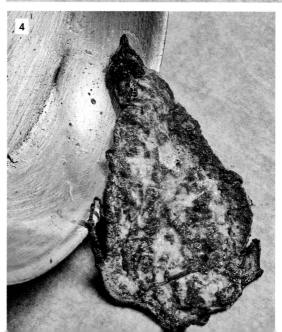

SINANGLAY NA ISDA

Red Snapper Wrapped in Collard Greens

THIS WHOLE SNAPPER is stuffed with herbs, wrapped in sturdy greens, and cooked in coconut milk. We first tried it in the province of Pampanga at a boutique Filipino cooking school and restaurant run by Lillian Borromeo, who is known as Atching Lillian—*atching* is a term of respect for a female elder. Atching Lillian cooks the traditional food of her region: in her version of this dish, the fish is wrapped in sturdy alagaw leaves from a tree growing right in her backyard; the leaves give the dish a natural lemony tartness. As a substitute, you can wrap the fish in thick collard greens and use a little lemon juice in the stuffing. You can also use several large napa cabbage leaves or taro leaf, if you prefer. **SERVES 4**

1 small tomato, diced

1 small white onion, diced

1 tablespoon fish sauce

Juice of 1 lemon

1 teaspoon freshly ground white pepper

1 bunch large collard greens

1 (1½-pound/680 g) whole red snapper or other white-fleshed fish, such as halibut, tilapia, or cod, cleaned

Kosher salt and freshly ground black pepper

2 tablespoons vegetable oil

4 garlic cloves, smashed with the side of a knife

1 tablespoon julienned fresh ginger

2 bay leaves

1½ cups (360 ml) coconut milk

4 to 6 cups (800 g to 1.2 kg) cooked white rice (see page 40), for serving

In a small bowl, combine the tomato, onion, fish sauce, and lemon juice and toss well. Season with white pepper and let sit for 10 minutes.

Meanwhile, bring a large pot of water just to a boil, then turn off the heat. Cut off the stem of each collard green at the base of the leaf. Plunge the collard greens into the hot water and soak until they soften enough to be pliable, just a few minutes, then remove them and pat them dry with paper towels.

Lay out 4 or 5 leaves (or enough to easily wrap the whole fish, though it's okay if the head and tail peek out) on a clean work surface, arranging them so that each leaf slightly overlaps the other. Place the fish in the center of the leaves.

Pat the fish dry and season the cavity liberally with salt and black pepper. Stuff the cavity with the tomato mixture.

> recipe continues →

SINANGLAY NA ISDA

Red Snapper Wrapped in Collard Greens

continued →

Wrap the fish tightly with the greens, drawing in the ends so that it is securely wrapped.

In a Dutch oven or a pot large enough to hold the wrapped fish, heat the vegetable oil over medium heat. Add the garlic and ginger and cook, stirring often, for 5 minutes, or until they begin to soften. Add the bay leaves and season with salt and black pepper as desired.

Add the wrapped fish to the bottom of the pan and pour in the coconut milk and 1 cup (240 ml) water. Raise the heat to high and let the liquid come to a boil. Reduce the heat to bring the liquid to a simmer, cover the pot, and cook for 20 minutes.

Transfer the fish to a serving platter. Meanwhile, simmer the coconut cooking liquid until it has thickened enough to coat the back of a spoon.

Cut the still-wrapped fish into pieces with a sharp knife and serve with rice, drizzling some of the sauce over the rice. Make sure to watch out for the bones.

GULAY AT BAGOONG ISDA

Stewed Greens with Fermented Anchovies

Note: Filipinos and other cultures cook with leaves from jute and sweet potato plants, and both are sold frozen and sometimes fresh in most Asian supermarkets. You'll also find frozen jute leaves in Middle Eastern stores, where they are labeled "molokheya." To use the leaves, let them defrost slowly in the refrigerator overnight and pour off any liquid if it accumulates. You can also substitute your own sweet potato leaves or any tender green, like chard or turnip greens; just blanch or lightly cook the fresh greens first, pour off any accumulated liquid, and measure out ½ cup (90 g).

LIKE PINAKBET TAGALOG (page 128), *gulay at bagoong isda* is a simply cooked vegetable dish that uses the complex flavors of bagoong, or fermented seafood paste, whose pungency gives life to a basic broth. You'll find similar preparations around the Philippines with names like *inabrau*, *dinengdeng*, *laswa*, and *bulanlang*. In this recipe, hearty mixed greens are served more like a soup or stew. Have a steaming bowl of greens alone or with a bowl of hot rice. **SERVES 4 TO 6**

1 medium tomato, cut into wedges

1 medium onion, quartered and sliced

4 whole garlic cloves, smashed with the side of a knife and peeled

½ pound (225 g) acorn squash, peeled, seeded, and cut into chunks

8 okra pods

½ pound (225 g) raw small shrimp, peeled and deveined (optional)

½ cup (15 g) fresh spinach

½ cup (90 g) thawed frozen sweet potato leaves (see Note)

½ cup (90 g) thawed frozen jute leaves (see Note)

½ cup (120 ml) bagoong balayan (see Key Ingredients, page 35)

4 to 6 cups (800 g to 1.2 kg) cooked white rice (see page 40; optional), for serving

Bring 6 cups (1.4 L) water to a boil in a stockpot. Add the tomato, onion, and garlic. Reduce the heat to medium, and simmer for 5 minutes.

Add the squash and cook for 4 minutes. Add the okra and cook for 3 minutes. Add the shrimp (if using), spinach, sweet potato leaves, and jute leaves. Simmer for about 3 minutes, or, if you are using the shrimp, until they are just cooked through.

Season with the bagoong and serve with rice, if desired.

GINATAANG TAMBO

Coconut-Stewed Bamboo Shoots with Jumbo Shrimp

BAMBOO grows throughout the Philippines. The shoots—the young sprouts of the plant—taste like a cross between hearts of palm and an artichoke heart. Canned bamboo shoots are fine to use here, but if you can find fresh—they occasionally show up in Asian markets—by all means, use those. Just blanch fresh bamboo first to tenderize the stalk and then cut it into thin slices. You can serve this as a side dish, but it's so delicious we prefer it as a main dish. **SERVES 4 TO 6**

2 tablespoons vegetable oil

1 tablespoon minced garlic

2 bird's-eye chiles (see Key Ingredients, page 37), minced

2 tablespoons minced fresh ginger

2 tablespoons diced white onion

2 cups (480 ml) coconut milk

1 pound (455 g) raw jumbo shrimp, peeled and deveined

1 teaspoon fish sauce

1 cup (130 g) canned bamboo shoots, cut into strips (see headnote)

Kosher salt and freshly ground black pepper

4 to 6 cups (800 g to 1.2 kg) cooked white rice (see page 40), for serving

In a large saucepan, heat the vegetable oil over medium heat. Add the garlic and cook, stirring often, until it is just beginning to brown, about 3 minutes.

Add the chiles, ginger, and onion and cook, stirring occasionally, for 3 minutes. Add the coconut milk and increase the heat to high to bring the coconut milk to a boil.

Reduce the heat to maintain a simmer, add the shrimp and the fish sauce, and cook just until the shrimp turn opaque, about 5 minutes. Stir in the bamboo shoots, turn off the heat, and season with salt and pepper as desired.

Serve hot over white rice.

LAING

Coconut-Stewed Taro Leaves

LAING IS MADE WITH A GINGER–COCONUT milk broth and the sturdy green taro leaves that are so abundant in tropical climates. Laing is from the region of Bicol, which is known for its use of coconut and chiles, both of which make this dish so delicious. It's a vegetable dish that is earthy, sweet, and slightly spicy from the ginger and the chiles, though you can alter the heat based on your preference. Heart-shaped taro leaves shouldn't be eaten raw. Like the edible tuber from which they sprout, they contain toxins that can result in an itchy throat. You can also substitute kale or collards; just remove the thick stems before you chop the leaves. **SERVES 4 TO 6**

½ cup (120 ml) vegetable oil

3 tablespoons minced garlic

3 tablespoons minced fresh ginger

1 bird's-eye chile (see Key Ingredients, page 37), minced

⅓ cup bagoong alamang (see Key Ingredients, page 35)

1½ cups (360 ml) coconut milk

2 pounds (910 g) fresh or dried taro leaves (see Note), coarsely chopped

4 to 6 cups (800 g to 1.2 kg) cooked white rice (see page 40), for serving

Note: The extra-large leaves of the taro plant are used throughout Asia, Africa, and the Caribbean—you'll sometimes see them sold as *colocasia* or *dasheen*. Fresh tastes best for this recipe, though traditionally cooks use dried taro leaves. Both are sold at South Asian and Indian markets and through online sources (see Resources, page 342).

In a large saucepan, heat the vegetable oil over medium heat. Add the garlic and cook, stirring often, until it is just beginning to brown, about 3 minutes.

Add the ginger, chile, and bagoong and cook, stirring occasionally, for 3 minutes. Add the coconut milk and increase the heat to high to bring the coconut milk to a boil.

Reduce the heat to maintain a low simmer and add the taro leaves, but do not stir them in—just let them wilt into the coconut milk. Cover the pot and cook for 1 hour.

Serve hot over white rice.

PINANGAT

Stuffed Taro Leaves Steamed in Coconut Milk

TO MAKE *PINANGAT*, whole taro leaves are stuffed with taro leaf ribbons, pork, and seasoned coconut milk. The origami-like packets are steamed in more seasoned coconut milk. As the coconut milk cooks, it creates coconut curds, which have a texture almost like that of soft-scrambled eggs. Spoon these curds over the cooked pinangat for an out-of-this-world meal. You can use kale or collards in place of the taro root leaves; remove the thick stems before you chop them. **SERVES 4 TO 6**

Notes: This recipe requires butcher's twine.

This recipe requires a pasta pot with a draining insert; you can also use a steaming basket in a regular pot to elevate the packets for cooking, though you might have to cook them in batches.

6 cups (1.4 L) coconut milk

3 tablespoons bagoong alamang (see Key Ingredients, page 35)

3 tablespoons minced fresh ginger

1 tablespoon minced garlic

Kosher salt and freshly ground black pepper

2 pounds (900 g) whole fresh taro leaves (see Note, page 143)

1 pound (455 g) pork belly, cut into 1-inch (2.5 cm) cubes

2 long green chiles (see Key Ingredients, page 37; optional)

In a medium bowl, stir together the coconut milk, bagoong, ginger, and garlic. Season with salt and pepper. (The coconut mixture should be on the saltier side. It will mellow during cooking.)

Set aside 18 whole taro leaves that are in good shape, with no bruises or tears. Coarsely chop the remaining taro leaves and set aside separately.

Place 3 whole taro leaves on top of one another and cup them in your hand or a small bowl. Fill the cup you've made with a small handful of the chopped taro leaves and ½ cup (120 ml) of the coconut milk mixture. Add 2 pieces of pork. Fold the leaves over themselves to form a square packet; tie with butcher's twine. The packet should be firm and secure but not overly tight. Set the packet aside on a plate. Repeat to make 6 packets total.

Put the remaining coconut milk mixture in a pasta pot that has a lid and draining insert (see Notes). Layer the packets neatly in the draining insert, then place the insert in the pot and cover with the lid. Bring the coconut milk mixture to a boil over medium-high heat, then reduce the heat to medium-low and simmer for 1½ hours.

Remove the pot from the heat and transfer the packets to a bowl (do not discard the coconut curds). Remove the twine from each packet with scissors.

To serve, place the packets into a bowl and spoon some of the coconut curds from the pot over the top.

PINANGAT ALLEY

In a small town in the region of Bicol, along the main highway, there are rows and rows of little shops that specialize in *pinangat*. A woman named Zeny and her husband provide many of the shops with the dish to sell, waking up at three o'clock in the morning to start the process, which begins with pressing fresh coconut milk. At lunchtime, the street is flooded with students and faculty from a nearby school enjoying this Bicolano dish.

NOODLES AND DUMPLINGS

THE CHINESE CONNECTION

FOR MANY, THE FIRST TASTE OF FILIPINO FOOD is actually Chinese influenced: thin, crispy-crunchy pork-filled spring rolls called *Lumpiang Shanghai* (page 152), or one of the many noodle stir-fries known as *pansit*. Those two dishes, along with chicken adobo (page 51), are the trifecta of globally recognized Filipino foods. This makes sense when you realize that the arrival of Chinese traders in the Philippines predates Spanish occupation by at least five hundred years, which had a significant impact on our earliest recipes. It's likely the Chinese were already doing business with Filipinos during the Tang Dynasty, which began way back in the seventh century. Along with those early exchanges of porcelain, silks, spices, and produce, the Chinese eventually moved to our archipelago.

Fast-forward some years later, and the Philippines had thriving Chinese neighborhoods like Binondo in Manila (it's the world's oldest Chinatown), Molo in Iloilo City (with remnants of old Chinese architecture), and another Chinese district in Cebu City. These Chinatowns came about when the Spanish arrived in the 1500s: they forced the non-Catholic Chinese to live only in certain districts, then known as ghettos or *pariáns*. Despite the closed-off communities, intermarriage between the Filipinos and Chinese was still very common. (*Tsinoy* is the word for those with Chinese-Filipino backgrounds; the Spanish used the term *mestizo de sangley*.) And of course, so was the blending of Chinese and Filipino cooking.

The Chinese influence is now so deeply rooted in our culture and cuisine that it is adapted and tweaked by cooks in nearly every province, and found at nearly every meal. It is Filipino: over the centuries, Chinese lo mein became our *pansit*, spring rolls are now our *lumpia*, and porky noodle soup is our very own *batchoy* (page 174), which is topped with crushed pork rinds and spiked with *bagoong*.

The most obvious connection to China is found in Binondo in Manila, which is the world's oldest Chinatown and is still a hub for working-class Chinese and Tsinoys. The area has largely remained unchanged over the decades. One alley has a little shop in the back serving burrito-size Chinese fresh lumpia (page 158); it has an art deco design that looks like a throwback to the movie *Chinatown*. Two Chinese restaurants compete for the title of oldest restaurant in the Philippines, one of which famously claims to have served the Filipino national hero José Rizal—a poet, writer, doctor, traveler, and advocate for political reform who was executed by Spain—his favorite meal, *pansit canton*. Throughout Binondo, bakeries sell the sweet Chinese pastries called *hopia* and steamed buns like *siopao* (page 163), both of which are nearly identical to their Chinese counterparts, though the fillings have more Filipino flavors like asado or ube.

LUMPIANG SHANGHAI
Pork and Beef Spring Rolls

THERE ARE MANY KINDS OF *LUMPIA—lumpia* being the general term for a wrapper of some kind rolled around a filling—but these slender little beauties are by far the most common. They're filled very simply with lightly seasoned pork and some carrot or onion, then rolled up tightly like little flutes before being plunged into hot oil. (The filling also gets some beef and a little more veg for extra moisture.) Like most Filipino Americans, my family always had a batch of lumpia in the freezer to be cooked up for afternoon snacks or a potluck contribution. **MAKES 30 LUMPIA**

Notes: Chinese Shaoxing wine is a Chinese rice wine with a taste that resembles dry or pale dry sherry like amontillado or manzanilla, both of which make fine substitutes. It's usually sold in 750 ml bottles in Asian markets.

You'll find the spring roll wrappers in the frozen section of Asian supermarkets and even some traditional supermarkets—the packages sometimes say "spring roll pastry" or "spring roll shells." For best results, let them slowly defrost in the refrigerator overnight. For sourcing suggestions, see Resources (page 342). You can make a vegan version of these by substituting cooked mushrooms for the meat in the filling and using a cornstarch slurry instead of egg to seal the wrappers.

FOR THE FILLING

1 pound (455 g) ground pork

1 pound (455 g) ground beef

1 tablespoon minced carrot

1 tablespoon minced celery

1 tablespoon minced water chestnut

1 tablespoon minced onion

2 teaspoons minced garlic

¼ cup (60 ml) white sugarcane vinegar (see Key Ingredients, page 42)

¼ cup (60 ml) Chinese Shaoxing cooking wine (see Notes)

⅓ cup (80 ml) soy sauce

1 tablespoon freshly ground black pepper

1 teaspoon kosher salt

TO ASSEMBLE

30 lumpia or spring roll wrappers (see Notes)

2 large eggs, beaten

FOR SERVING (OPTIONAL)

White sugarcane vinegar (see Key Ingredients, page 42)

Freshly ground black pepper

Sawsawan (see page 34)

Prepared sweet-and-sour sauce or Asian sweet chili sauce

Vegetable oil, for greasing and frying

Make the filling: In a large bowl, combine all the ingredients for the filling and use your clean hands to mix until everything is evenly blended. Cover and refrigerate the filling for 2 hours.

Assemble the lumpia: Line a baking sheet with parchment paper. Lay a wrapper out on a clean work surface and spread a heaping tablespoon of the filling along the bottom of the wrapper. Brush the edges of the wrapper with some of the beaten egg and then roll it up tightly in the shape of a flute. Repeat with the remaining wrappers and filling, placing them on the baking sheet as you go. (Some or all can be frozen at this point in an airtight container for up to a month. Fry them directly from the freezer.)

In a heavy-bottomed skillet, heat 2 to 3 inches (5 to 7.5 cm) of vegetable oil over medium heat until it registers 275°F (135°C) on an instant-read thermometer. Line a plate with paper towels and set it nearby.

Working in batches, add the lumpia to the hot oil, being careful not to crowd the pan, and fry them, flipping them every few minutes so they cook evenly on all sides, until golden brown and crispy, about 10 minutes. Use tongs or a spider to transfer them to the paper towel–lined plate to drain. Repeat with the remaining lumpia.

Serve the lumpia hot or at room temperature, with a little white vinegar mixed with black pepper, any sawsawan you like, or even sweet-and-sour or Asian sweet chili sauce.

> The *hiya* piece is the last bite of any shared meal. *Hiya* is the Tagalog word for "shame," so eating that last piece of lumpia on the plate meant having no shame! Usually, someone with gumption will pick up the last piece and decide who gets it—it typically goes to the oldest or youngest person at the table. Another option is to divvy up the last bite so everyone can enjoy it, which is a kind gesture that leads to *kapwa*, or togetherness.

LUMPIANG PRITO
Vegetable Spring Rolls

THE KEY TO THESE LARGE, VEGGIE-FILLED FRIED *lumpia* is their delicate homemade wrapper, made from a sticky beaten wheat and rice flour dough. After an overnight rest, you spread the dough around a hot griddle to make each wrapper. Fried, they are crispy and crunchy, a perfect foil for the vegetable filling of smoked tofu and carrots, lots of crunchy bean sprouts, plus onions, cabbage, and *kamote*, also known as mountain yams, or sweet potatoes. Of course, you can try filling them with whatever vegetables you like. **MAKES ABOUT 10 LARGE LUMPIA**

Notes: You can skip the homemade wrappers and use store-bought spring roll wrappers like the ones used for Lumpiang Shanghai (page 152).

A shortcut for cutting the vegetables is to use a mandoline, which will do most of the work for you.

FOR THE WRAPPERS

2½ cups (315 g) all-purpose flour

2 tablespoons rice flour

1 teaspoon salt

FOR THE FILLING

3 tablespoons vegetable oil

1 cup (110 g) diced white onion

2 tablespoons minced garlic

2 cups (280 g) kamote or sweet potato matchsticks (see Notes)

2 cups (260 g) carrot matchsticks

1 cup (250 g) finely crumbled smoked or extra-firm tofu

2 cups (140 g) thinly sliced napa cabbage

6 cups (540 g) mung bean sprouts

½ teaspoon kosher salt

½ teaspoon freshly ground black pepper

Fish sauce (optional)

Vegetable oil, for greasing and frying

Sawsawan (see page 34), for serving (optional)

Prepare the wrappers: In a large bowl, stir together both flours and the salt. Stir in 3½ cups (180 ml) water and, using your hands or two wooden spoons, work the dough by lifting and slapping it against the sides of the bowl until it is elastic and well mixed. (The batter should be a little lumpy; if it is too stiff, add water a tablespoon at a time.) Cover and refrigerate overnight.

The next day, when you are ready to make the wrappers, remove the dough from the fridge and let it warm up for about 30 minutes. Work the dough with two spoons in the same manner as the day before until the dough is smooth but still very sticky **(see page 157, photo 1).**

Heat a 10-inch (25 cm) skillet or crepe pan over low heat. Grab the ball of dough in your hand and, using a fast, circular motion, rub the dough all over the pan and remove it quickly, almost as if it were a rag you were using to clean the pan **(2).** (It is important to use low heat, because the batter won't stick to the pan if it is too hot, and it's important not to press down too hard when you smear the dough or you'll end up with fewer wrappers that are too thick.) The dough should leave a perfectly thin layer on the pan; this is your wrapper (3). When the edges of the wrapper begin to lift up—in just a few seconds, normally—it is done. Remove it from the pan with your fingers or a spatula (4) and set it aside on a plate. Repeat (5) until you have used all the dough, stacking the wrappers on top of one another on the plate as you finish them (6). You should have at least 20 wrappers.

Make the filling: In a large skillet, heat the vegetable oil over medium heat. Add the onion and garlic and cook until it is just beginning to soften, about 2 minutes.

Add the sweet potato and carrot to the skillet and cook until they just begin to soften, about 2 minutes. Add the tofu and cabbage and cook until the cabbage is just beginning to soften, about 2 minutes.

Add the bean sprouts and ½ cup (120 ml) water. Cook, stirring almost continuously, for 5 minutes more.

Add the salt and pepper, taste, and season with fish sauce, if needed. Transfer the vegetables to a colander set over a bowl or in the sink and let the filling completely drain and cool before filling the wrappers.

Assemble the lumpia: Line a baking sheet with parchment paper.

Lay two wrappers out on a clean work surface, one on top of the other. Place 3 tablespoons of the vegetable filling in the center of the bottom wrapper and spread it out slightly horizontally into a rectangular shape. Fold up the bottom over the filling and roll it from the bottom up like a cigar. Place the lumpia on a baking sheet and repeat with the remaining wrappers and filling.

Meanwhile, fill a Dutch oven or large heavy-bottomed pot about halfway with vegetable oil and heat it over medium-high heat until it registers 350°F (175°C) on an instant-read thermometer or just begins to shimmer. Line a plate with paper towels and set it nearby.

Working in batches, add the lumpia to the hot oil, being careful not to crowd the pot, and fry, flipping them every few minutes so they cook evenly on all sides, until they are golden brown on all sides, about 5 minutes. Use tongs or a spider to transfer them to the paper towel–lined plate to drain. Repeat with the remaining lumpia.

Serve them hot or at room temperature, with sawsawan, if you like.

MAKING FRESH WRAPPERS FOR LUMPIA

CHINESE FRESH LUMPIA

Fresh Spring Rolls with Rice Noodles and Peanuts

IN MANILA THERE'S A TINY DELI-CUM-GROCERY that is the closest approximation of a New York City bodega I've ever seen. It's brimming with Chinese-labeled ingredients—noodles and sausages, lotions and potions and medicinal ointments—that are the draw for both metropolitan foodies and Filipino-Chinese descendants, or Tsinoys. From a small corner of the shop they sell prepared foods like Chinese fresh *lumpia* ("fresh" essentially meaning "not fried"). The lumpia are the size of a California burrito, and I've never seen them like this outside of the Philippines. Use the homemade wrappers from the Lumpiang Prito (page 154), but make them a little larger and don't fry them. Left pliable, they are wrapped around a robust, earthy, crunchy mix of chopped vegetables, cooked and fried rice noodles, dried seaweed, and sugarcoated roasted peanuts. The salty-sweet-fresh flavors make this a very different kind of lumpia. It might be tempting to cook all the vegetables together, but sautéing them separately ensures that each is perfectly cooked. **MAKES 8 LUMPIA**

Notes: *Bihon*, or thin rice noodles, are commonly found in the Asian foods section of most supermarkets and are often labeled "rice vermicelli" or "rice stick noodles." For this recipe, follow the package directions to cook the noodles, or boil them in water until just soft, 2 to 3 minutes, then drain and let cool.

For the lumpia wrappers, follow the recipe on page 154, using a 12- or 14-inch (30 to 36 cm) skillet to make the wrappers wider but of the same thickness.

FOR THE SAUCE

1 cup (220 g) packed light brown sugar

1½ tablespoons cornstarch

2 tablespoons minced garlic

FOR THE LUMPIA

Vegetable oil

1 cup (170 g) minced shallots

2 tablespoons minced garlic

½ cup (125 g) crumbled smoked or extra-firm tofu

1½ (210 g) cups finely diced carrots

1 cup (70 g) diced white button mushrooms

1 cup (70 g) thinly sliced napa cabbage

2 cups (250 g) diced water chestnuts

1 cup (110 g) thinly sliced green beans

2 cups (250 g) cooked bihon, or thin rice noodles (see Notes)

8 fresh lumpia wrappers (see Notes)

8 (4-inch/10 cm) square sheets dried seaweed (nori)

8 green lettuce leaves, washed and dried

2 cups (290 g) honey- or sugarcoated roasted peanuts

Prepared sweet-and-sour sauce, banana ketchup (see page 316), or simple sawsawan (see page 34), for serving

Make the sauce: In a small saucepan, whisk together the brown sugar, cornstarch, garlic, and 1 cup (240 ml) water and heat the mixture over medium heat. Continue to whisk until the sauce thickens, about 5 minutes. Turn off the heat and keep the sauce covered and warm while you make the filling.

Make the filling: In a large skillet or wok, heat 1½ tablespoons vegetable oil over medium-high heat. Add the shallots, garlic, and tofu and cook until the shallots just begin to soften, about 3 minutes. Transfer the shallot-tofu mixture to a bowl and set it aside.

In the same pan, cook the carrots over medium-high heat for 3 minutes. (Be careful not to overcook them; you want them to retain a little bite.) Transfer the carrots to the bowl with the shallots and tofu.

In the same pan, heat 1 tablespoon vegetable oil over medium-high heat. Add the mushrooms. Cook for 3 minutes, then transfer to the bowl with the rest of the vegetables. Add the cabbage and water chestnuts, mix them together, then set the bowl aside.

In the same pan, cook the green beans over medium-high heat for 3 minutes. (Be careful not to overcook them; you want them to retain a little bite.) Transfer the beans to a separate bowl.

In the same pan, heat ¼ cup (60 ml) vegetable oil over medium-high heat. Line a plate with paper towels and set it nearby. Add the cooked noodles slowly, stirring them continuously with a wooden spoon or tongs to keep them from clumping and to make sure they cook evenly. Cook until the noodles are golden brown, just a few minutes, then use tongs or a slotted spoon to transfer them to the paper towel–lined plate.

Assemble the lumpia: Lay out a wrapper on a clean work surface. Add a piece of dried seaweed, then a lettuce leaf (it will overflow), then layer on 6 tablespoons of the vegetable mixture and 1 tablespoon of the green beans. Add a sprinkle of the fried noodles and a sprinkle of the sugared peanuts, then drizzle a little lumpia sauce across the top of everything.

Fold in the sides of the wrapper and roll it up over itself into a tube, like a burrito. Serve it right away with sweet-and-sour sauce, banana ketchup, or simple sawsawan.

LUMPIANG SARIWA
Savory Fresh Vegetable Crepes

LUMPIANG SARIWA are usually eaten for *meryenda*, the Filipino-Spanish tradition of taking a small afternoon meal (see page 271). A handmade crepe is filled with vegetables and baby shrimp and drizzled with a mild tangy-sweet sauce.

The flavors here are not as bold as in most other Filipino dishes—the main selling points here are freshness and crunch. The crepe, technically a handmade lumpia wrapper or skin, is thicker and sturdier than the one used for the Lumpiang Prito (page 154), so it won't disintegrate when folded around crisp vegetables. Once you get the hang of making the crepes, try adding flavorings like spices or finely chopped herbs to the batter. **SERVES 4 TO 6**

FOR THE CREPES

½ cup (80 g) rice flour

½ cup (65 g) all-purpose flour

2 tablespoons cornstarch

Pinch of kosher salt

3 large eggs, beaten

1 cup (240 ml) coconut milk

FOR THE SAUCE

¼ cup (30 g) cornstarch

1 cup (240 ml) vegetable stock

½ cup (95 g) muscovado or brown sugar

2 tablespoons soy sauce

FOR THE FILLING

2 tablespoons vegetable oil

1 large carrot, shredded

2 teaspoons minced garlic

1 small white onion, chopped

2 cups (180 g) bean sprouts

¼ head napa cabbage, thinly sliced

3 scallions, thinly sliced

1 cup (250 g) small-diced smoked or extra-firm tofu

⅓ cup (50 g) thinly sliced hearts of palm

½ pound (225 g) cooked baby shrimp or roughly chopped small to medium shrimp

Fish sauce

Kosher salt and freshly ground black pepper

TO ASSEMBLE

1 head leaf lettuce, leaves separated, washed, and dried well

½ cup (70 g) crushed roasted peanuts (optional)

Note: You can make the crepes a few hours in advance, but don't make them the day before or they'll get dry and brittle. And don't fill them until you are ready to serve them or they'll quickly get soggy. Instead, line each wrapper with waxed paper and store them in an airtight container or ziplock bag with a slightly damp kitchen or paper towel so they don't dry out.

> recipe continues →

LUMPIANG SARIWA

Savory Fresh
Vegetable Crepes

continued →

Make the crepes: In a large bowl, stir together both flours, the cornstarch, and the salt. Add the eggs, coconut milk, and ¼ cup (60 ml) water and whisk until smooth.

Heat a nonstick skillet over medium-low heat. Working quickly, use a ladle to add ¼ cup (60 ml) of the batter to the pan, then quickly swirl the pan around so the batter completely coats the bottom and pour the excess back into the bowl.

Return the pan to the heat and cook until the crepe is dry and cooked through and slides around in the pan. Transfer the crepe to a sheet of waxed paper. Repeat with the remaining batter, separating each wrapper with a layer of waxed paper. Cover loosely with a clean damp kitchen towel while you prepare the sauce and the filling.

Make the sauce: In a small bowl, whisk together the cornstarch and ½ cup (120 ml) water to form a slurry. Set aside.

In a small saucepan, combine the stock, sugar, and soy sauce and bring just to a boil, then reduce the heat to medium. Slowly stir the slurry into the sauce and simmer for about 5 minutes, or until the sauce begins to thicken. Turn off the heat and keep the sauce covered and warm while you make the filling.

Make the filling: In a large skillet, heat the vegetable oil over medium heat. Add the carrot, garlic, onion, bean sprouts, and cabbage. Cook, stirring often, until the vegetables are just wilted but still crisp, about 3 minutes. Remove from the heat and let cool, then stir in the scallions, tofu, hearts of palm, and shrimp and season with fish sauce, salt, and pepper. Set the filling aside.

Assemble the crepes: Lay one crepe flat on your work surface and place a lettuce leaf in the center. Put 2 to 3 tablespoons of the filling on top of the lettuce and then roll the crepe up tightly like a tube, starting from one side. Set the filled crepe seam-side down on a platter. Repeat with the remaining crepes, lettuce, and filling.

Top the rolled crepes with the warm sauce and a sprinkle of peanuts, if desired, and serve immediately.

SIOPAO

Steamed Buns

SIOPAOS—BASICALLY "HOT DUMPLINGS" in Chinese—are soft, fist-size, bright white steamed buns filled with meat and often a sliver of salted egg (see page 41). Steamed buns came to the Philippines in the 1920s courtesy of Ma Mon Luk, a Chinese immigrant hoping to raise enough money selling them to curry favor with his future in-laws. (It worked.)

The bun dough must be left to rise three times, so be sure to set aside at least three to four hours for the process. **MAKES 10 BUNS**

1 cup (240 ml) warm milk
(70° to 80°F/21° to 26°C)

2 teaspoons active dry yeast

½ cup plus 2 tablespoons
(125 g) sugar

½ teaspoon salt

2 cups (250 g) all-purpose flour

2 teaspoons baking powder

2 tablespoons vegetable oil,
plus more for greasing

Juice of ½ lime

1½ cups (300 g) Adobong Manok
Dilaw (page 60), tocino (see Notes),
or the filling of your choice

2 tablespoons distilled white vinegar

Notes: If you don't have a steamer pot, you can set a metal colander (or even a wire rack, if you have one that fits) into a large spaghetti or soup pot with a lid.

Tocino is typically made with pork. It's a close cousin to the Chinese *char siu* or red-cooked pork, but it gets its red coloring from annatto seeds.

In a small bowl, combine the milk, yeast, 2 tablespoons sugar, and salt. Whisk vigorously to make sure everything is dissolved, about 5 minutes. The mixture should be frothy. Set it aside.

In the bowl of a stand mixer fitted with the dough hook, combine the flour, baking powder, remaining ½ cup (100 g) sugar, and the vegetable oil and beat on low speed until thoroughly mixed, about 1 minute.

Increase the mixer speed to medium and slowly add the milk mixture, then add the lime juice and mix for 5 to 7 minutes, until the dough is smooth and elastic, not sticky. Form the dough into a ball.

Grease a large bowl with vegetable oil. Place the dough in the greased bowl, turning the dough a few times to coat it with oil. Cover the bowl with plastic wrap and set aside in a dry, warm place to rise until it has doubled in size, usually about 2 hours; start checking it after 30 minutes.

Line a baking sheet with parchment or waxed paper.

Once the dough has doubled in size, punch it down, invert it onto a clean work surface, and form it into a log. Divide it into 10 equal pieces, roll them into balls, and place them on the prepared baking sheet, making sure to allow space between them because they will increase in size. Cover the dough balls with

> recipe continues →

SIOPAO

Steamed Buns

continued →

a clean damp kitchen towel and set them aside in a warm place to rise for about 1 hour, or until they have increased in size by 50 percent.

To make the buns, cut ten 5-inch (13 cm) squares of parchment paper.

Use a rolling pin to flatten each dough ball into a 5-inch (13 cm) round disc. Place 1½ tablespoons of the adobong manok dilaw or your desired filling in the center of each (see below, photo 1), and then pinch the edges together up and over the filling (2). Once all the edges are pinched together, twist them tightly to seal (3), then place the bun seam-side down on a square of parchment paper (4). Repeat with the rest of the dough. Cover the buns with a damp kitchen towel and let them rest in a warm place for at least 30 minutes, or until they have doubled in size.

Fill a steamer pot with a couple of inches of water (making sure it won't touch the steam basket) and bring the water to a boil. Add the vinegar. Place the filled buns in the steamer basket, making sure they do not touch (you may need to do them in batches), cover, and steam them for 20 minutes. Let them rest for 3 minutes before serving.

FILLING AND FORMING THE SIOPAO

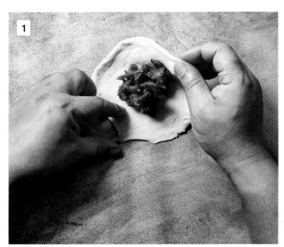

I AM A FILIPINO

PANSIT PALABOK
Rice Noodles with Shrimp Sauce

PANSIT (PRONOUNCED *PAN–SIT*) SIMPLY MEANS "NOODLE." It's the word that follows *pansit* that tells you either the type of noodle in the dish or the style of preparation. Here *palabok* refers to both. *Pansit palabok* is a luscious, buttery, bisque–like shrimp sauce tossed with white rice noodles and topped with *tsitsaron*, crisp-fried pork rinds. Loosely translated, *palabok* means "sauce," and the original dish was made from ground shrimp heads and shells blended with annatto seeds, water, and cornstarch. I grew up with the kind that was made by opening a seasoning packet labeled "palabok." You added water to make a gelatinous sauce that tasted mildly like shrimp. This version takes at least an hour and begins with an annatto-shrimp stock that is the foundation of the sauce. The traditional flavorings, which are sometimes referred to as *sahog*, include not just the pork rinds but also smoked fish, eggs, and scallions. To make the dish ultra decadent, you can add sea urchin, or *hayop ng siotsin*; the urchin's rich, buttery flavor and bright orange color make the finished dish even more divine. **SERVES 4 TO 6**

½ cup (1 stick/115 g) unsalted butter

¾ cup (95 g) all-purpose flour

2 to 3 cups (480 to 720 ml) warm shrimp stock (recipe follows)

Fish sauce

2 tablespoons vegetable oil

1 tablespoon minced garlic

1 pound (455 g) raw jumbo shrimp, shells removed and reserved, shrimp halved lengthwise and deveined (see Notes)

1 pound (455 g) squid bodies, cut into thick rings

1 pound (455 g) palabok noodles (see Notes), cooked, drained, and kept warm

¼ cup (25 g) crushed pork rinds

1 cup (300 g) diced smoked tofu

¼ cup (2.5 g) tinapa or bonito flakes (see Notes, page 130)

1 lemon, cut into quarters

Notes: Ideally you would use the shells from the shrimp to make the stock: peel the shrimp, then refrigerate both the shrimp and shells separately until you are ready to use them.

Palabok noodles, or cornstarch noodles, are found in Filipino supermarkets and are often labeled "special palabok cornstarch noodles." If you can't find them, use thick rice flour noodles, also called rice stick noodles. Cook in a large pot of boiling water until they are just al dente, then drain and keep warm until ready to use.

In a small saucepan, melt the butter over medium heat, then whisk in the flour and cook, whisking continuously, until the flour and butter are totally combined and have turned a light blond color.

Immediately whisk in 2 cups (480 ml) of the warm stock and bring the mixture to a boil, then stir and simmer over low heat until the sauce thickens, about 10 minutes. If it gets too thick, add a little more stock. Season with fish sauce, then set the sauce aside and keep hot.

> recipe continues →

In a large skillet, heat the vegetable oil over medium heat. Add the garlic and cook, stirring continuously, for 1 minute. Add the shrimp and squid and cook, stirring often, until the shrimp begin to curl and turn pink, about 5 minutes. Turn off the heat.

Put the warm cooked noodles on a serving platter and spoon the warm sauce over the center of the platter. Top the noodles with the cooked shrimp and squid, alternating shrimp and squid around the platter. Sprinkle on the crushed pork rinds, smoked tofu, and tinapa.

Serve immediately with lemon wedges.

SHRIMP STOCK

MAKES ABOUT 10 CUPS (2.4 L)

Note: Crab paste with bean oil is sold in jars in Chinese or Southeast Asian supermarkets.

2 tablespoons vegetable oil

1 large white onion, sliced

2 tablespoons minced garlic

Shrimp shells from 1 pound (455 g) shrimp (see Notes, page 167)

½ cup (140 g) annatto seeds (see Key Ingredients, page 35)

4 ounces (115 g) crab paste with bean oil (see Notes, page 167)

3 tablespoons fresh lemon juice

1 tablespoon fish sauce

3 bay leaves

2 tablespoons whole black peppercorns

In a stockpot, heat the vegetable oil over medium heat. Add the onion and cook, stirring occasionally and making sure not to let it brown, for 4 minutes, or until soft. Add the garlic and shrimp shells and cook, stirring continuously, until the shells turn pink.

Add the annatto seeds, crab paste, lemon juice, fish sauce, bay leaves, peppercorns, and 12 cups (3 L) water and raise the heat to high. Bring to a boil, reduce the heat to medium, and simmer for 1 hour. Strain the stock, discarding the solids, and set it aside until ready to use or refrigerate it overnight. Reheat it gently before making the sauce.

Leftover stock can be stored in an airtight container in the refrigerator for up to 1 week or in the freezer for up to a month.

PANSIT ISABELA

Egg Noodles in Broth with Pork and Poached Eggs

NORTHEAST OF THE SIERRA MADRE, the longest mountain range in the Philippines, you'll find a cooler climate, remote highlands, and a unique *pansit* dish called *pansit Cabagan*. The beauty of the dish is not only its deep, layered flavors—pork and beef and runny egg, with the crackle of pork rinds and the crunch of blanched vegetables—but also in the way you eat it. You mix in the toppings, letting them flavor the broth as you slurp. You get two portions of broth; the second is added after you've eaten most of the noodles so you can enjoy the remnants of egg yolk, red onion, and pork in your bowl. Our friend Cocoy (see page 100) introduced us to the dish in Cabagan, a town in his home province of Isabela, which is why we call our version Pansit Isabela. You don't have to use *all* the toppings if you want to make a slightly easier version, but it is amazing if you go all out. **SERVES 4**

Kosher salt

½ cup (70 g) diced carrot

½ cup (35 g) thinly sliced Napa cabbage

½ cup (55 g) diced long beans or green beans

2 tablespoons vegetable oil

½ pound (225 g) crumbled cooked longanisa hamonado (see Key Ingredients, page 39)

8 cups (2 L) beef stock

2 tablespoons soy sauce

¼ cup (60 ml) oyster sauce

1½ teaspoons cornstarch, dissolved in 1 tablespoon cold water

½ pound (225 g) miki noodles (see Notes)

4 poached eggs (recipe follows)

½ cup (25 g) pork rinds, coarsely crushed

4 teaspoons minced Chinese garlic chives (see Notes)

½ cup (55 g) minced red onion

4 quail eggs, hard-boiled, peeled, and thinly sliced (see Notes)

¼ cup (60 ml) garlic oil (see page 183; optional)

Notes: *Miki* noodles (see Key Ingredients, page 39) are a type of pansit made with eggs and wheat flour. They're not easy to find outside of Filipino stores, but chow mein noodles or "Hong Kong–style" egg noodles—both widely available at Chinese markets—are good substitutes.

Chinese chives have long flat leaves and a slightly garlicky flavor. They are sold by the bunch in the produce section of Asian markets. If you can't find them, use regular chives. Same goes for the quail eggs—if you can't find them, just hard-boil one regular egg.

Bring a large pot of salted water to a boil. Fill a bowl with ice and cold water and set it nearby. Plunge the carrots into the boiling water and cook for 2 minutes. Remove them with a strainer and transfer to the ice water. Let them sit for a minute or two, until they are cool to the touch, then remove them with a strainer and set them aside in a bowl. Repeat this process with the cabbage and the beans, putting each in a separate bowl.

> recipe continues →

PANSIT
ISABELA

Egg Noodles in
Broth with Pork
and Poached Eggs

continued →

In a large saucepan, heat the vegetable oil over medium-high heat. Add the longanisa and cook for 2 minutes, just until it starts to brown. Add 4 cups (1 L) of the beef stock, the soy sauce, and the oyster sauce and bring to a boil.

Reduce the heat slightly so the stock simmers and cook for about 5 minutes, or until the longanisa is cooked through. Remove it with a slotted spoon or tongs and set aside in a bowl or on a plate.

Add the cornstarch slurry to the broth and cook over high heat for 2 to 3 minutes, until the liquid just begins to thicken. Add the noodles, tearing them apart with your hands if needed and stirring them into the broth so they begin to soften. Reduce the heat slightly and cook the noodles at a simmer, gently stirring them into the sauce the whole time, until they are cooked through and tender.

Serve the noodles piled into four large soup bowls, topping each with a quarter of the sauce. Add 1 poached egg to the middle of each bowl, then place a quarter of the cooked pork on one side of each bowl. Top each bowl evenly with the carrot, pork rinds, chives, red onion, cabbage, long beans, and quail eggs, adding each topping in a small pile rather than sprinkling them over. Drizzle each bowl with garlic oil, if desired, and serve hot, encouraging your guests to stir the ingredients so they get a little of everything in each bite.

If desired, once you've eaten most of the noodles and toppings, top off each bowl with a cup (240 ml) or so of the remaining broth, heated to a simmer in a saucepan, for a "second" meal.

POACHED EGGS

1 teaspoon distilled white vinegar   **4 large eggs**

Fill a medium saucepan about two-thirds full of water and bring it to a hard simmer over medium heat. Add the vinegar.

Crack each egg into an individual small cup or ramekin. Swirl the water with a chopstick or teaspoon to make a whirlpool, then immediately but gently pour the egg from the cup into the middle of the swirl. Cook for 3 minutes, then remove it with a slotted spoon and set it aside on a plate. Use a spoon or scissors to trim up any rough edges of the whites.

Repeat with the remaining 3 eggs. (You can poach more than one at a time, as long as you keep plenty of room between the eggs and the sides of the pot.)

Use right away or store the poached eggs in the refrigerator for 2 to 3 days, then gently reheat them, but you will need to quickly cool them in a bowl of chilled water when you remove them from the simmering water.

PANSIT PUSIT

Rice Noodles with Squid Ink

THE DEEP BLACK SQUID INK in this simple noodle dish is one of the hallmarks of the province of Cavite, an hour south of Manila. The squid ink adds a faint funk, a taste of the ocean, and color to the noodles. In the small *karinderia* in Cavite's public market, cooks serve the *pansit* in rolled-up newspapers lined with banana leaves. But our favorite version is at Asiong's, a multigenerational restaurant run by Chef Sonny, who garnishes his with thin slices of fresh *kamias*, a sweet-tart vegetable also called *bilimbi* or tree cucumber. If you can't find kamias, you can use thin slices of kumquat, or even unripe strawberries or pineapple. **SERVES 4 TO 6**

Note: Most fish markets sell squid ink in small packets.

1 pound (455 g) cleaned small squid, including tentacles

2 tablespoons vegetable oil

2 garlic cloves, minced

2 bay leaves

1 finger-size knob fresh ginger, peeled and cut into matchsticks

3 tablespoons finely diced white onion

1 teaspoon squid ink (see Note)

2 tablespoons fish sauce

½ cup (120 ml) fish stock (see page 95)

3 cups (525 g) soaked and drained bihon, or thin rice noodles (see Notes, page 158)

1 bird's-eye chile (see Key Ingredients, page 37), thinly sliced

Kosher salt and freshly ground black pepper

½ cup (70 g) thinly sliced kumquats or other sour fruit, for serving

Slice the squid bodies about ¼ inch (6 mm) thick. Set them aside with the tentacles.

In a skillet or wok, heat the vegetable oil over medium heat until it begins to shimmer, about 3 minutes. Add the garlic and the bay leaves. Cook, stirring occasionally, until the garlic browns slightly, 3 to 5 minutes (do not let it burn).

Add the ginger and onion to the pan and cook, stirring for 1 minute.

Add the squid and cook, stirring often, until it is tender, about 3 minutes. Add the squid ink, fish sauce, and stock, increase the heat to high, and bring the liquid to a boil. Immediately reduce the heat to medium-high, add the noodles, and cook, stirring so that they are coated with the sauce, until nearly all the liquid in the pan is gone. Add the chile, season with salt and pepper, and stir.

Transfer the noodles and squid to a serving platter and garnish with the sliced kumquats.

Philippine G

Philippine Gardens comes out every first Saturday of the month. For comments and sug

2015

Medinilla xFlorin

Medinilla

menco"

We spell *pansit* with
an *s*, instead of the
more common spelling,
pancit, because
the original Filipino
languages didn't have
the letter *c*.

BATCHOY
Pork Noodle Soup

BATCHOY IS A HEARTY, PORKY noodle soup created in the La Paz public market in the 1930s. Two popular styles are served there: one has a broth that's sweet with the funk of offal, and the other is savory. This version is a blend of both. **SERVES 4**

Notes: You should be able to order tripe and calf's liver at a butcher shop. If you can't find them or don't want to use them, leave them out, but be sure to use pork stock (see page 107) if you do, so the broth has a porky flavor. In that case, use 10 to 12 cups (2.4 to 2.8 L) pork stock and let it simmer and reduce to 8 cups (2 L) before continuing with the recipe.

It is easier to slice the pork butt if you freeze it for an hour or two first.

¼ pound (115 g) cleaned honeycomb beef tripe, cut into ½-inch-wide (1.5 cm) strips (see Notes)

8 cups (2 L) pork stock (see page 107) or chicken stock (see page 179)

½ pound (225 g) calf's liver (see Notes)

1 to 2 tablespoons fish sauce

¼ cup (60 ml) bagoong guisado (page 36)

½ pound (225 g) miki noodles (see Key Ingredients, page 39)

2 tablespoons vegetable oil

1 tablespoon minced garlic

¼ pound (115 g) pork butt, cut into thin strips and then squares (see Notes)

½ cup (25 g) garlic chips (see page 183)

1 cup (50 g) pork rinds, finely crushed

2 large scallions, thinly sliced on an angle

Fill a large saucepan with water and add the tripe. Bring the water to a boil and cook for 10 minutes. Pour off all the water and add the stock. Bring to a boil, then reduce the heat and simmer until the tripe is very tender, 2 hours.

When the tripe is tender, add the calf's liver and simmer until just cooked through, 5 to 7 minutes. Transfer the liver to a plate and set it aside to cool slightly. Stir the fish sauce and the bagoong into the stock. Keep hot.

Fill another large saucepan with water and bring it to a boil. Cook the noodles according to the package directions, usually 3 to 5 minutes. Drain and set aside.

In a large skillet, heat the vegetable oil over medium-high heat. Add the garlic. Cook, stirring, until the garlic begins to brown, about 2 minutes, then add the pork slices. Cook until the pork is cooked through, 5 to 7 minutes. Transfer to a plate.

Slice the calf's liver into ¼-inch-thick (6 mm) slices.

Divide the noodles among four bowls. Fill each bowl with the stock, making sure each one gets some tripe. Add a few slices of calf's liver and top with some pork. Sprinkle the garlic chips, pork rinds, and scallions across the top and serve hot.

PANSIT MOLO

Wonton Soup

THE DUMPLINGS ARE THE MOST IMPORTANT part of this soup, and the key is to use the thinnest wrappers you can find; once cooked, they should almost feel like a sheet of silk. The wrappers enclose a seasoned chicken meatball, which gets a slight crunch from the addition of water chestnuts. (You could also fill them with shrimp and pork; see the variation.) According to folklore, these dumplings are folded in a very specific way—to resemble the habits of the Dominican order of nuns from a nearby Catholic church in Molo. This soup is best with a rich, collagen-filled broth, so use homemade chicken stock made from roasted chicken bones. Finish the soup with a sprinkle of white pepper. **SERVES 4 TO 6; MAKES ABOUT 36 DUMPLINGS**

FOR THE DUMPLINGS

½ pound (225 g) ground chicken

1 teaspoon minced fresh ginger

½ teaspoon minced garlic

½ teaspoon porcini mushroom powder

A pinch of freshly ground white pepper

1 tablespoon fish sauce

A pinch of kosher salt

2 tablespoons thinly sliced scallions

1 tablespoon minced water chestnuts

50 thin Shanghai-style dumpling wrappers (see Note)

FOR THE SOUP

8 cups (2 L) chicken stock (see page 179)

1 tablespoon fish sauce

Freshly ground white pepper

1 scallion, finely sliced, for garnish

Note: The wrappers should be the extra-thin version also called "Shanghai style." They usually come frozen in packs of 50, and you will likely need to defrost them overnight. You can use thicker ones if that's all you can find, but the dumplings just won't have the same delicateness.

Make the dumplings: In a large bowl, combine the ground chicken, ginger, garlic, mushroom powder, white pepper, fish sauce, salt, scallions, and water chestnuts. Mix together with your hands until everything is incorporated.

Fill a small bowl with water and set it nearby.

Take 1 teaspoon of the filling and place it in the middle of a wrapper **(see page 178, photo 1)**. Arrange the wrapper point-side up, so that it is a diamond

› recipe continues →

rather than a square, and fold the bottom point up over the filling, leaving ½ inch (1.5 cm) of space exposed along the top two sides of the diamond shape; now the wrapper looks like a triangle **(2)**. Dip your finger in the water and gently moisten the exposed wrapper along the top two edges.

Fold the two outer points of the triangle tightly up over the filling, one on top of the other **(3, 4)**. The wrapper will look like a nun's habit or a pope's hat—tall with a point on the top. Place the dumpling on a large plate or baking sheet. Repeat with the remaining wrappers and filling (don't let them touch as you place them on the plate or baking sheet).

Cook or freeze the Molo immediately. To freeze, place the baking sheet directly in the freezer and freeze the dumplings for 4 hours. Working quickly, remove the dumplings from the baking sheet with a spatula, place them in freezer-safe ziplock bags or airtight containers, and return them to the freezer. Use within 6 months; do not defrost them before you cook them.

Make the soup: In a stockpot, heat the stock over high heat. Stir in the fish sauce and let the stock come to a boil.

Add the dumplings, stirring gently so they don't stick together. Let the broth come back to a boil, then reduce the heat to medium and cook at a simmer for 3 minutes, or until the dumplings rise to the top and are just cooked through. (To check, remove one dumpling and cut it in half.)

Serve immediately, ladled into bowls and garnished with a dusting of white pepper and a sprinkle of scallion.

VARIATION

Shrimp and Pork Dumpling Filling

This filling will make a dumpling more similar to a traditional Chinese wonton. Use it instead of the chicken filling in the first step of the recipe for *pansit Molo*.

4 ounces (112 g) minced raw shrimp

2 ounces (56 g) ground pork

1½ teaspoons minced fresh ginger

¼ cup (32 g) minced water chestnuts

¼ teaspoon kosher salt

¼ teaspoon freshly ground black pepper

In a large bowl, combine the ground shrimp, pork, ginger, water chestnuts, salt, and pepper. Mix everything together with your hands until evenly incorporated. Use to fill the dumplings following the process on page 175.

> recipe continues →

FILLING AND FORMING MOLO DUMPLINGS

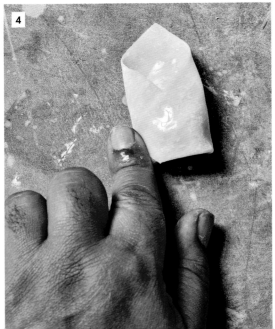

CHICKEN STOCK

This deeply flavored stock is rich with collagen thanks to the chicken bones and will improve almost any recipe that calls for chicken stock, though you can of course use store-bought or bouillon cubes in a pinch. **MAKES 8 CUPS (2 L)**

5 pounds (2.3 kg) chicken bones (see Note)

1 large carrot, halved

2 celery stalks, each cut into 3 pieces

2 large white onions, quartered

2 teaspoons whole black peppercorns

4 bay leaves

¼ cup (10 g) cilantro stems

Note: You should be able to get chicken bones from any butcher, though you will likely need to call ahead. A little meat left on is fine. You can also use bones left over from roasted, fried, baked, or any other chicken dish— you can keep them tightly sealed in the freezer until you collect enough to make the stock.

Preheat the oven to 350°F (175°C).

Place the chicken bones on a rimmed baking sheet and roast, turning them occasionally with tongs, until they are nicely browned on all sides, about 1 hour. Drain off any fat that may have accumulated in the pan and reserve it for another use, such as for roasting vegetables or making fried rice.

Transfer the bones to a large stockpot and add the carrot, celery, onions, peppercorns, bay leaves, cilantro stems, and 5 quarts (5 L) water. Bring to a boil over high heat, then reduce to medium-low so the stock cooks at a simmer. Simmer for at least 2 hours and up to 3 hours.

Strain the stock through a fine-mesh sieve, discarding the solids. Store the stock in airtight containers in the refrigerator for up to 1 week or in the freezer for up to several months.

Molo, the part of Iloilo City on the southeastern tip of Panay Island, was once a *parián*, an area where all the Chinese in the region were forced to live. Like Binondo, the Chinatown in Manila, it is a place where it's easy to see the imprint of Chinese culture on Philippine architecture, cuisine, and commerce. Some Chinese eventually intermarried and moved out of Molo and into the rest of Iloilo City, many becoming part of the city's upper class. Today, remnants of that community still stand, including fantastic dishes heavily influenced by the early Cantonese settlers, not to mention a few incredible (though fading) Chinese-influenced mansions hidden behind modern buildings.

HUMBA
Braised Pork Belly

THIS SLOW-COOKED, DEEPLY SPICED PORK BELLY dish varies from region to region, and devotees of *humba* famously debate its proper ingredients. Most agree it is Chinese in origin, first made in the Visayans and in Mindanao (see page 189), but it's now cooked and eaten country-wide, and has been adapted by travels, migration, or marriage. Think of it as a cross between adobo and the Chinese "red-cooked" soy-braised pork dish called *hong ba* (which is one possible source for humba's name). This recipe came to us from a Filipino friend who recommended the addition of Chinese fermented black beans and soybean paste. (Soybean paste isn't traditional in Pinoy recipes, though it is in spirit, since you find influences from Japan, China, Spain, plus all the countries along the Silk Road in Filipino cooking.) You'll first blanch the pork, which makes it easier to score the skin and lets the meat soak up the marinade. It's traditional to serve this with rice, but you can also give a nod to humba's roots and serve it in a split-open steamed Chinese bun topped with slaw and fried garlic chips (see page 183). **SERVES 4 TO 6**

Note: American butcher shops typically sell pork belly that is much leaner, with a thinner fat cap, and they usually sell whole pork belly without the bone—though at a good butcher shop or counter you can ask for it with the bone. For best results, though, you'll want to seek out an Asian butcher shop, which generally sources meat with more fat, as their customer base prefers, or heritage breeds of pork, which have the fat cap, but at a premium price.

2½ pounds (1.1 kg) bone-in, skin-on pork belly (see Note)

½ cup (120 ml) white sugarcane vinegar (see Key Ingredients, page 42)

½ cup (95 g) muscovado or brown sugar

⅓ cup (80 ml) soy sauce

1 tablespoon red soybean or miso paste

1 tablespoon Chinese fermented black beans (see Notes, page 106)

3 bay leaves

7 star anise pods

¼ cup (35 g) raw peanuts (optional)

6 garlic cloves

1 teaspoon freshly ground black pepper

4 to 8 cups (1 to 2 L) pork stock (see page 107) or chicken stock (see page 179)

4 cups (800 g) cooked white rice (see page 40), for serving

Sawsawan (see page 34), for serving

Bring 1 gallon (4 L) water to a boil in a large pot, add the pork belly, and blanch for 10 minutes. Remove the meat from the pot and let cool on a plate.

When the meat is cool enough to handle, use a sharp knife to score the skin into a crosshatch pattern.

In a large ziplock bag, combine the vinegar, sugar, soy sauce, red soybean paste, fermented black beans, bay leaves, star anise, peanuts (if using), garlic, and pepper, add the pork belly, seal the bag, and marinate in the refrigerator overnight or for up to 24 hours.

When ready to cook the pork belly, preheat the oven to 350°F (175°C).

Pour the pork and the marinade into a Dutch oven or large flameproof roasting pan, add enough of the stock to cover, and simmer over medium-low heat for 2 to 2½ hours, until the pork is fork-tender.

Transfer the pork belly to a platter and set the roasting pan on the stovetop over medium-high heat. Bring the liquid to a simmer and cook until it is thick enough to coat the back of a spoon, 5 to 7 minutes.

To serve, cut the cooled pork into 2- to 3-inch (5 to 7.5 cm) pieces, then gently rewarm it in the thickened sauce. Serve immediately, with rice and sawsawan.

Portmanteaus, or words derived by blending two or more others, are plentiful in Tagalog. *Humba* might be an example. Some folklore traces the dish's namesake from stringing the first two letters of the first and last words in the phrase *humot nga baboy* together. (*Humot* can mean "sweet smelling" or "delicious smell"; *baboy* means "pork" or "pig.") Another theory is that it derives in the same way from *humok nga baboy*, where *humok* means "soft and tender." All of the above apply, as humba is tender, soft, and sweet, smells divine, and melts in your mouth.

SINANGAG

Garlic Fried Rice

BREAKFAST IN THE PHILIPPINES is built on *sinangag*, or cooked rice tossed with garlic and oil. For us, the smell of sinangag cooking is better than waking up to the aroma of coffee. This recipe may garner some raised eyebrows from knowledgeable Filipino cooks because we don't use leftover rice to make it and we don't use a rice cooker. Instead, we cook the rice in a pot on the stove over very low heat. The rice kernels stay intact and even a bit dry—much like day-old rice—and thus they hold up to the additions of garlic chips and homemade garlic oil, which make the rice more robust and flavorful. **SERVES 2 TO 4**

FOR THE GARLIC OIL AND CHIPS

1 cup (240 ml) vegetable oil

1 cup (135 g) garlic cloves, sliced paper thin

4 cups (800 g) freshly cooked jasmine rice (see page 40), kept hot

Kosher salt

FOR SERVING (OPTIONAL)

2 to 4 large eggs, fried or sunny-side up (see Notes)

Notes: You can also make sinangag using rice left over from your meal from the previous day. Just heat the rice in a pan with a tablespoon or two of garlic oil. When the rice is hot, add 2 tablespoons of the garlic and a drizzle of garlic oil.

Add eggs and the sweet Filipino cured meat called *tocino* or the garlicky sausages called *Lucban longanisa* for a *silog*; it's an excellent breakfast. Include the Classic Ensalada (page 122) or cucumber relish (see page 123), too.

In a medium saucepan, heat the vegetable oil over medium heat until the oil begins to shimmer. Line a plate with paper towels and set it nearby.

Carefully pour the garlic into the hot oil and stir continuously until the garlic is just beginning to lightly brown. Remove the pan from the heat and use a slotted spoon to transfer the fried garlic onto the paper towel–lined plate; reserve the oil. Set both the garlic and the oil aside while you make the rice. (You can store the garlic chips and oil in separate airtight containers in the refrigerator for up to a week.)

Fluff the hot rice with a fork and toss it with ¼ cup (60 ml) of the garlic oil and ½ cup (40 g) of the fried garlic chips. (You will have leftover oil and chips for more rice; or try them on the pansits and soups on pages 167–169.)

Season the rice with salt and serve right away or at room temperature, with the eggs, if desired.

Silog is a portmanteau: *sinangag* is the "*si–*" and "egg" ("it log") is the "*–log*." Then, you attach a prefix based on what protein you're adding: *Spamsilog* for Spam, *longsilog* with sausage, *tocilog* with the tocino, and so on.

ARROZ CALDO
Savory Rice Porridge

ARROZ CALDO—RICE SIMMERED WITH A LITTLE ginger, garlic, and chicken stock until soft and supple—ranks with *tinola* (page 110) as an excellent cold remedy. The Chinese likely introduced it to us as the similar dish called congee. Some scholars theorize that our Spanish colonizers didn't care to learn the Chinese names of things, so they renamed them in their own language, hence *arroz caldo*, which means "rice broth" in Spanish. In some parts of the Philippines, the same dish is also known as *lugaw* or *goto*. No matter what you call it, arroz caldo is a perfect lunch or *meryenda* snack; serve it with a splash of lemon juice and fish sauce.

This porridge is made with two types of rice—equal parts jasmine and glutinous rice (a trick I learned from my father). The glutinous rice will hold its shape longer than regular rice throughout the simmering process. Try experimenting with whatever toppings you like, from scallions to roasted Brussels sprouts to shaved raw beets. **SERVES 4 TO 6**

Note: Some people like to cook their arroz caldo until the grains of rice have started to break down and disintegrate, but we like them to retain just a little bit of texture. If they do get too soft, it's okay—the dish will still taste good.

8 cups (2 L) chicken stock (see page 179)

2 cups (370 g) uncooked jasmine rice or equal parts jasmine and glutinous rice (see Note)

¼ cup (35 g) minced garlic

¼ cup (25 g) minced fresh ginger

Kosher salt

1 lemon, quartered, for serving (optional)

Fish sauce, for serving (optional)

In a large saucepan or stockpot, stir together the stock, rice, garlic, and ginger. Bring to a boil over medium-high heat, stirring occasionally to make sure the rice doesn't stick to the bottom, then reduce the heat until the liquid is just at a simmer. Cook, uncovered, stirring frequently, until the arroz caldo is thick and starchy, and the rice is soft but the individual grains are still distinct, at least 30 minutes, or more, if necessary.

Season with salt and serve hot with a squeeze of lemon and a splash of fish sauce, if desired.

SPICE AND BURNT COCONUT

THE FOOD OF THE MUSLIM SOUTH

THE SOUTHERNMOST section of the Philippines—home to Mindanao, the second-largest island in the archipelago—stands distinct from the rest of the country. In nearly every other province, Filipino food means a mixture of traditions built from the cross-pollination of indigenous customs layered with influences from the Spanish, the Chinese, the Americans, and others. But the south has a different history: seven centuries ago, these islands became home to Arab traders and Malay tribes, most of whom were Muslim, from other nearby Southeast Asian islands. Throughout the centuries, the people of this region have been protective of their territory and culture, asserting their political and religious autonomy, somehow resisting many of the rules and restrictions of Spanish colonization and American occupation and even modern governance. Their independence is reflected in their recipes, which are rarely found outside the region, and it is fascinating to consider that some of the foods from this region are the closest approximation to Filipino cuisine before the influence of the Spanish, Chinese, and Americans.

Today, provinces like Maguindanao, Lanao del Sur, Sulu, and Tawi-Tawi are still staunchly Muslim, meaning there are celebrations for Islamic holidays like Ramadan and an absence of pork. Both Arabic and Malay roots also mean the iconic dishes from this region have unique flavors and techniques, like a penchant for curry-like sauces with layered spices and even unsweetened chocolate (see the exquisite Mindanao version of adobo on page 54). Some tribes eat diced cassava root instead of rice; others use fresh turmeric to give their dishes an earthy tang, and toast or burn coconut to impart its nutty flavor to stews and sauces like Zamboanga Sauce (page 195). *Palapa*—a paste of pounded coconut, ginger, chiles, and spring onions—is used as a condiment, seasoning, or side dish. Some of the most distinctive dishes in the Philippines come from the Muslim regions, and they're a living connection to our precolonial past.

For decades those from the central or northern part of the country have stayed away from visiting the southernmost islands of the Philippines, discouraged by true stories of violent vigilantes and the ongoing war for independence between some of the Moros—the term for Muslim Filipinos in the south—and the Philippine government. Moro is a collective term for the many native ethnic groups or tribes that still exist in this part of the Philippines, like the Maranao described on page 194. In fact, at the far southwestern tip of the country there is the Autonomous Region in Muslim Mindanao, or ARMM, a region with its own government; we've traveled there and found excellent food we had never had before, beautiful mosques, and friendly locals.

PIAPARAN MANOK

Chicken Wing Stew with Ginger, Scallions, and Chiles

VELVETY AND SWEET YET EARTHY, this chicken-and-coconut stew comes from the Maranao tribe in the province of Lanao del Sur on the island of Mindanao and is often served during the fast-breaking celebration at the end of Ramadan. The Maranao are known for their use of *palapa*, a wonderfully fragrant spice paste made with ginger, chile, and a local variety of scallion called *sakurab* that is more like a spring onion. Much like a *sofrito* in Spanish cuisine, palapa is the cornerstone of Maranao cooking, and no meal or dish is complete without it on the table in some form. It can be served on its own as an appetizer, or blended with grated coconut to make a chunky condiment, or even dried. The trick is to sauté it for a minute before using it, which removes the bitterness of the raw scallion and helps prevent the ginger from losing its potency. It's usually made in advance and kept in the refrigerator as a base for soups, marinades, or stews like this one—and, in fact, you can double or triple the spice recipe if you want to keep it on hand. (It can be refrigerated for up to a week or frozen for several months.) For this stew, we use chicken wings, which don't have a lot of meat but do provide deep flavor and lusciousness to the sauce. **SERVES 4 TO 6**

FOR THE PALAPA SPICE PASTE

¼ cup (25 g) minced fresh ginger

½ cup (15 g) toasted coconut flakes

½ cup (30 g) spring onions or minced scallions (white part only)

1 large bird's-eye chile (see Key Ingredients, page 37), seeded and minced

1 teaspoon vegetable oil

Kosher salt

Sugar

FOR THE CHICKEN STEW

3 tablespoons vegetable oil

1½ pounds (680 g) skin-on chicken wings

½ cup (55 g) diced white onion

1½ tablespoons minced garlic

2 thumb-size pieces fresh turmeric, peeled and diced (see Note)

½ cup (90 g) diced tomato

1 (13-ounce/385 ml) can coconut milk

½ cup (30 g) thinly sliced scallions

1 cup (145 g) chopped red bell pepper

1 cup (85 g) unsweetened shredded coconut

2 tablespoons fish sauce

Freshly ground black pepper

FOR SERVING

4 to 6 cups (800 g to 1.2 kg) cooked white rice (see page 40)

Sawsawan (see page 34)

Note: For more about fresh turmeric, see page 60. Fresh is best for this dish, but if you can't find it, substitute 2 teaspoons ground turmeric.

> recipe continues →

PIAPARAN MANOK

Chicken Wing Stew with Ginger, Scallions, and Chiles

continued →

Make the palapa spice paste: In a bowl, stir together the ginger, toasted coconut flakes, scallions, chile, vegetable oil, and ½ teaspoon salt. Working in batches, if necessary, use a mortar and pestle to crush and grind the mixture into a rough paste. (You could also use a blender or a food processor; just be careful not to overprocess the mixture—you want it to be rough, not totally smooth.)

Heat a medium skillet over medium-high heat. When the pan is hot, add the spice paste and cook, stirring occasionally, for 1 minute. Stir in salt and sugar to taste. Set the palapa aside.

Make the stew: In a Dutch oven or large saucepan, heat the vegetable oil over medium-high heat. Place the chicken wings in the pot, skin-side down, in a single layer. (If they don't fit in one layer, cook them in batches.) Cook until they are browned on both sides, about 5 minutes per side. Remove the chicken wings from the pot and set them aside.

Add the onion, garlic, and turmeric to the pot and cook, stirring occasionally, until the onion is soft and translucent, 3 to 5 minutes. Add the tomato and cook, stirring occasionally, until soft, 3 to 5 minutes.

Stir in the coconut milk and return the browned chicken wings to the pot. Bring the coconut milk mixture to a boil. Reduce the heat slightly, cover the pot, and simmer for about 25 minutes, or until the chicken is cooked through. Turn off the heat, remove the cooked chicken wings from the pan, and set aside in a deep bowl, but don't discard the coconut milk sauce.

In the same pan, cook the palapa over medium heat, stirring often, for 5 minutes. Stir in the scallions, bell pepper, and shredded coconut. Simmer for 5 minutes, or until the coconut milk mixture starts to reduce and the mixture thickens slightly. Add the fish sauce and black pepper to taste, then pour the sauce over the cooked chicken wings.

Serve the wings with the sauce from the bowl, with rice and sawsawan on the side.

The Maranao tribe are the largest group of Muslims in the Philippines. They live around Lake Lanao, which is why they're also known as the "People of the Lake." The Maranao once ran their own kingdom, known for its rich culture with its own distinct music, clothing, and food.

ZAMBOANGA SAUCE WITH TALANGKA

Crabs in Toasted Coconut Sauce with Cinnamon, Turmeric, and Nutmeg

THIS IS A RIFF on a well-known dish from the famous Alavar Seafood Restaurant in Zamboanga City, which sits at the end of the Zamboanga peninsula. If you ever visit the region, you'll no doubt be told that you have to stop by Alavar to try their pumpkin-orange Alavar sauce served over *curacha* (also known as spanner or red frog crab), a giant crab indigenous to the region.

In addition to sweet roasted onions and warm spices like nutmeg and cinnamon, the real secret to the sauce is the Mindanao innovation of toasting coconut meat to make toasted coconut milk. It forms an extraordinary base for what is essentially a curry. We cook the split live blue crabs, or *talangka*, directly in the sauce because the crabs, especially the females, which also have bright orange roe, or eggs, open up to release their fat and juices, giving the sauce an extra richness. That said, this sauce is also delicious over steamed crabs, or any kind of steamed, grilled, or sautéed seafood, like lobster or shrimp. **SERVES 4 TO 6**

FOR THE ZAMBOANGA SAUCE

3 medium white onions

Vegetable oil

1 pound (455 g) unsweetened shredded or grated coconut

5 cups (1.2 L) coconut milk

2 tablespoons minced fresh turmeric (see Note, page 193)

4 garlic cloves, smashed with the side of a knife

2 tablespoons minced fresh ginger

2 long red chiles (see Key Ingredients, page 37), thinly sliced

½ cup (115 g) Achuete Butter (recipe follows)

Kosher salt and freshly ground black pepper

FOR THE CRABS

2 tablespoons vegetable oil

4 live medium blue crabs, preferably female (see Notes)

2 tablespoons minced garlic

2½ tablespoons minced fresh ginger

¾ cup (95 g) minced white onion

½ teaspoon fish sauce, plus more if needed

¾ teaspoon ground cinnamon

1 teaspoon freshly grated nutmeg

FOR SERVING

4 to 6 cups (800 g to 1.2 kg) cooked white rice (see page 40)

Sawsawan (see page 34)

> recipe continues →

Notes: The sauce for this dish takes 2 to 3 hours to make, but it can be prepared in advance and kept in the refrigerator for up to 1 week or in the freezer for up to 1 month. It can also easily be multiplied, if you wanted to make a large batch to keep on hand.

To cut live crabs in half, refrigerate or cool them over ice for just a few hours before you prepare them. The ice will make the crabs lethargic and easier to handle. But if you keep the crabs below 50°F (10°C) for too long, you'll kill them, so only place them on ice just before you're going to cook them. Rinse them off; then, working with one at a time, place them on their backs on a cutting board. Working quickly and using a large, sturdy knife, cut vertically through the crabs. It's helpful to place your other hand on top of the knife for more leverage.

ZAMBOANGA SAUCE WITH TALANGKA

Crabs in Toasted Coconut Sauce with Cinnamon, Turmeric, and Nutmeg

continued →

Make the Zamboanga sauce: Preheat the oven to 350°F (175°C).

Place the onions in a small baking dish and drizzle all over with vegetable oil, turning them as you do so that they are well coated. Cover the dish with aluminum foil and roast for 45 minutes to 1 hour, or until they are soft and easily pierced all the way through with the tip of a knife. Set aside.

When the onions are done, increase the oven temperature to 450°F (230°C). Sprinkle the shredded coconut in an even layer on a rimmed baking sheet and toast in the oven for 5 to 10 minutes, or until the coconut flakes are a deep golden brown. The timing can vary widely depending on the accuracy of your oven and other factors, so it's important to watch the coconut as it cooks and stir it every few minutes to make sure it doesn't burn. Set aside 3 tablespoons of the toasted coconut for the finished dish and place the rest in a blender.

Add 3 cups (720 ml) of the coconut milk to the blender and puree until the mixture is as smooth as you can get it.

Working over the sink, strain the pureed coconut mixture through a fine-mesh sieve or double layer of cheesecloth set over a bowl. Use your clean hands to squeeze all the liquid out of the coconut. Reserve the toasted coconut milk and discard the solids.

In a large skillet, heat 2 tablespoons vegetable oil over medium heat. Add the turmeric, garlic, ginger, and chiles and cook, stirring often, until the vegetables are soft, about 10 minutes.

Coarsely chop the roasted onions and add them to the skillet. Cook for a minute or two, until they are warmed through. Add the toasted coconut milk and the remaining 2 cups (480 ml) plain coconut milk and raise the heat to medium-high to bring the mixture to a simmer. Cook for 10 minutes, stirring often so the milk does not burn.

Turn off the heat and stir in the achuete butter, stirring until it is incorporated into the sauce. Let cool slightly.

Transfer the sauce to a blender and puree until smooth. Taste and season with salt and black pepper as desired. Set aside while you make the crabs, or refrigerate for up to 1 week or freeze for up to 1 month until ready to use.

Make the crabs: In a large skillet or wide, deep pan, heat the vegetable oil over medium-high heat. When the oil is hot, cut the crabs in half with a large chef's knife (see Notes). Add the crab halves and ¾ cup (180 ml) water to the pan (be careful, as the oil may spatter) and cook, stirring often, until the water evaporates, about 10 minutes. (If your pan is not large enough to fit all the crabs, cook them two at a time.)

Reduce the heat to medium and add the garlic, ginger, and onion. Cook, stirring and tossing the crabs, until the onion is soft and translucent. Add about 2 cups (480 ml) of the Zamboanga sauce, the fish sauce, and the reserved 3 tablespoons toasted coconut and stir to cover the crabs.

Add the cinnamon and nutmeg and cook, stirring continuously, for another minute or two, until the sauce is thick and the crabs are coated. Taste and add more fish sauce as needed.

Serve immediately, with rice and sawsawan on the side. You can refrigerate or freeze any remaining Zamboanga sauce—but not the crabs—or heat it and serve it on the side.

ACHUETE BUTTER

Richly flavored and brilliant orange-red in color, this butter recipe can be scaled up or down as needed. **MAKES ½ CUP (115 G)**

1 tablespoon annatto seeds (see Key Ingredients, page 35)

½ cup (1 stick/115 g) unsalted butter, cut into 3 pieces

Place the seeds in a skillet or small saucepan over medium heat. Once the seeds start to pop, about 3 minutes, add the butter and stir continuously until it has melted and is just beginning to bubble. Turn off the heat and let the mixture sit for 5 minutes.

Strain the butter through a fine-mesh sieve into a glass jar or plastic storage container and discard the seeds. Use right away, or cover and refrigerate for about 1 week; it can also be frozen for up to 1 month.

BAKA TULA-SOG

Beef in Spiced Chocolate Sauce

NO ONE KNOWS FOR SURE WHETHER this Mindanao stew of beef, sweet potato, and bananas, whose sauce is similar in spirit to multilayered moles from Mexico, came from cross-pollination between Filipinos and Mexicans during the Spanish colonial era (see page 217) or is just a coincidence, given the spice-rich sauces from this region of the Philippines. As with *mole poblano*, unsweetened chocolate (which has been produced in the Philippines for four centuries, thanks to its introduction by the Spanish) is one ingredient used to flavor the savory sauce, along with ginger, chiles, peanut butter, fish sauce, and vinegar. **SERVES 4 TO 6**

Note: This recipe calls for rustic Filipino *tsokolate tableya*. Known as *tableya* for short, it's a full-flavored Filipino style of chocolate, which is usually made into hot chocolate drinks or used to flavor rice pudding called *champorado*. You can find it at any Filipino market (see Resources, page 342). It's famously made in the province of Batangas, which is known for the quality of its shade-grown cacao beans. They're roasted, ground into a paste, then formed into thick rounds or balls or often the tablet shapes from which they get their name: *tableya* means "tablet." If you can't find it, just use good-quality unsweetened cocoa powder instead.

4 tablespoons (60 ml) vegetable oil

1 pound (455 g) rib-eye steak, pounded thin and cut into 1½-inch-wide (4 cm) strips

Kosher salt and freshly ground black pepper

1 Japanese or baby sweet potato, peeled and cut into ½-inch-thick (1.5 cm) slices

4 Saba bananas (see page 252) or 2 yellow plantains, peeled and cut into ½-inch-thick (1.5 cm) slices

1 cup (115 g) thinly sliced onion

2 tablespoons minced fresh ginger

1 tablespoon minced garlic

1 teaspoon muscovado or brown sugar

¼ cup (85 g) grated tableya (see Note) or unsweetened cocoa powder

2 teaspoons fish sauce

1½ tablespoons natural peanut butter

1 long green chile (see Key Ingredients, page 37), seeded

1 cup (240 ml) chicken stock (see page 179)

1 tablespoon white sugarcane vinegar (see Key Ingredients, page 42)

¼ cup (35 g) crushed roasted peanuts, for garnish

4 to 6 cups (800 g to 1.2 kg) cooked white rice (see page 40), for serving

Sawsawan (see page 34), for serving

In a large skillet, heat 2 tablespoons of the vegetable oil over medium-high heat. Season the steak on all sides with salt and pepper. When the oil is almost smoking, add the steak to the pan and cook, undisturbed, for 3 minutes. Flip the slices and cook on the second side for 3 minutes more.

> recipe continues →

BAKA TULA-SOG

Beef in Spiced Chocolate Sauce

continued →

Transfer the steak to a bowl or plate and reduce the heat under the pan to medium-low. Add the sweet potato and bananas. Cook, stirring occasionally, for about 10 minutes, until the vegetables are brown on all sides and the sweet potato is tender when pierced with a knife. Transfer the contents of the pan to the bowl with the steak.

Wipe out the skillet, return it to the stovetop, and heat the remaining 2 tablespoons oil over medium heat. Add the onion, ginger, and garlic and cook for 3 to 5 minutes, until the onion is soft and translucent. Add the sugar and the tableya and cook, stirring, until the onion mixture is completely coated with the chocolate.

Transfer the onion mixture to a blender and add the fish sauce, peanut butter, chile, and stock. Blend until completely pureed.

Transfer the puree back to the skillet and simmer over medium-low heat until slightly reduced and thickened enough to coat the back of a spoon. Stir in the vinegar and cook for 1 minute more. Add the vegetables and steak to the pan and toss to coat them in the sauce. Cook until heated through, 3 to 5 minutes.

Serve the stew in bowls, garnished with a sprinkle of crushed peanuts, with rice and sawsawan alongside.

SATTI NA CURRY

Barbecued Skewers with Rice Cakes and Curry Sauce

SATTI IS THE MINDANAO SISTER OF satay, the Thai and Malaysian dish of skewers of grilled meats served with a dipping sauce on the side. But where the Thai and Malaysian versions are peanut-heavy and sweet, satti is silkier and spicier, and served with the pillowy steamed rice cakes called *puto*. Though some people dunk their puto in the sauce just like the skewers, others like to submerge the puto so they soak up the sauce and turn from a snack into a hearty meal. Try it both ways. In Zamboanga, you'll find satti stands on the street from the wee hours until sunrise, set up around makeshift patios meant for communal dining. This being a Muslim dish, you'll find the skewers made only with chicken or beef: no pork here. **SERVES 4 TO 6**

FOR THE MARINADE

2 tablespoons calamansi juice

½ cup (120 ml) coconut milk

2 tablespoons brown sugar

FOR THE CURRY SAUCE

½ cup (75 g) thinly sliced bird's-eye chiles (see Key Ingredients, page 37)

¾ cup (75 g) thinly sliced fresh ginger

4 thumb-size pieces fresh turmeric (see page 60), peeled and minced

1 medium white onion, thinly sliced

1 teaspoon dried oregano

2 tablespoons vegetable oil

½ teaspoon bagoong (see Key Ingredients, page 35)

1 tomato, finely diced

1½ cups (300 g) sugar

½ cup (65 g) cornstarch

½ cup (65 g) all-purpose flour

1 tablespoon kosher salt

¼ cup (25 g) ground annatto seed (see Key Ingredients, page 35)

6 cups (1.4 L) chicken stock (see page 179)

½ cup (120 ml) coconut milk

2 teaspoons curry powder

FOR THE SKEWERS

1 pound (450 g) boneless lean sirloin or chuck, cut into large cubes

1 pound (450 g) boneless chicken thighs, cut into large cubes

½ cup (120 ml) vegetable oil

Kosher salt and freshly ground black pepper

8 to 12 freshly cooked Puto (page 277)

Note: If you are using wooden skewers, soak them in warm water for 15 to 30 minutes before you add the meat so they don't burn as you cook the meat.

> recipe continues →

In a large mixing bowl, combine the calamansi juice, coconut milk, and brown sugar. Toss the meat in the marinade and let sit, refrigerated, for 1 to 2 hours.

Make the curry sauce: In a blender, combine the chiles, ginger, turmeric, onion, oregano, and 1 cup (240 ml) water. Process until smooth and set the mixture aside.

In a medium skillet, heat the vegetable oil over medium-high heat. Add the bagoong and the tomato and cook, stirring occasionally, for 3 minutes. Stir in the chile-ginger puree, reduce the heat to medium, and cook, stirring occasionally, until almost all the liquid has reduced, about 10 minutes. Set this aside.

In a small bowl, combine the sugar, cornstarch, flour, salt, and annatto. Whisk in 1 cup (240 ml) water until there are no lumps. Set this aside.

In a pot, bring the stock to a boil. Add the coconut milk and curry powder and stir until well combined. Add the bagoong mixture. Reduce the heat to medium-low and simmer for 15 minutes.

Add the cornstarch mixture to the pot, stir, and cook for 15 minutes more, until the sauce has thickened. Season with the salt and keep warm while you grill the skewers.

Make the skewers: Heat a grill pan over high heat or heat a charcoal or gas grill to medium. Thread 3 or 4 skewers with the beef cubes, then do the same with the chicken cubes. Brush them on all sides with the vegetable oil and sprinkle all sides with salt and pepper.

Place the skewers on the grill pan or grill and cook, flipping them once or twice, until the beef is cooked through to your liking, about 8 minutes for medium-rare, and the center of a piece of chicken registers 165°F (75°C) on an instant-read thermometer, between 8 and 15 minutes, depending on your cooking surface. Set the skewers aside on a serving platter when done.

To serve, put a few ladles of curry sauce in individual bowls and serve the skewers and puto family-style on large platters with the bowls of curry sauce alongside for dunking.

SATTI NA CURRY

Barbecued Skewers with Rice Cakes and Curry Sauce

← continued

MANOK SA TSOKOLATE

Chocolate Chicken

LIKE *BAKA TULA-SOG* (page 200), *manok sa tsokolate* is a stew made with the distinctive chocolate called *tableya*. It's like a cross between a Filipino adobo and a Mexican mole, which is why some refer to this dish as *adobong manok sa tableya*. The combination of star anise and rustic chocolate is a masterful one, which highlights the spice blending that is a hallmark of the Muslim region of the Philippines. **SERVES 4 TO 6**

1 cup (240 ml) white sugarcane vinegar (see Key Ingredients, page 42)

½ cup (120 ml) soy sauce

6 garlic cloves, smashed with the side of a knife

6 whole cloves

3 bay leaves

3 star anise pods

1½ tablespoons sugar

1 teaspoon whole black peppercorns

3 pounds (1.4 kg) skin-on chicken thighs and drumsticks

3 tablespoons vegetable oil

1 cup (130 g) grated tableya (see Note, page 200) or 1 cup (95 g) unsweetened cocoa powder

4 to 6 cups (800 g to 1.2 kg) cooked white rice (see page 40), for serving

Sawsawan (see page 34), for serving

In a nonreactive bowl, combine the vinegar, soy sauce, garlic, cloves, bay leaves, star anise, sugar, and peppercorns. Transfer the marinade to a ziplock bag or nonreactive plastic container, add the chicken, and marinate in the refrigerator for at least 1 hour and preferably up to 4 hours.

Remove the chicken and garlic cloves from the marinade and set them aside, then strain the marinade through a fine-mesh sieve into a bowl and set it aside.

In a large saucepan or Dutch oven, heat the vegetable oil over medium heat. Add the chicken pieces and the garlic cloves to the pan, making sure the chicken is skin-side down. Cook, stirring occasionally, until both the chicken and the garlic are browned, 7 to 10 minutes.

Add the strained marinade to the pot, along with 4 cups (1 L) water, and stir to combine. Bring to a boil, then reduce the heat slightly and cook at a simmer for 30 to 40 minutes, until the sauce is thick enough to coat the back of a spoon. Stir in the grated tableya and simmer for 5 minutes more.

Serve immediately, with rice and sawsawan.

TIULAH ITUM

Burnt Coconut Beef

TIULAH ITUM IS A RICH STEW made with the local technique of burning coconut meat to give the dish a unique smokiness and a mild, nutty sweetness that has no substitute. Unlike the coconut in the Zamboanga sauce (see page 195), here the coconut meat is not toasted but truly charred, traditionally over real flames most likely made from burning coconut husks. It's easy to char the coconut in a modern kitchen, too; watch it closely to make sure it doesn't go from charred to fully burnt and bitter. **SERVES 4 TO 6**

1 whole coconut or 3 cups (255 g) unsweetened coconut flakes

6 tablespoons vegetable oil

2 pounds (910 g) beef rump roast, cut into 1-inch cubes

Kosher salt and freshly ground black pepper

1 medium white onion, diced

½ cup (50 g) minced fresh ginger

5 tablespoons (45 g) minced garlic

4 lemongrass stalks, outer leaves removed

1 pound (455 g) taro root (see Note), peeled and diced

4 bird's-eye chiles (see Key Ingredients, page 37), seeded and thinly sliced

3 cups (720 ml) beef broth

3 cups (720 ml) coconut milk

¼ cup (60 ml) fish sauce

3 tablespoons soy sauce

2 tablespoons white sugarcane vinegar (see Key Ingredients, page 42)

4 to 6 cups (800 g to 1.2 kg) cooked white rice (see page 40), for serving

Sawsawan (see page 34), for serving

Note: Taro root is a brown-skinned tuber found at Asian, Caribbean, and Indian markets and, these days, many mainstream supermarkets.

If using the whole coconut, break it open and scoop out the meat (**see page 208, photo 1**). Place the meat in a mortar and char it using a kitchen torch **(2)**, then pound it with a pestle **(3)** for 5 to 8 minutes until all the pieces have broken down and are fully blackened **(4)**.

If using coconut flakes, heat your largest skillet over high heat and add the coconut flakes. (Work in batches if they do not easily fit in the pan all at one time.) Toast, stirring the flakes often, until they are charred and very deep black-brown but not fully blackened and burnt—this will take at least 10 minutes.

Set 1 cup (85 g) of the charred flakes aside and place the other 2 cups (170 g) in a blender with 3 tablespoons vegetable oil. Blend into a chunky paste. Set this aside.

> recipe continues →

TIULAH ITUM

Burnt Coconut
Beef

continued →

In a large bowl, season the beef cubes with salt and pepper. Toss the beef cubes with the charred coconut puree and marinate at room temperature for 1 hour.

When the beef is almost fully marinated, in a large saucepan, heat the remaining 3 tablespoons vegetable oil over medium-high heat. Add the onion and ginger and cook just until they begin to soften, about 2 minutes. Add the garlic and cook until lightly browned, about 5 minutes.

Smash the lemongrass stalks with the side of a chef's knife and add them to the pan. Stir in the taro, chiles, and the marinated beef, making sure to scrape any leftover coconut puree from the sides of the bowl into the pan. Cook, stirring occasionally, until the beef begins to brown, 5 to 7 minutes.

Add the broth and coconut milk and bring everything to a boil. Reduce the heat so that the mixture cooks at a simmer and cook for 30 minutes, or until the beef is tender.

Remove the lemongrass stalks from the pan. Take ½ cup (120 ml) of the broth from the pot and transfer it to a blender with the reserved 1 cup (85 g) charred coconut flakes. Puree until the mixture is smooth, then return the mixture to the pan.

Stir in the fish sauce, soy sauce, and vinegar, and taste for seasoning. Serve immediately in deep bowls, with rice and sawsawan.

CHARRING COCONUT MEAT

BALBACOA
Stewed Cow's Foot and Oxtails

DAVAO, IN MINDANAO, IS HOME TO open-air street vendors, many of which sell *balbacoa*. The stew is luscious and savory, made with cow's foot and oxtails that contain plenty of cartilage that helps create a thick broth. You need about three hours of cooking to tenderize tougher off-cuts like cow's foot or oxtails. Both cuts may be difficult to find, but a butcher or nearly any Latin or Asian meat market should have them. **SERVES 4 TO 6**

8 cups (2 L) beef stock

2 thumb-size pieces fresh ginger, smashed with the side of a knife

6 garlic cloves, smashed with the side of a knife, plus 2 tablespoons minced garlic

4 shallots, cut into eighths

4 star anise pods

1 long green chile (see Key Ingredients, page 37)

1 pound (455 g) oxtails

1 pound (455 g) cow's foot

2 tablespoons vegetable oil

2 tablespoons minced white onion

1 cup (155 g) cooked or canned white beans, such as navy or cannellini

¼ cup (40 g) fermented black beans (see Notes, page 106)

½ pound (225 g) Saba bananas (see page 252) or yellow plantains, sliced into 1-inch-thick (2.5 cm) rounds

1 tablespoon fish sauce

Kosher salt and freshly ground black pepper

4 to 6 cups (800 g to 1.2 kg) cooked white rice (see page 40), for serving

Sawsawan (see page 34), for serving

In a stockpot or Dutch oven, combine the stock, ginger, smashed garlic, shallots, star anise, and chile. Bring the mixture to a boil over medium-high heat.

Add the oxtail and the cow's foot and pour in enough water to cover both. Bring the liquid to a boil. Reduce the heat to low so that it cooks at a simmer and cook for 3 hours, or until the meat is tender.

After about 2½ hours, in a medium saucepan, heat the vegetable oil over medium heat. Add the onion and minced garlic and cook until they begin to soften, about 3 minutes. Add the white beans and cook, stirring occasionally, for 10 minutes. Set this aside.

When the oxtail and cow's foot are tender, add the white bean mixture to the pot along with the fermented black beans, bananas, and fish sauce.

Cook for 10 minutes more, or until the bananas are just tender, and season with salt and pepper. Serve with rice and sawsawan.

TOMATOES AND TAMALES

THE SPANISH-MEXICAN INFLUENCE

THE CONNECTION between Spain and the Philippines is a deep and complicated one, thanks to more than three hundred years of Spanish rule over the country, which began when Ferdinand Magellan claimed the Philippines as a Spanish colony in 1521. The Spanish influence—you might even say supremacy—touches every aspect of Filipino culture, starting with the fact that the very country is named after a Spanish king. Many Filipinos have Spanish last names, the language is strewn with Spanish terms, and the majority of the population is Catholic.

Spain is, of course, present in Filipino cooking, beginning with the many garlic-onion-tomato sauces (such as the *afritada* on page 224) you'll see throughout this chapter. The Spanish influence is behind the use of raisins in menudo (page 225) and the olives that brighten up the goat stew *kaldereta* (page 226). You can see the Spanish influence on the sausage filling in *rellenong manok* (stuffed chicken, page 232), as well as the reason for making it: to celebrate the birth of Jesus on Christmas Eve. There's a common perception that all Southeast Asian food is spicy. Save for a few regions, this is not true of the Philippines, a fact that might also be attributed to the Spanish dominion over the islands.

Still, when we talk about the Spanish influence, we must broaden the story to include Mexico, which was also a Spanish colony. Direct trade between those two countries (see page 217) meant the transfer and mixing of language, people, plants, and dishes between the Philippines and Mexico as well as Spain: the banana leaf–wrapped tamale filled with pork, salted egg, and rice flour dough on page 218 is a beautiful example.

Between 1565 and 1815, Spanish trading ships known as the Manila Galleons sailed often between Manila and Acapulco in Mexico, connecting the two countries. Transfer of culture between our two countries thrived during this time, and in fact, Spanish leaders in Mexico were given authority over the Philippines, because Mexico's west coast was so much closer to us than Spain. Food historians now see that many of the Filipino dishes we assume have Spanish roots—tomato sauces, pico de gallo–like salad (page 122), chocolate in the sauce of *baka tula-sog* (page 200)—may have come from cross-pollination with Mexico. The flow of influence is not just one way: some old stories say the famous Mexican mole was originated by a Filipina, a Pueblan nun named Catarina de San Juan, who arrived in Mexico as a slave from Southeast Asia in the 1600s and eventually converted to Catholicism. Most reports say she was Vietnamese or Cambodian or Indian, but others say she came from Muslim royalty in what is now Mindanao. Connections like these—culinary and beyond—are only just beginning to be explored.

ROBINSON'S TAMALES

CAVITE, my father's hometown province, is heavily influenced by Spain, and Spain's former colony of Mexico, due to its role as a port for Spanish galleon trade starting in the sixteenth century. Though lesser known for its Spanish-accented cuisine than highly regarded Pampanga, another port city, the greater province of Cavite is also a culinary destination. One of the must-try dishes in this area is Robinson's Tamales, which supposedly take their name from the American great-grandfather of the city's most famous maker of these Filipino-style tamales. (Robinson was said to be a U.S. soldier stationed there in the early twentieth century who married a local.) There are various kinds of tamales in the Philippines, and though they share the same style of wrapping and steaming, most similarities end there. Robinson's tamales are wrapped in banana leaves and filled with leftover cooked pork or chicken, a slice of salted egg, and two different colors of toasted rice flour masa, one sweet and one orange thanks to a little peanut butter and achuete oil. You could make these vegetarian or vegan using vegetables like roasted chiles or mushrooms instead of chicken or pork and egg; you can add some pickled hot chiles, too. **MAKES ABOUT 8 TAMALES**

Notes: You will need butcher's twine to tie the tamales.

If you don't have a steamer pot, you can set a metal colander (or even a wire rack, if you have one that fits) into a large spaghetti pot or soup pot with a lid.

Leftover roasted or boiled pork or chicken is perfect for this dish.

2 cups (370 g) uncooked jasmine rice

6½ cups (1.6 L) coconut milk, plus more as needed

Kosher salt and freshly ground black pepper

½ cup (120 ml) natural peanut butter

2 tablespoons Achuete Oil (page 58)

1 tablespoon fish sauce

1 cup (125 g) chopped roasted peanuts

1 (1-pound/450 g) package frozen banana leaves (see Key Ingredients, page 36), defrosted

1 cup (140 g) shredded cooked pork or chicken (see Notes)

2 salted eggs (see page 41) or hard-boiled eggs, peeled and sliced lengthwise into 8 pieces

In a large dry skillet, toast the rice over medium-high heat until all the grains have turned white, watching and stirring continuously to make sure they don't burn. (It's okay if a few of the grains begin to brown, but you don't want a lot of brown grains.)

Immediately remove the pan from the heat and transfer the rice to a blender or food processor. Process until you have a coarse powder and set it aside. (This can be done several days in advance; just keep the flour in a tightly sealed container.)

In a large saucepan, bring the coconut milk to a low boil over medium heat and season it well with salt and pepper. Turn off the heat and stir in 2 cups (200 g) of the rice flour, adding it half a cup at a time. Make sure it is totally incorporated, with no lumps—the mixture should have the consistency of

> recipe continues →

continued →

mashed potatoes or polenta: smooth and soft, but stiff enough to hold a peak. Add more rice flour or coconut milk as needed.

Take a little more than half the rice flour mixture out of the pan and set it aside in a bowl.

Add the peanut butter, achuete oil, fish sauce, and peanuts to the rice flour mixture remaining in the pan and stir until they are totally incorporated. Set aside.

Trim off the brown edges of the banana leaves and cut the leaves into 8-inch (20 cm) squares. You will need about 16 squares (you will have some leaves left over).

Take two banana leaf squares and set them down on a clean work surface. Add 3 tablespoons of the white rice flour dough to the middle of the banana leaf and press it down into a rectangular shape. There should be a border of at least 2 inches (5 cm) of banana leaf on all sides.

Top the rice flour dough with about 2 tablespoons of the shredded pork or chicken, placing it along the center of the masa. Top this with 3 tablespoons of the peanut butter rice flour dough, pressing it down into a rectangular shape and covering the chicken and white rice flour dough. Gently press 1 slice of egg into the top.

Fold up the sides of the banana leaf over the filling as if you were wrapping a gift, then tie it shut with butcher's twine, making sure the string wraps around all four sides. Set the tamale aside on a plate or baking sheet. Repeat with the rest of the banana leaves and filling. (At this point, the tamales can be frozen for up to 1 month, then cooked straight from the freezer as directed below.)

Fill a steamer pot with a couple inches of water (making sure it won't touch the steam basket) and bring the water to a boil. Place the tamales in the steamer basket, cover, and steam them for 1½ hours. Remove the tamales from the pot to drain.

You can serve the tamales hot, warm, or at room temperature: place a tamale on a plate, snip the twine with scissors, and fold open the banana leaf.

Until 1986, Filipino Spanish—similar to Mexican Spanish, thanks to the galleon trade during the Spanish colonial era (see page 218)—was an official language of the Philippines, along with English and Tagalog. But the language was no longer officially recognized after the People Power Revolution in 1986 brought the country a new democratically elected government. Yet in the southern part of the country (see page 189), and in other sparsely populated areas, an older, Spanish-based Creole dialect called Chavacano is still an official language: a sign at one of the airports in Mindanao announcing "hello" in many languages reads *bienvenidos* for those who speak Spanish and Chavacano.

DAMPA FRY NA ESCABECHE

Whole Fried Fish with Sweet-and-Sour Sauce

IN THE PHILIPPINES, the *dampa* is an open-air food market, surrounded by rows of small casual restaurants. In most of them, you can bring the cooks the whole fish or fresh seafood you just bought and they will quickly clean it and cook it to your liking. (There are many Filipino and Asian markets in the States, particularly in California, that will do this, too.) There is nothing like the taste of fresh, crispy fried fish from the dampa; it's great on its own with rice and *sawsawan*, or with a classic *escabeche*, a Spanish sweet-and-sour sauce with wilted red and green peppers. (Though the cornstarch dredge used here actually makes it Spanish-Chinese-Filipino.) The recipe is remarkably simple and light, and the fish is so crispy, you can eat it gill to tail. **SERVES 4 TO 6**

FOR THE FISH

1 cup (240 ml) white sugarcane vinegar (see Key Ingredients, page 42)

1 cup (240 ml) soy sauce

¼ cup (35 g) minced garlic

¼ cup (25 g) minced fresh ginger

3 lemongrass stalks, thinly sliced

4 (1- to 1½-pound/455 to 680 g) whole red snappers, cleaned and gutted (see Note)

FOR THE ESCABECHE SAUCE

1 cup (240 ml) fish stock (see page 95)

½ cup (120 ml) white sugarcane vinegar (see Key Ingredients, page 42), plus more to taste

½ cup (90 g) muscovado or brown sugar

¼ cup (30 g) cornstarch

1 tablespoon vegetable oil

2 tablespoons diced red bell pepper

2 tablespoons diced green bell pepper

Vegetable oil, for frying

3 cups (390 g) cornstarch

¼ cup (45 g) kosher salt

2 tablespoons freshly ground black pepper

1 tablespoon paprika

4 to 6 cups (800 g to 1.2 kg) cooked white rice (see page 40), for serving

Sawsawan (see page 34), for serving

Note: The recipe calls for red snapper—which has a sweet white flesh—but you can substitute any mild-fleshed whole fish you prefer. You could use fewer large fish or more small fish, or even one whole fish, if it fits easily in the pot you'll be using to deep-fry. The fish will taste best if it's allowed to marinate overnight.

> recipe continues →

Marinate the fish: In a large ziplock bag or nonreactive container, combine the vinegar, soy sauce, garlic, ginger, and lemongrass. Score the fish on the diagonal two or three times on both sides, making cuts that go all the way to the bone. Place the fish in the bag or container, making sure they are covered in marinade on all sides, and marinate in the refrigerator for at least 2 hours and preferably overnight.

Make the sauce: In a medium saucepan, combine the stock, vinegar, and sugar and bring to a boil, then reduce the heat to low.

Meanwhile, in a small bowl, whisk together the cornstarch and 1 cup (240 ml) water to form a slurry. Slowly stir the slurry into the sauce, stirring until it thickens. Keep warm.

In a large skillet, heat the vegetable oil over medium heat. Add the bell peppers and cook, stirring occasionally, until they have softened slightly but still have some texture, about 5 minutes. Add them to the sauce with more vinegar to taste, if desired.

Cook the fish: When you're ready to fry the fish, fill a large stockpot or Dutch oven about halfway with vegetable oil and heat the oil over medium heat until it registers 350°F (175°C) on an instant-read thermometer or just begins to lightly shimmer.

While the oil heats, in a wide shallow bowl or baking dish, whisk together the cornstarch, salt, black pepper, and paprika.

Dredge the fish on all sides in the cornstarch mixture and set them on a plate or baking sheet.

Add the fish to the hot oil one or two at a time, so as not to crowd the pot, and fry, flipping the fish once, until crispy and golden brown on both sides, about 4 minutes per side. (You can tell the fish is done when the coating in the scored part starts to color and flake, and the rest of the fish is golden brown and feels crisp to the touch.) Remove the fish from the oil with tongs or a slotted spoon and set it on a plate or platter. Repeat with the remaining fish.

To serve, drizzle the fried fish generously with the sauce. Serve hot, with rice and sawsawan.

DAMPA FRY NA ESCABECHE

Whole Fried Fish with Sweet-and-Sour Sauce

← continued

AFRITADA MANOK
Chicken Stew with Tomatoes and Garlic

AFRITADA MANOK IS ONE OF MANY similar Spanish-influenced tomato stews that is a staple at fiestas; others include menudo, *kaldereta*, and *mechadong* mackerel (all of which can be found on the following pages). They're all variations on the same theme; this one is mild and very simple to make. **SERVES 4 TO 6**

Vegetable oil

3 bone-in, skin-on chicken thighs

3 bone-in, skin-on chicken drumsticks

Kosher salt and freshly ground black pepper

1 large onion, diced

2 tablespoons minced garlic

2 cups (480 ml) tomato puree

2 large carrots, cubed

2 potatoes, peeled and cubed

¼ cup (60 ml) fish sauce

2 tablespoons soy sauce

Juice of 2 lemons

4 to 6 cups (800 g to 1.2 kg) cooked white rice (see page 40), for serving

Sawsawan (see page 34), for serving

In a Dutch oven or large heavy-bottomed pot, heat ¼ cup (60 ml) vegetable oil over medium-high heat. Season the chicken with salt and pepper.

When the oil is hot and just begins to send up wisps of smoke, place the chicken in the pot in a single layer, skin-side down, and reduce the heat to medium. (You may need to do this in batches.) Cook the chicken until well browned, 5 to 7 minutes. Flip the chicken over and cook on the other side for 5 minutes more, then remove the chicken to a large plate.

Add more oil, if necessary, so there are at least 3 tablespoons in the pot. Add the onion and garlic and cook, stirring occasionally, until the garlic starts to brown, 2 to 3 minutes.

Add the tomato puree and 3 cups (720 ml) water, stirring so they are well combined, then return the chicken to the pot. The liquid should nearly cover the chicken; if not, add more water as needed.

Increase the heat and bring the liquid to a boil, then reduce the heat so it cooks at a simmer. Cover and cook for 20 minutes, then add the carrot and potato to the pot. Cover again and cook for 20 minutes more, or until the chicken is just cooked through and the carrots and potatoes are tender.

Stir in the fish sauce, soy sauce, 1½ teaspoons black pepper, and the lemon juice. Cook for 5 minutes more.

Serve hot, with rice and sawsawan.

MENUDO
Duck Leg Stew

FILIPINO MENUDO IS DIFFERENT FROM THE Mexican soup of the same name, but is equally beloved as a comfort food. It's made with plenty of tomato, garlic, and ginger, plus a touch of liver paste. Menudo is often made with pork, but we prefer duck legs for extra richness. **SERVES 4 TO 6**

6 bone-in, skin-on duck legs

1 cup (110 g) diced white onion

¼ cup (35 g) minced garlic

1 tablespoon minced fresh ginger

½ cup (120 ml) liver paste or liverwurst (see Key Ingredients, page 39)

4 cups (1 L) tomato sauce

5 cups (1.2 L) chicken stock (see page 179)

2 Idaho potatoes, peeled and cubed

2 carrots, cubed

1 cup (145 g) black raisins

1½ cups (205 g) frozen or fresh green peas

¼ cup (60 ml) fish sauce

3 tablespoons soy sauce

½ teaspoon freshly ground black pepper

Fresh lemon juice

4 to 6 cups (800 g to 1.2 kg) cooked white rice (see page 40), for serving

Sawsawan (see page 34), for serving

Preheat the oven to 375°F (190°C).

Heat a Dutch oven or large heavy-bottomed pot over medium-high heat. Place the duck legs in the pot skin-side down and cook until browned, 6 to 8 minutes. Flip the duck legs over and cook on the other side for 2 minutes more. Remove the duck legs to a large plate.

Drain off all but 1 tablespoon of the duck fat from the pot. Reduce the heat to medium and add the onion, garlic, and ginger. Cook, stirring frequently, until the onion is soft and the garlic is just beginning to brown, 3 to 5 minutes. Stir in the liver paste and cook for 3 minutes.

Whisk in the tomato sauce and the stock until combined. Stir in the potatoes, carrots, and raisins and cook for 10 minutes, or until tender. Return the browned duck legs to the pot. Once the liquid begins to simmer, cover the pot and place it in the oven. Cook for 45 minutes to 1 hour, or until an instant-read thermometer inserted into the thickest part of a duck leg reads 165°F (75°C).

Stir in the peas, fish sauce, soy sauce, and pepper and cook for a minute or two, just until the peas are cooked through, then add the lemon juice.

Serve hot, with rice and sawsawan.

KALDERETA

Goat in Tomato Stew with Olives

YOU CAN MAKE A *KALDERETA* with any meat, like beef or pork, but in the Philippines, goat kaldereta (technically *kaldereta kambing*; *kambing* means "goat") is usually reserved for special occasions. Olives are typical in this dish, which makes it different from other Filipino stews. We thicken and smooth out the sauce with a little liver paste and mild goat cheese, though some use Edam cheese, canned cheddar, or peanut butter. Most kaldereta recipes would have you stew the olives along with the goat, but we add them later as a garnish so you have a slightly briny bite to balance out the rich sauce. **SERVES 4 TO 6**

3 tablespoons vegetable oil

2 pounds (910 g) boneless, skinless goat meat, cut into bite-size chunks

4 garlic cloves, smashed with the side of a knife

1 small white onion, quartered

4 bay leaves

1 tablespoon whole black peppercorns

¼ cup (60 ml) tomato paste

2 cups (480 ml) tomato sauce

2 tablespoons fish sauce

1 long green chile (see Key Ingredients, page 37; optional)

¼ cup (60 ml) liver paste or liverwurst (see Key Ingredients, page 39)

2 small red potatoes, quartered

1 large carrot, diced

2 bell peppers, one red and one green, coarsely chopped

2 ounces (56 g) mild fresh goat cheese, at room temperature

1 cup (155 g) pitted Spanish green olives

4 to 6 cups (800 g to 1.2 kg) cooked white rice (see page 40), for serving

Patis (see page 35), for serving

In a Dutch oven or large heavy-bottomed pot, heat the vegetable oil over medium-high heat. Add the goat meat and cook, turning the pieces once or twice, until browned on all sides, 7 to 10 minutes. Remove the goat meat from the pot and set it aside on a large plate.

Reduce the heat to medium and add the garlic cloves. Cook until they begin to brown, about 2 minutes. Add the onion and cook, stirring occasionally, for 3 minutes, then add the bay leaves and the peppercorns. Stir in the tomato paste and let it brown slightly, stirring often, about 3 minutes.

> recipe continues →

Add the lemon slices, tomato sauce, stock, soy sauce, and bay leaves. Stir to combine thoroughly, and raise the heat to high. Once the liquid is bubbling, reduce the heat so the liquid cooks at a simmer and cook until the sauce is thickened, about 30 minutes.

Meanwhile, take each mackerel and use a knife or kitchen shears to butterfly them open, leaving the two sides attached at the tail. Remove the spine by running your finger underneath it, then pulling it out, making sure to keep the two sides attached at the tail. (You may have to use kitchen shears or a knife to get it out.) Repeat for all 6 mackerel.

Once the mackerel are butterflied, fill each one with an equal amount of the crispy bacon. Fold the two sides back together.

In a large skillet, heat the remaining 2 tablespoons oil over medium-high heat. When the oil begins to lightly smoke, add the mackerel. Do not overcrowd the pan; if necessary, work in batches. Cook until the fish are browned on the first side, 3 to 5 minutes, then flip them and cook for 3 to 5 minutes more, until the other side is brown. Remove the fish from the pan and set aside on a plate. Repeat with the remaining mackerel.

When the sauce is thickened, stir in the fish sauce and season with salt and black pepper. Once all the mackerel are browned, place them in the pot with the sauce and cook until heated through, about 5 minutes. Taste and season with lemon juice.

Serve the mackerel right away, with the sauce, rice, and sawsawan.

MECHADONG MACKEREL

Bacon-Stuffed Mackerel in Tomato Sauce

← continued

FILLING AND FORMING RELLENONG MANOK

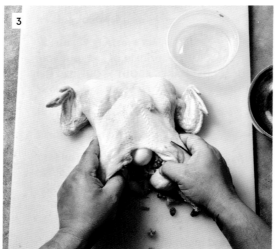

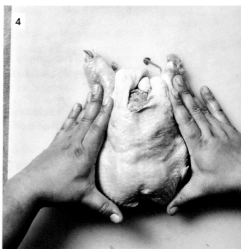

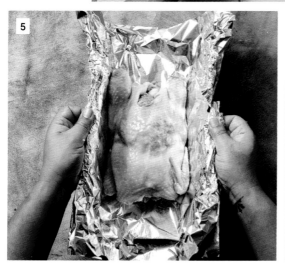

SARSIADO ISDA

Fried Fish Fillets with Tomatoes and Eggs

SARSIADO IS A SIMPLE, HOMEY DISH of fried fish in a tomato and scrambled egg sauce. (*Sarsiado,* meaning "cooked in a thick sauce," is thought to be derived from the Spanish word for "salsa.") After the fish is fried, it's topped with a unique sauce: eggs are gently scrambled into a fresh tomato sauce seasoned with onions and garlic. Mixing the eggs into the sauce is a clever way to use up the leftovers you'll have from battering the fillets. You can eat the fish on its own, over rice, or tucked into a *pandesal* (page 298). **SERVES 4**

FOR THE SAUCE

2 tablespoons vegetable oil

1 medium yellow onion, diced

3 garlic cloves, minced

2 medium tomatoes, diced

1½ tablespoons fish sauce

1½ teaspoons kosher salt, plus more as needed

½ teaspoon freshly ground black pepper, plus more as needed

FOR THE FISH

4 (½-pound/225 g) tilapia, catfish, or whitefish fillets

Kosher salt and freshly ground black pepper

¼ cup (30 g) all-purpose flour

2 large eggs, beaten

¼ cup (45 g) fine cornmeal

Vegetable oil, for frying

2 tablespoons thinly sliced scallion

Make the sauce: In a Dutch oven, heat the vegetable oil over medium heat. Add the onion and garlic and cook, stirring occasionally, until the garlic is just beginning to brown and the onion is soft and translucent, about 10 minutes.

Add the tomatoes and cook over medium heat for 1 minute. Add ¾ cup (180 ml) water and the fish sauce and bring the mixture to a boil. Reduce the heat to low and simmer for 5 to 7 minutes, until the tomatoes have softened but not totally broken down. Season with the salt and pepper, taste, and add more as desired. Set the sauce aside while you fry the fish.

Make the fish: Season the fillets with salt and pepper on both sides and let them sit for 10 minutes.

Place the flour, the beaten eggs, and the cornmeal in three separate shallow bowls. Dredge each seasoned fillet in the flour, dip it into the egg, letting the excess drip back into the bowl, then roll it in the cornmeal. Set the battered fillets on a clean plate or baking sheet. Reserve the eggs for the sauce.

Fill a Dutch oven or heavy-bottomed pot about halfway with vegetable oil, and heat the oil over medium-high to high heat until it is just barely shimmering or registers 350°F (175°C) on an instant-read thermometer. (You can also fry the fish in a large skillet, but be careful: they'll splatter.)

Fry the fillets one or two at a time—or as many as will fit without touching—flipping them once or twice, until they are golden brown and crispy on both sides, about 8 minutes. Set the fried fillets aside while you finish the sauce.

Return the sauce to medium-low heat and bring it to a low simmer. Add the reserved beaten egg and cook, stirring continuously, for 1 minute. Add the scallion and cook for a minute or two, until it has just wilted and the eggs are cooked through in the sauce; you want the eggs to be light and fluffy.

Top each fillet with a quarter of the sauce and serve immediately.

PANSIT GALLEON

Noodles with Sausage, Chicken, and Shrimp

SLENDER SPANISH *FIDEO*—skinny noodles that look like pieces of cut spaghetti—are typically toasted in oil before they are cooked in liquid. Here we apply the same technique to make a *pansit galleon*. Like other pansits, this is a quick noodle stir-fry loaded with toppings, from meat and seafood to crushed pork rinds, scallion, and tomato, which is a nod to Spain and Mexico. It's possible that some of the inspiration for fideo may have gone from the Philippines to Spain, considering that the Chinese brought the noodles that became pansit to the Philippines some five hundred years before the Spanish arrived. This pansit is our own creation, inspired by the overlapping influences in our cuisines. **SERVES 4 TO 6**

Notes: Fideo, sometimes called fidelini, are very thin, short vermicelli noodles that look like miniature pieces of spaghetti. They are widely sold in mainstream supermarkets, sometimes in the Latin foods section. If you can't find them, break up very thin vermicelli into small pieces.

Clean mussels by gently scrubbing the shells under running water to remove any leftover slime or seaweed. To debeard the mussels, look for any hairy membranes hanging out of the shell and use your fingers to grasp them and pull them out.

4 tablespoons (60 ml) vegetable oil

1 pound (455 g) fideo noodles (see Notes)

4 garlic cloves, minced

2 tablespoons minced fresh ginger

½ cup (90 g) diced tomato

3 ounces (85 g) diced cooked Vigan longanisa (see Key Ingredients, page 39)

4 ounces (115 g) sliced raw chicken breast

4 ounces (115 g) raw small shrimp, peeled and deveined

12 mussels, cleaned and debearded (see Notes)

2 to 3 cups (480 to 720 ml) chicken stock (see page 179)

¼ cup (12 g) coarsely crushed pork rinds, for garnish

1 scallion, thinly sliced, for garnish

In a large, deep-sided skillet or saucepan, heat 2 tablespoons of the vegetable oil over medium heat until it begins to shimmer. Add the noodles and toast them in the oil, stirring continuously, until they are golden brown, about 5 minutes. Remove the noodles from the pan and set them aside.

Add the remaining 2 tablespoons oil, the garlic, and the ginger to the pan. Cook, stirring occasionally, for 1 minute. Add the tomato and longanisa and cook, stirring occasionally, for 3 minutes. Add the chicken and cook, stirring occasionally, until it is cooked through, about 4 minutes.

Add the shrimp, mussels, toasted noodles, and 2 cups of the stock. Cook, stirring occasionally, until the mussels have opened, most of the liquid has been absorbed, and the noodles are al dente. (You may need to add more stock and cook for a few minutes more, if the noodles are not yet cooked through.) Discard any mussels that have not yet opened.

Top with the pork rinds and scallion and serve immediately.

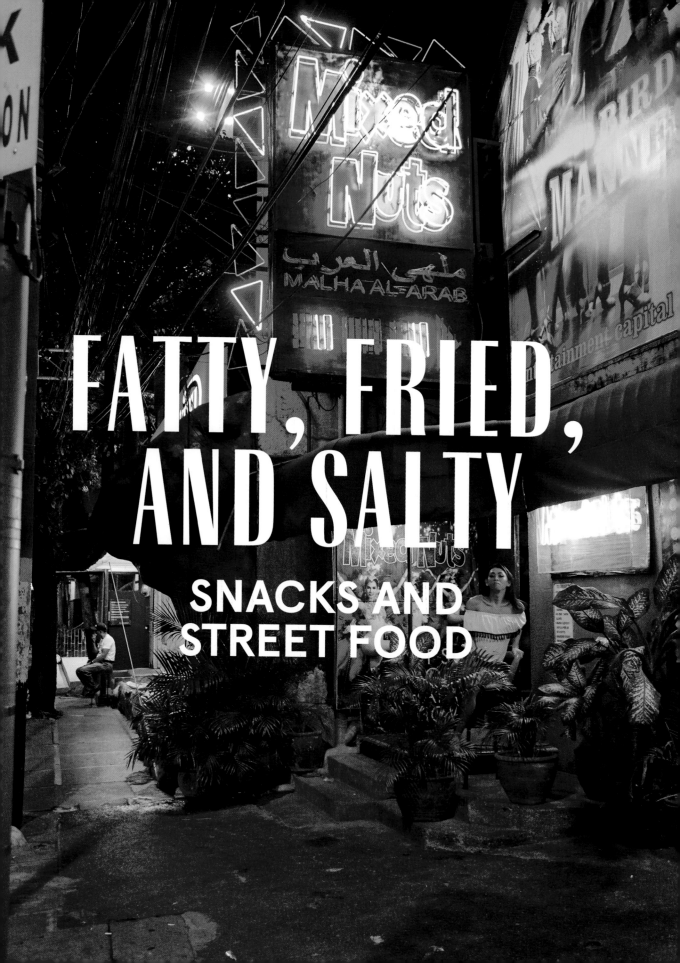

FATTY, FRIED, AND SALTY

SNACKS AND STREET FOOD

THE HARDEST-WORKING DISHES in Filipino cuisine are found on the street, at backyard parties, and served in *karinderia*s, little cafeteria-like stalls with a few seats. Indeed, snacking is an art: vendors selling fried bites of fish or dough or skewers of smoky grilled meats to eat on the run dot Philippine plazas and parks, line the main streets of smaller villages, and are even found on college campuses and in the open-air markets where we buy our fresh foods.

The salt, fat, crunch, and tang found in these snacks are the flavors and textures that so many of us crave. In fact, many of the foods in this chapter are often eaten, not surprisingly, with a cold beer, so much so that we even have a special word for things served with alcohol: *pulutan*. (It's from the root word *pulot*, meaning "to pick up.")

It follows that these snacks are the hallmarks of any social event, when you gather with friends and family. So invite your *barkada* (posse) to your place for a backyard barbecue and serve any of the recipes from this chapter, from crispy fried anchovies (page 246) and sweet-charred chicken barbecue (page 258) to deep-fried, long-marinated pig's foot and its oh-so-crackly skin (page 262).

Inihaw, or grilled meat stands (*inihaw* means "grilled"), are everywhere in the Philippines—on the street, in alleys, on college campuses, in the middle of parks, and on beaches. Meats and fish become so flavorful when cooked over charcoal or, better still, the smoking embers of burnt coconut husks. Usually you order very specifically by the part or the cut; you can find everything from fish collar to pork intestine to chicken wings and it will be served to you three or four on a skewer. Some dishes were given special or funny names in the 1980s, like Betamax (chicken-blood cake), Walkman (grilled pork ears), Adidas (chicken feet), and pope's nose (chicken butts).

PRITONG DILIS
Fried Anchovies with Spicy Rémoulade

THIS DISH IS INSPIRED by both fried tawilis (sardines) and crispy *dilis* (anchovies). Dilis are eaten as an everyday snack in the Philippines, and are perfect dipped in spicy rémoulade and served with cold beer. **SERVES 6**

Note: Maggi seasoning sauce is like liquid umami: a dash or two will perk up almost anything, from broth to noodles to adobos. Used and sold around the world, especially in Asia, formulas vary slightly by country. Any type will work here—you'll often find it in grocery stores sold beside the HP, A1, Worcestershire, and soy sauces—though you can sometimes find the Filipino version, which has a little calamansi juice added, in Asian supermarkets.

FOR THE SPICY RÉMOULADE

10 bird's-eye chiles (see Key Ingredients, page 37)

2 teaspoons Maggi seasoning sauce (see Note)

1 cup (240 ml) mayonnaise

¼ cup (60 ml) white sugarcane vinegar (see Key Ingredients, page 42)

FOR THE DILIS

Vegetable oil, for frying

1 pound (455 g) cleaned whole anchovies

3 cups (390 g) cornstarch

2 tablespoons kosher salt

2 tablespoons freshly ground black pepper

1 tablespoon paprika

Maldon sea salt (optional)

Make the spicy rémoulade: Heat the chiles in a cast-iron skillet over high heat until they are lightly charred on all sides, 7 to 10 minutes. Watch them carefully and flip them often to make sure they do not totally burn.

Let the chiles cool slightly, then transfer them to a food processor and add the Maggi, mayonnaise, and vinegar. Pulse until they are well incorporated, then set the spicy rémoulade aside while you prepare the fish. (It will keep in an airtight container in the refrigerator for 7 days.)

Make the dilis: Fill a Dutch oven or heavy-bottomed pot about halfway with vegetable oil, and heat the oil over medium-high heat until it is just barely shimmering or registers 350°F (175°C) on an instant-read thermometer.

Pat the fish dry with paper towels, then set them aside on a paper towel–lined plate.

In a large bowl, stir together the cornstarch, kosher salt, pepper, and paprika. Line another plate or a separate large bowl with paper towels.

Working with one handful of fish at a time, toss them in the seasoned cornstarch mixture. Shake off any excess and fry them in the hot oil until they are golden brown and the bubbling around their edges stops, 2 to 3 minutes. Fry them just 10 seconds more, then use a slotted spoon to transfer them to the paper towel–lined plate or bowl. Repeat with the remaining fish.

Serve hot, with the spicy rémoulade and a sprinkle of sea salt.

ENSALADA MANGGA

Green Mango Salad

FILIPINO SNACK VENDORS sell wedges of unripe mango in a plastic Baggie with a side of *bagoong*, or fermented seafood paste. But near the mountainous region of Baguio, there is one impressive mango stand that offers an array of bagoong flavors for dipping or combining: from spicy and sweet to funky and garlicky. This green mango salad is inspired by those combinations. Once you've tried this, you can easily adjust the dressing with more heat or more tartness, depending on your preference. **SERVES 4 TO 6**

Note: This snack is best made with Filipino-style mangoes—the ones found in the States are never quite as tart—but you can make this salad with any firm, unripe mango (see Key Ingredients, page 38) you can find.

¼ cup (60 ml) fresh lemon juice

¼ cup (60 ml) fresh lime juice

3 tablespoons bagoong alamang (see Key Ingredients, page 35)

1 tablespoon Dijon mustard

1 tablespoon white sugarcane vinegar (see Key Ingredients, page 42)

1½ cups (360 ml) extra-virgin olive oil

2 medium to large green mangoes (see Note), pitted, peeled, and coarsely chopped

1 cup (145 g) cherry tomatoes, halved

⅓ cup (45 g) coarsely chopped peeled jicama

1 shallot, sliced paper thin

2 tablespoons thinly sliced scallion (green part only)

Kosher salt and freshly ground white pepper

In a small bowl, whisk together the lemon juice, lime juice, bagoong, mustard, and vinegar until thoroughly combined. While whisking, slowly stream in the olive oil and whisk until the mixture is emulsified. Set aside while you prepare the salad.

In a salad bowl, combine the mangoes, cherry tomatoes, jicama, shallot, and scallion. Toss to combine.

Drizzle the bagoong-citrus vinaigrette over the salad to taste. (You may have some left over; the vinaigrette will keep, covered, in the refrigerator for up to a week.) Mix well, taste, and add salt, if needed, then season with white pepper. Serve immediately.

UKOY
Vegetable and Shrimp Fritters

FILIPINO FRITTERS are made with many different vegetables and in many different sizes, though usually they contain small head-on or dried whole shrimp. We first tried this recipe using jumbo shrimp with the heads left on (the heads are great when fried), but we realized that it's easier both to cook and eat the fritters when the shrimp are smaller, cleaned, and peeled (though if you're up for it, try the recipe with the jumbos—the crunch and juiciness are amazing). *Ukoy* can be made in any size you like, from one large family-style fritter, which you cut or tear into pieces, to small individual-size pieces.

To make small fritters, use two extra-large slotted spoons, moving the shrimp to the middle as you form the fritters so that when they cook, the shrimp are protected by a cage of crispy vegetables. (The slotted spoons also help to remove any excess batter.) Whatever size you go with, don't crowd the pan—the fritters will steam rather than fry, and the oil won't stay hot. In the Philippines, ukoy are mostly served at room temperature, crispy and delicious. **SERVES 4 TO 6**

1 cup (130 g) cornstarch

1 cup (130 g) cake flour

1 teaspoon kosher salt, plus more as needed

1 cup (240 ml) shrimp stock (see Note) or water

1 Japanese sweet potato, peeled and cut into matchsticks

2 large carrots, peeled and cut into matchsticks

4 scallions, sliced lengthwise and then into 2-inch (3 cm) pieces

1 medium white onion, peeled and cut into matchsticks

Freshly ground black pepper

⅓ cup (80 ml) vegetable oil, plus more as needed

1 pound (455 g) raw small shrimp, peeled and deveined (see Note)

Maldon sea salt, for sprinkling

Pinakurat (page 34), for serving

Note: Flavor the batter with shrimp stock of some kind, even just a stock made by soaking dried baby shrimp in hot water. You can also make a quick shrimp stock by simmering the peels and heads from the shrimp in 1½ cups (360 ml) water for about 15 minutes.

In a large bowl, whisk together the cornstarch, cake flour, and kosher salt. Stir in the stock and mix well.

In another large bowl, use your hands to mix together the sweet potato, carrot, scallion, and onion. Season with kosher salt and pepper. Add the vegetables to the batter, mixing so that the veggies are just coated. The batter should be thick but loose enough to coat the vegetables. If it is too thick, add a little water.

> recipe continues →

UKOY

Vegetable and Shrimp Fritters

continued →

In a large sauté pan, wok, or cast-iron skillet, heat the vegetable oil over medium heat until it begins to shimmer, or registers 350°F (175°C) on an instant-read thermometer. Line a baking sheet with paper towels and set it nearby.

Using two large slotted spoons, make the ukoy by mounding some of the batter-coated vegetables onto the bowl of one spoon. Use your fingers to tuck a few shrimp into the middle of the nest, then top it off with more vegetables. Invert the other spoon over the pile, and gently shake off any excess batter into the bowl.

Working carefully, slide the ukoy off the spoons into the oil—it will be a little messy, but that's okay. Cook a few ukoy at a time, being careful not to crowd the pan, for 3 to 5 minutes, until the bottoms begin to crisp and turn golden brown. Flip and cook the ukoy for 3 to 5 minutes more, until crispy and golden brown on the second side.

Remove the fritters to the paper towels, sprinkle the tops with sea salt, and serve hot or at room temperature, with a small bowl of pinakurat for dipping.

PINASUGBO

Banana Fritters

PINASUGBO IS LONG, THIN SLICES OF banana that are fried, coated in dark caramel candy, and topped with a crown of white sesame seeds. In the Philippines, you would use a small, firm, locally grown, especially flavorful variety of banana called Saba, which is generally cooked rather than eaten raw, much like a plantain. Yellow but still firm plantains make an excellent substitute for Sabas, which are rarely found in the United States. For the caramel candy coating, you'll need a candy thermometer and the patience to watch the simmering brown sugar to make sure it doesn't burn. **SERVES 4 TO 6**

⅓ cup (80 ml) vegetable oil, plus more as needed

4 Saba bananas (see headnote) or firm yellow plantains, peeled

2 cups (440 g) packed brown sugar

1 cup (150 g) sesame seeds

In a large sauté pan, wok, or cast-iron skillet, heat the vegetable oil over medium heat until it begins to shimmer or registers between 275°F and 325°F (135°C and 160°C) on an instant-read thermometer. Line a baking sheet with paper towels and set it nearby.

While the oil heats, use a mandoline or a sharp knife to slice the bananas lengthwise (from tip to stem) into long slices about 1/16 inch (2 mm) thick.

When the oil is ready, add a handful of banana slices at a time, being careful not to crowd the pan, and fry until golden brown and crisp, 2 to 3 minutes. Use a slotted spoon or strainer to transfer them to the prepared baking sheet, and repeat until you have fried all the banana slices.

To make the caramel candy coating, in a large saucepan with a candy thermometer clipped to the side, combine the brown sugar and ¼ cup (60 ml) water and heat over medium-high heat. Cook, stirring continuously with a nonstick spatula, until the mixture registers 305°F (150°C). (The water will bubble out and the mixture will darken—that's okay.)

Working as quickly as you can, add the fried banana slices right into the caramelized sugar mixture and toss them until they are well coated. Use tongs to remove the bananas from the sugar one at a time, dipping one end of each slice into the sesame seeds. Place the fritters on a cooling rack set over a baking sheet, making sure they don't touch.

Let the banana fritters cool before serving. These will last for a week in an airtight container.

In Iloilo there is a mini factory behind an enclosed basketball court and down a narrow walkway where workers make *pinasugbo*. Huge woks are set over open fires and filled with blackened caramel that spills onto the floor. If you find these sweets in a Philippine airport, they most likely came from this little operation, which packages and labels the treats for other vendors, selling them for 50 pesos (approximately one U.S. dollar) for a pack of twelve.

EMPANADA DE KALISKIS

Pork and Vegetable Empanada

THIS FLAKY, BUTTERY, CRUSTY PASTRY filled with meat and raisins is a labor- and time-intensive thing to make, but it is worth the effort. One of the beautiful features of this empanada, which hails from the Bulacan province, is the layers of dough that fan out along the top. (*Kaliskis* is a Tagalog term for "fish scale," which is what it resembles.) You create the top layer by making two doughs: One is soft and pliable and known as the water dough; the other, called the oil dough, is crumbly and dry. You fold the water dough around the oil dough, then fold and roll, fold and roll, fold and roll, resulting in the special ruffled kaliskis crust. You can serve these plain or with banana ketchup (see page 316). **SERVES 4 TO 6**

FOR THE FILLING AND FRYING

3 tablespoons vegetable oil, plus more for frying

1 cup (125 g) finely diced white onion

1 tablespoon minced garlic

2 pounds (910 g) ground pork

1 cup (140 g) finely diced potato

1 cup (140 g) finely diced carrots

1 cup (170 g) canned green peas

1 cup (145 g) raisins

1 teaspoon calamansi juice (see Key Ingredients, page 37) or fresh lime juice

Fish sauce

FOR THE WATER DOUGH

1 cup (125 g) all-purpose flour, plus more for dusting

2 tablespoons sugar

1 teaspoon kosher salt

¼ cup (50 g) cubed cold pork lard (see Note)

½ teaspoon distilled white vinegar

FOR THE OIL DOUGH

1½ cups (190 g) all-purpose flour

½ cup (100 g) cubed cold pork lard

Note: You can find pork lard, or pork fat, at butcher shops, many mainstream supermarkets, and most Latin or Hispanic markets, where it is often labeled "manteca." It is usually a thick paste with the texture of Crisco when cold but quickly melts to liquid at room temperature.

Make the filling: In a large skillet or saucepan, heat the vegetable oil over medium heat. Add the onion and garlic and cook, stirring often, until the onion is translucent, about 7 minutes. Add the pork and cook, stirring often, until it is lightly browned, about 7 minutes.

Reduce the heat to low and add the potato, carrots, peas, and raisins. Add ½ cup (120 ml) water to the pan and cook until the water has evaporated, the pork is tender, and the vegetables are cooked through, about 10 minutes.

> recipe continues →

**EMPANADA
DE KALISKIS**

Pork and
Vegetable
Empanada

continued →

Mix in the calamansi juice; taste and season with fish sauce. Transfer the filling to a bowl and let cool in the refrigerator until you're ready to fill the empanadas.

Make the water dough: In a medium bowl, combine the flour, sugar, and salt. Add the cubed lard and, using your fingertips, work it in until you have pea-size crumbles. Make a well in the center of the dry ingredients, then add the vinegar and ½ cup cold water, a little at a time, mixing with a wooden spoon and then your clean hands, until the dough forms a smooth, cohesive ball. Wrap the dough ball in plastic and refrigerate it for 30 minutes.

Make the oil dough: In a clean medium bowl, combine the flour and cubed lard and mix it together with your fingertips until you have pea-size crumbles. Cover the bowl with plastic wrap and refrigerate for 15 minutes.

Lightly flour a large work surface and a rolling pin. Roll the water dough out into an even, flat circle about ⅛ inch (3 mm) thick, making sure the dough doesn't tear **(see opposite, photo 1)**.

Place the oil dough (it will be crumbly) on one half of the water dough **(2)**. Press it down so it covers the half, leaving about ¼ inch (6 mm) of the water dough uncovered around the outer edges. Fold the top of the water dough over the oil dough. Press it down all over, making sure there are no air bubbles, and press the edges to seal **(3)**. The oil dough should be completely sealed inside the water dough.

Fold the dough over on itself **(4)**, then use a rolling pin to flatten it into a long rectangle. Fold the dough over on itself twice, rotate it 90 degrees, then roll it out again into a long rectangle **(5)**. Repeat this twice more, folding the dough over on itself twice again, then rotating it 90 degrees, then flattening it into a long rectangle **(6)**.

Take the long side of the rectangle and use your hands to roll the dough up like a rough jelly roll. Cut the roll crosswise into circles 1 inch (2.5 cm) thick **(7)**, set the slices on their sides, then roll out each circle to a diameter of about 4 inches (10 cm) **(8)**. (You should be able to see the spiraled lines in each disc.)

Place 1½ tablespoons of the filling in the middle of each circle **(9)**. Wet the edges of half of the circle **(10)**, then fold it over on itself into a half-moon and pinch the edges together, making a decorative pattern, if you like **(11)**. There should be no air bubbles, and the empanadas must be completely sealed so the filling doesn't come out when you fry them **(12)**. Place the filled empanadas on a baking sheet and refrigerate for 30 minutes.

When you're ready to fry the empanadas, fill a Dutch oven or heavy-bottomed pot about halfway with oil, and heat the oil over medium-high heat until it is just barely shimmering or registers 350°F (175°C) on an instant-read thermometer.

Fry the empanadas one or two at time in the hot oil for 7 to 10 minutes, flipping them once or twice, or until they are golden brown on all sides. Transfer them to paper towels to drain and cool completely before serving, so that the flaky "scales" will fully develop.

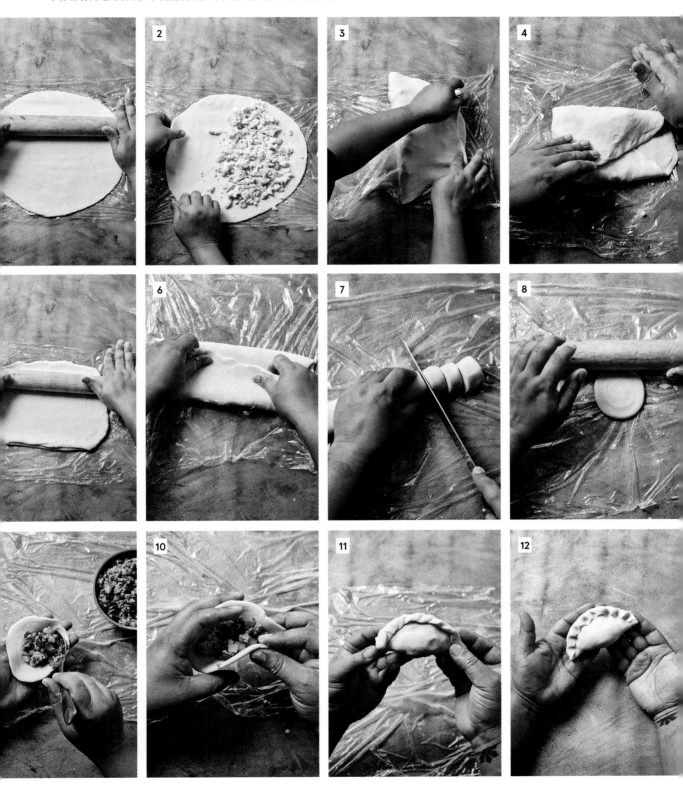

INIHAW NA MANOK

Chicken Barbecue

BARBECUED CHICKEN SKEWERS are both a backyard staple and a street food treat, and it seems like everyone has their own secret method for the marinade: It can be salty or sour, sweet, or loaded with garlic. For us the perfect barbecue sauce for chicken is made with banana ketchup, soy sauce, sugarcane vinegar, and 7UP. It's slightly sticky when cooked and develops a nice char as the sugars in the soda and ketchup caramelize, while the dark thigh meat (a must) stays tender and juicy. Serve the skewers alone or over *sinangag* (page 183), with *sawsawan* made of diced onions, crushed garlic, black pepper, and a bit of fish sauce, soy sauce, and vinegar. **SERVES 4 TO 6**

Note: If you are using wooden skewers, soak them in warm water for 15 to 30 minutes before you add the chicken so they don't burn as you grill.

2¼ cups (540 ml) banana ketchup (see page 316)

1 cup (240 ml) 7UP

½ cup (120 ml) fresh lemon juice

½ cup (120 ml) soy sauce

½ cup (120 ml) white sugarcane vinegar (see Key Ingredients, page 42)

½ cup (110 g) packed brown sugar

¼ cup (35 g) minced garlic

3 pounds (1.4 kg) boneless, skinless chicken thighs, cut into 1-inch pieces

Cooking spray or vegetable oil, for greasing

Sawsawan (see page 34), for serving

In a large nonreactive bowl, storage container, or ziplock bag, mix together the banana ketchup, 7UP, lemon juice, soy sauce, vinegar, brown sugar, and garlic until the sugar has dissolved.

Add the chicken pieces and toss. Cover the bowl or container or seal the bag and marinate in the refrigerator for at least 1 hour and preferably overnight.

When you are ready to cook the meat, heat a grill pan over high heat or heat a charcoal or gas grill to medium.

Reserving the marinade, thread 3 or 4 pieces of chicken on each skewer, letting the pieces touch slightly, and set them on a plate or baking sheet.

Pour the marinade into a saucepan and bring it to a simmer over medium-high heat. Reduce the heat to medium and cook for 10 minutes; set it aside.

Spray the pan or grill grate lightly with cooking spray. Place the skewers on the grill pan or grill and cook, turning them and basting them often with the heated marinade, until they are cooked through or the center of a piece of chicken registers 165°F (75°C) on an instant-read thermometer. This should take between 8 and 15 minutes, depending on your cooking surface. (Discard any leftover marinade.)

Transfer to a platter and serve immediately, with sawsawan.

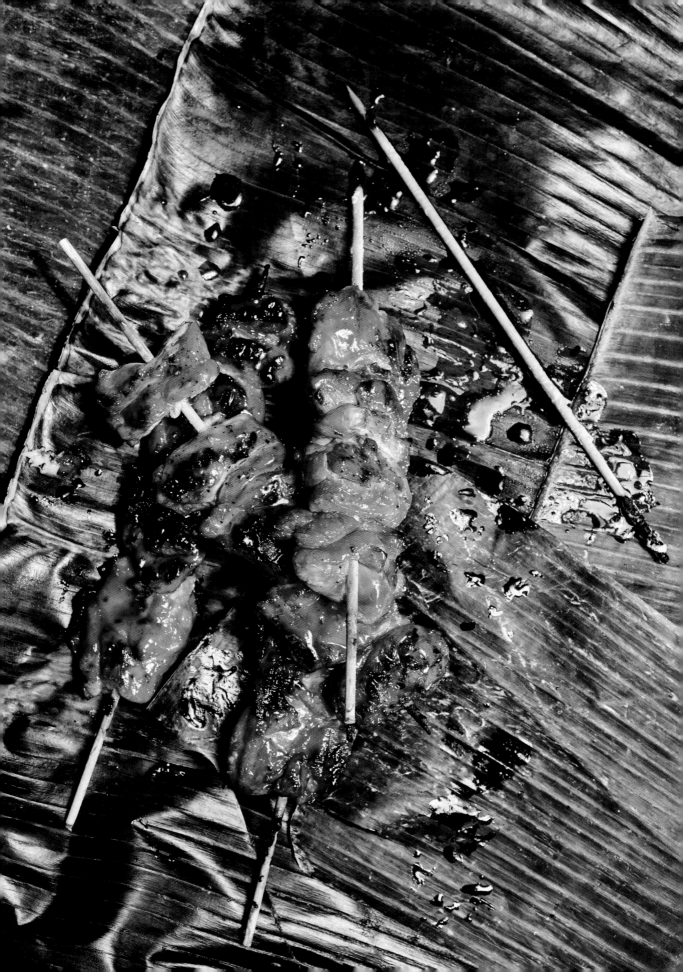

INIHAW NA LIEMPO
Grilled Pork Belly

PORK BELLY IS UBIQUITOUS throughout the Philippines; the fat is glorious and tastes great grilled. Getting a nice char on the fatty bits is important, as it adds another level of flavor to the salty-sour-tart-sweetness of the soy-calamansi marinade. This is a versatile dish: You can enjoy it as is with a side of *sawsawan* or the spiced vinegar called *pinakurat*. Or you can add it to stews and soups for extra flavor, or even to our version of ceviche (see page 67). For this recipe, you'll need to marinate the pork belly overnight, so plan ahead. **SERVES 4 TO 6**

1 cup (240 ml) soy sauce

1 cup (240 ml) calamansi juice
(see Key Ingredients, page 37)

1 tablespoon minced garlic

1 teaspoon freshly ground
black pepper

2 pounds (910 g) skinless pork belly,
sliced lengthwise into 1-inch-thick
(2.5 cm) strips

Sawsawan (see page 34) or pinakurat
(page 34), for serving

In a large nonreactive bowl, storage container, or ziplock bag, mix together the soy sauce, calamansi juice, garlic, and pepper.

Add the pork belly slices, toss so they are well coated in the marinade, cover the bowl or container or seal the bag, and marinate in the refrigerator overnight.

When you are ready to grill the pork, heat a gas or charcoal grill to medium or heat a grill pan or cast-iron skillet over medium-high heat.

Discard the marinade and grill the pork slices, turning them once or twice, for 3 to 5 minutes, until they are cooked through and slightly charred around the edges.

Transfer to a platter and serve with sawsawan or pinakurat.

LECHON KAWALI
Wok-Fried Crispy Pork Belly

KAWALI MEANS "WOK," and *lechon* usually refers to crispy-skinned roast pork. The key to this recipe is in the days of prep work before the belly is fried. First, you'll cure the pork for three days in a spice mix rich with coriander and cumin seeds, then gently poach the belly, and finally let it air-dry in the refrigerator overnight. These last two steps ensure that the belly cooks flawlessly and extra moisture is removed from the skin, which makes the belly juicy and flavorful on the inside and extra crispy on the outside. **SERVES 4 TO 6**

1 pound (455 g) kosher salt

½ cup (140 g) coriander seeds

½ cup (140 g) whole black peppercorns

½ cup (140 g) cumin seeds

6 bay leaves, crushed

2 pounds (910 g) bone-in, skin-on pork belly (see Note, page 180)

Vegetable oil, for frying

Pinakurat (see page 34), for serving

In a large bowl, whisk together the salt, coriander, peppercorns, cumin, and bay leaves.

Lay down a double layer of plastic wrap on a baking dish and place the pork belly on top of the plastic. Cover all sides of the pork belly with the spice mix, then wrap it tightly in the plastic wrap. Set a weight like a brick or a pot filled with water on top of the plastic-wrapped pork and refrigerate for 3 days.

Rinse the pork belly well with cold water and place it in a medium pot. Add water to cover the pork completely and bring to a boil. Reduce the heat to medium-low and simmer for 2 hours, or until the bone pulls out easily.

Transfer the pork to a baking dish and refrigerate, uncovered, overnight. (You're trying to dry it out; if you don't have time to dry it overnight, you can speed up this process by placing the pork on a table in front of a fan for 2 hours.)

When you're ready to fry the pork, fill a wok, Dutch oven, or heavy-bottomed pot about halfway with vegetable oil, and heat the oil over medium-high heat until it is shimmering or registers 375°F (190°C) on an instant-read thermometer. Line a plate with paper towels and set it nearby.

Cut the pork belly into 3-inch-wide (7.5 cm) portions and score the skin crosswise. Working in batches, fry the pork for 6 minutes, or until the skin is very crispy. (Allow for room between the pieces as you fry them.) Use tongs to transfer the pork belly to the paper towel–lined plate. Repeat with the remaining pork.

Serve immediately, with pinakurat on the side for dipping.

Lechon kawali can sometimes be interchangeable with the northern Filipino version of crispy pork belly called *bagnet*, though this fried pork belly is slightly different. Bagnet is a slab of boneless pork belly that is cooked three times: boiled, fried, and then fried again to order. The result is a superthick, ruffled crust on the top layer of skin that looks more like chicharrón. In the north, bagnet is typically served with the vegetable dish *pinakbet* (page 128).

CRISPY PATA
Crispy Pig's Foot

PATA, OR PORK SHANK, is decadent to eat, with its layers of fat, meat, and crunchy skin. We prepare pata like duck confit. First, cook the shank in pork fat, ensuring deep flavor and plenty of moisture. Then fry it to guarantee the best part—that crispy skin! Despite the French technique, you can still serve this dish the traditional way: whole and on the bone. You'll want to use a steak knife to break into the crackling skin. For a complete meal, serve it with hot white rice and Classic Ensalada (page 122). **SERVES 4**

2 skin-on pork shanks,
about 1½ pounds (680 g) each

4 bay leaves

10 garlic cloves, peeled and
smashed with the side of
a knife

5 whole black peppercorns

10 coriander seeds

6 cups (1.2 kg) melted pork lard
(see Note, page 255)

Vegetable oil, for frying

4 cups (800 g) cooked white rice
(see page 40), for serving

Sawsawan (see page 34),
for serving

Preheat the oven to 275°F (135°C).

In a Dutch oven or roasting pan, place the pork shanks, bay leaves, garlic, peppercorns, and coriander. Pour in the lard, making sure it covers the shanks. Cook in the oven, covered, for 2 to 3 hours, until the pork is tender and pulling away from the bone.

Remove the shanks from the fat and let them cool, reserving the fat for another use. (You can complete this step a day or two ahead. Store the shanks in the fat, then bring them to room temperature and remove from the fat before frying them.)

When you're ready to fry the pork, fill a Dutch oven or heavy-bottomed pot about halfway with oil, and heat the oil over medium-high heat until it is just barely shimmering or registers 350°F (175°C) on an instant-read thermometer.

Fry the pork shanks one at time in the hot oil for about 10 minutes, or until they are browned and crispy on all sides.

Transfer them to a platter and serve them whole, with bowls of rice and sawsawan on the side for dipping.

SIZZLING SISIG

Pork Cooked Three Ways, with Chile, Egg, and Onion

SISIG MIGHT BE THE BREAKOUT STAR of Filipino cuisine; it's an addictive chopped mix of pig's head (*maskara* in Tagalog) and other pig parts that are either chargrilled or fried, then seasoned with citrus, onion, and chile peppers. Our favorite sisig is served at Aling Lucing, the namesake restaurant of Pampangan chef Aling Lucing, who first served sisig at the table in a sizzling pan in the 1970s. But sisig wasn't always made with meat or even cooked: it was originally a chopped salad of sour fruits dressed in vinegar. It's unclear when the dish morphed from an *ensalada* to a *porkissimo* dish, but one theory is that it happened during the American occupation, when Army Air Corps soldiers on the military base in the province of Pampanga threw out the heads of the pigs they purchased. Filipino cooks are said to have turned the discarded pigs' heads into the sisig we know today.

Sizzling is the way this sisig should be served; it's a mix of fried (the fatty pork belly), grilled (chewy ears and snouts), and creamy (pureed chicken livers). Top it off with calamansi juice, onions, chiles, and raw eggs, which you can scramble into the blazing-hot pork either right before serving or at the table. It's crunchy, chewy, sour, fatty, and smoky all at once. Serve it with Garlic Fried Rice (page 183) and beer. **SERVES 4**

Note: You may be able to find pigs' ears and snouts at Asian or Latin meat markets; otherwise, special order them from a butcher.

2 pounds (910 g) bone-in, skinless pork belly (see Note, page 180)

¼ pound (115 g) pig's ears (see Note)

¼ pound (115 g) pig's snout (see Note)

1 tablespoon whole black peppercorns

3 bay leaves

6 bird's-eye chiles (see Key Ingredients, page 37; optional)

Vegetable oil

5 garlic cloves, minced

1 medium red onion, diced

¼ pound (115 g) chicken livers, pureed

¼ cup (60 ml) white sugarcane vinegar (see Key Ingredients, page 42)

2 tablespoons calamansi juice (see Key Ingredients, page 37) or lime juice

Kosher salt and freshly ground black pepper

4 large eggs

In a large pot, combine the pork belly, ears, and snout and pour in enough water to cover. Add the peppercorns, bay leaves, and 3 of the chiles (if using) and simmer over medium-high heat until the pork is tender, 2 to 3 hours. Let the belly, snout, and ears cool in the liquid, then transfer them to a platter and set aside. (You can reserve the cooking liquid for later use, if desired.)

Heat a grill pan or cast-iron pan over medium heat. Grill the snout and ears over medium heat for about 3 minutes on each side, or until they begin to char. Dice and set aside.

In a large skillet, heat 2 tablespoons vegetable oil over medium-high heat. Dice the pork belly and fry until it is light golden brown, then set it aside.

Dice the remaining 3 chiles, if you want extra heat, and set them aside.

Wipe out the skillet and heat 2 tablespoons oil over medium heat. Add the garlic and all but one-quarter of the red onion and one-quarter of the diced chiles (if using) and cook, stirring often, for about 4 minutes, or until soft. (The reserved onion and chiles will be used to garnish the dish.)

Stir in the chicken liver puree and cook, stirring often, until cooked through, about 3 minutes. Add the pork belly, snout, and ears and cook, stirring continuously, for 1 minute. Add the vinegar and calamansi juice and season with salt and pepper. Set this mixture aside.

In a cast-iron pan or heavy-bottomed (not nonstick) skillet, heat 2 tablespoons oil over high heat. Once the oil is very hot, add the pork mixture—be careful, as it will sizzle. Crack the eggs directly on top of the meat and sprinkle on the reserved onion and chiles (if you used them).

Serve the dish immediately. Place the skillet directly on a trivet at the table and use two serving spoons to stir in the eggs, making sure they are well mixed with the meat.

Aling Lucing

THE SISIG QUEEN EST. SINCE 1974

With dishes like *sisig*, which has changed so much over time with only inherited stories left to confirm its past, it's a race against time to learn about the dish from aging cooks. The tastes of the old, the new, the blended, the hyperregional, the artisanal, and the agricultural are emerging at a rapid pace. It's important to document and archive a culinary history that is disappearing.

SWEETS

MERRY MERYENDA

VISIT A FRIEND IN THE PHILIPPINES, and after pleasantries are exchanged, the first question is always some variation of "Are you hungry?" It's not unheard-of in the Philippines to eat possibly seven or even eight times a day: It starts with a little pre-breakfast snack, maybe of *pandesal* and fruit; then comes breakfast, followed by a post-breakfast nibble. At around noon there's lunch, then a small afternoon snack break, followed by dinner, and finally a little snack before bedtime.

Meryenda is the term Filipinos use for the post-breakfast and afternoon snacks, or meals three and five, if you follow the list in the previous paragraph. These lighter meals are often one form of a subtly sweet rice-based treat collectively called *kakanin*, like the steamed rice cakes known as *puto* (page 277). Other snacks might include the rounds of soft sweet yeast bread called pandesal (page 298), or a butter-and-cheese-topped *ensaymada* (page 303). Meryenda also includes nearly anything else that's sweet, from the shaved ice sundae known as *halo-halo* (page 294) to the caramel-topped *leche* flan (page 288). Traditionally, sweets are saved for in between breakfast, lunch, and dinner—though really anything can be called meryenda so long as it doesn't involve a whole meal.

Meryenda is enjoyed in many parts of the world (although it goes by different names and appears in other forms), including Spain, which gifted the Philippines the term *merienda* during the Spanish colonial era. (Their merienda is not about eating sweets, but is often bread, cheese, fruit, or another small snack.) In Britain, it takes the form of afternoon tea with sandwiches or scones. Meryenda—whether eaten in the morning or the afternoon—is a moment to relax and recharge or an excuse to chat with family or friends. It can lift your spirits and energy, while also tiding you over during the arduous task of waiting for the next meal.

If the French have patisserie, Filipinos have *kakanin*. Our pastries are made from starchy ingredients like rice or rice flour and root vegetables like cassava or taro, and usually include coconut milk. Though the pastries vary widely in shape and form, kakanin are typically chewy and sticky, only subtly sweet, and often wrapped in banana leaves and steamed or baked. They're sold either by the piece—about the size of baklava, a little bit of a pick-me-up just heavy enough to keep you from starving—or by the *bilao*, or platter. Some of the most popular kakanin in the Philippines include *suman* (page 275), *bibingka* (page 282), *puto* (page 277), and *palitaw* (page 281).

SUMAN
Steamed Rice Cakes

THINK OF *SUMAN* AS THE FOUNDATION or introduction to *kakanin*, a diverse category of Filipino sweets. While many kakakin are multilayered and complicated, suman are straightforward: sticky rice cooked with coconut milk and a little sugar, then steamed in a banana leaf or sometimes a palm leaf, depending on the region of the Philippines in which they're being made. Suman, like most kakanin, are not overly sugary. Their charms include a nutty aroma from the banana leaf, a chewy texture from the sticky rice, and a subtle sweet creaminess from the coconut milk. When they're freshly made and still soft and warm, you can just peel back the banana leaf and snack away, or dip the suman in the caramelized coconut milk curds called *latik*, brown sugar, or toasted coconut flakes. After they have cooled or have been refrigerated, suman are best eaten panfried, then topped with ice cream and a dusting of confectioners' sugar. **MAKES ABOUT 15**

2 cups (400 g) white glutinous rice (see Key Ingredients, page 40)

1½ (13.5-ounce/400 ml) cans coconut milk

¼ cup (60 ml) rum

½ cup (100 g) granulated sugar

1 teaspoon kosher salt

1 (16-ounce/455 g) package frozen banana leaves (see Key Ingredients, page 36), defrosted

FOR SERVING (OPTIONAL)

Latik (see page 307), brown sugar, or toasted coconut flakes

Vegetable oil, for panfrying

Confectioners' sugar

Ice cream

Notes: If you don't have a steamer pot, you can set a metal colander (or even a wire rack, if you have one that fits) into a large spaghetti or soup pot with a lid.

You can keep these in the fridge for up to 1 week before serving them, but once refrigerated, they should be panfried to get the best texture, as they toughen up over time.

Wash the glutinous rice: Put the rice in a colander (make sure the holes are small enough that the rice doesn't slip through) and rinse it under cold running water until the water runs clear, using your clean hands to massage the rice kernels as the water runs over them. Shake the colander a few times to get rid of excess water, then let the rice drain in the sink while you heat the coconut milk.

In a large heavy-bottomed saucepan, heat the coconut milk and rum over medium heat, stirring it until it is very smooth and just begins to steam.

Add the drained rice, granulated sugar, and salt and stir until the sugar and salt have dissolved and the rice is totally coated in the coconut milk.

> recipe continues →

SUMAN

Steamed
Rice Cakes

continued →

Increase the heat to high and bring the mixture just to a boil, then immediately lower the heat to medium so the mixture cooks at a simmer. Cook, uncovered, stirring almost continuously, for about 30 minutes, or until the liquid has been absorbed and the rice is tender. (Test it by tasting a grain.) It will be sticky and look like rice pudding.

Spread the hot rice out on a baking sheet and let cool until you can handle it.

Meanwhile, remove the tough outer spine of the banana leaves—you can pull it like a string, the way you would remove the strings from a piece of celery or a banana.

Take one banana leaf and use your fingers to tear it into thirty ¼-inch-long (6 mm) ribbons. You will use these or butcher's twine to tie the suman shut.

Cut the remaining banana leaves into about fifteen 5 by 7-inch (12.5 by 17.5 cm) rectangles. Working with one at a time, hold each leaf with tongs and gently pass it over the burner on a gas stovetop. (If you have an electric stove, bring a large pot of water to a boil and, working in batches, dip the leaves into the water for just a few seconds.) This step makes the leaves shiny and pliable.

Place a soft banana leaf on a clean work surface so that one long side is facing you. Place ½ cup (90 g) of the rice mixture in a rectangular shape (about 3 by 5 inches/7.5 by 12.5 cm) in the center of the banana leaf, leaving several inches uncovered on all sides. (The long side of the rice rectangle should be along the long side of the banana leaf.)

Fold the long side of the banana leaf over the rice and then roll it up like a burrito or a cigar, folding the two loose ends of the leaf into and over the middle. Tie those two flaps down at either end with a strip of banana leaf. Repeat with the remaining banana leaves and filling.

Fill the bottom of a steamer pot (see Notes) with a few inches of water (be sure it doesn't touch the bottom of the steamer basket). Arrange the suman in the steamer basket, piling them on top of one another. Cover the pot and steam over medium heat for 1½ hours.

Remove the suman from the steamer. You can eat them immediately, just as they are, by unwrapping and discarding the banana leaf. Alternatively, while they are still warm, you can dip the suman in a little latik, brown sugar, or toasted coconut flakes.

The suman will keep at room temperature for up to 3 days or in the refrigerator for 1 week. Keep them wrapped in the banana leaves until you serve them. At this point, they are much better fried. To fry the suman, let them come to room temperature if they've been refrigerated, then peel away the banana leaves. In a large skillet, heat ½ inch (1.5 cm) of vegetable oil over medium to medium-high heat. Cook a few suman at a time, flipping them occasionally until they are golden brown and crispy on all sides, 3 to 5 minutes.

Use a slotted spoon to transfer the suman to a plate. While they are still warm, dust them with confectioners' sugar and/or serve them topped with ice cream.

PUTO
Steamed Rice Cakes

PUTO IS EATEN AS A QUICK snack or as a side dish with the stew called *dinuguan* (page 71) or with *batchoy* (page 174), a noodle soup. These small fluffy cakes of steamed rice flour are very mildly flavored, like plain Chinese steamed buns, and are usually served instead of white rice with rich stews. They are also extremely easy to make: mix the ingredients together in a blender, pour the batter into small ramekins, and steam them. **MAKES ABOUT 25**

2 large egg whites

¼ cup (60 ml) whole milk

1¾ cups (230 g) cake flour

1 cup (200 g) sugar

2 tablespoons baking powder

½ teaspoon kosher salt

Cooking spray, for greasing

Banana leaf (see Key Ingredients, page 36; optional)

Notes: We make puto in 2-ounce (60 ml) metal ramekins, but any size that fits into your steamer pot will work, and if you do not have ramekins, you can be creative and cook the puto in any heatproof container, like cupcake tins, egg poachers, or small heatproof bowls.

If you do not have a steamer pot, you can set a metal colander (or even a wire rack, if you have one that fits) into a large spaghetti or soup pot with a lid.

In a blender, combine the egg whites, milk, and 1½ cups (360 ml) water and blend on medium speed until the ingredients are well combined.

Slowly add the flour, sugar, baking powder, and salt and blend on medium speed until well combined.

Coat lightly with cooking spray as many ramekins as will fit in your steamer pot at one time. Fill the steamer pot with a couple of inches of water (be sure the water does not touch the bottom of the steamer basket) and bring to a simmer over medium-high heat.

Pour the puto batter into the prepared ramekins to fill them about halfway. Lay the banana leaf in the steamer basket, if desired (it will impart a uniquely aromatic flavor to the puto), and place the ramekins on top. Set the basket in the pot, cover, and cook for 7 minutes, or until a toothpick inserted into the center of a puto comes out clean.

Remove the ramekins from the pot with tongs and let the puto cool for 1 minute before inverting them onto a plate or into a basket. Repeat with the remaining batter, respraying the ramekins and checking to make sure there is water in the steamer pot before each batch.

Puto can be served hot, warm, or at room temperature, and are best eaten the day they are made.

Puto are related to the *putto* or *putti* made in the southern Indian state of Kerala. The Keralan versions are laced with grated coconut and steamed in a bamboo stalk. Filipinos also make coconut versions, as well as many other flavors of puto.

BANAUE RICE TERRACES

Rice has played a major role in Filipino culinary history. Though many other countries in Southeast Asia, like Thailand and Vietnam, have grown rice for centuries, it is thought that the Philippines developed the complex techniques of planting rice on steep terraces carved into the mountainside, with a sophisticated irrigation system. The ancient Banaue Rice Terraces on the island of Luzon are feats of engineering and were the product of the Ifugao people, a minority ethnic group. In recent decades, younger generations have opted out of rice farming and moved into more modern jobs, leaving the future of these rice terraces in question. At the top of these mountains are the area's last five remaining *mumbakis*, or village shamans, whose disappearing traditions include the practice of "reading" the blood of sacrificed chickens to predict the season's harvest.

PALITAW

Sweet Rice Dumplings

LIKE *SUMAN* (page 275) and *puto* (page 277), *palitaw* are a simple *kakanin*. Small sticky rice flour dumplings, palitaw are eaten dusted with toasted coconut flakes, sesame seeds, and the caramelized coconut milk curds called *latik*. They get their name from how you make them: the word *palitaw* is derived from *litaw*, meaning "to surface." When you boil the palitaw to cook them, you can tell they're done when they float to the top of the pot. The shape of these dumplings is more like a rough round patty, and they don't need to be perfect. It's easiest to form them in the palm of one hand, using the fingers of your other hand to press them into shape. **MAKES ABOUT 20**

2 cups (320 g) glutinous rice flour (see Key Ingredients, page 40)

1 cup (240 ml) hot tap water (not boiling)

1 cup (85 g) sweetened coconut flakes, toasted

½ cup (75 g) black sesame seeds, toasted

½ cup (65 g) confectioners' sugar

½ cup (75 g) Latik (see page 307), for garnish (optional)

Bring a large pot of water to a boil over medium-high heat.

Meanwhile, in a medium bowl, stir together the rice flour and the hot tap water. When all the water has been incorporated, knead the mixture by hand in the bowl until the dough is smooth and comes away cleanly from the sides.

Use your hands to form 1 tablespoon of the dough into a ball. Place the ball in the palm of one hand and use the thumb or fingers of your other hand to flatten it into a thin (about ¼-inch/6 mm), roughly shaped oval or patty that holds its shape.

Drop it into the boiling water and cook until it rises to the surface, about 3 minutes. (It will still be pliable.) Remove it from the pot with a slotted spoon, shaking off any excess water, and let it dry on a clean kitchen towel or wire rack. While the first one boils, form 2 or 3 more palitaw and drop them into the pot, making sure you don't crowd the water, and scoop them out as they rise to the surface. Repeat, working in batches of about 3, until all the palitaw have been formed, cooked, and drained.

When all the palitaw have been cooked and while they're still warm, place the toasted coconut on one shallow plate and the sesame seeds on another. Dredge the palitaw in the toasted coconut, then in the sesame seeds, and finally dust both sides with confectioners' sugar.

Garnish the tops with latik, if desired, and serve right away. Palitaw are best eaten the day they are made.

BIBINGKA
Coconut Rice Cake

IT IS DIFFICULT TO RESIST the dreamy *bibingka* you find at streetside shacks in the province of Laguna. The buttery, fluffy, salty-sweet, banana leaf–wrapped cakes are cooked in flat-bottomed woks over coconut husk fires, then handed over to customers in little smoky bundles. The homemade version can be almost as addictive, especially when baked in a cast-iron skillet and eaten warm, while still slightly gooey on the inside. As with most Filipino recipes, there are many different variations of this cake: this is our favorite approach; it calls for a generous portion of salted egg and grated cheese, which provide the savoriness that defines Filipino pastries. Serve the cake with the ginger tea called *salabat*. **SERVES 4 TO 6**

Butter or cooking spray, for greasing

1 banana leaf (see Key Ingredients, page 36), washed and dried

1 cup (160 g) glutinous rice flour (see Key Ingredients, page 40)

1 cup (200 g) sugar

2½ teaspoons baking powder

⅛ teaspoon kosher salt

1 cup (240 ml) coconut milk

¼ cup (60 ml) whole milk

3 tablespoons unsalted butter, melted

3 large eggs

1 salted egg (see page 41) or hard-boiled egg, peeled and sliced

3 tablespoons condensed milk

½ cup (55 g) grated Edam cheese

Salabat (recipe follows), for serving (optional)

Preheat the oven to 350°F (175°C). Grease a 9-inch (23 cm) cast-iron skillet or baking dish with butter or cooking spray and line it with the banana leaf. Trim the edges of the leaf so that it hangs over the skillet or dish by only an inch or two, then coat the leaf with more butter or spray.

In a large bowl, stir together the rice flour, sugar, baking powder, and salt.

In a medium bowl, beat together the coconut milk, whole milk, melted butter, and raw eggs until well combined.

Slowly mix the wet ingredients into the dry ingredients, making sure they are well incorporated.

Pour the batter into the prepared skillet or baking dish and top it with the salted egg slices.

Bake for 20 minutes, or until a toothpick inserted into the center comes out clean. Brush the top with condensed milk and sprinkle with the cheese. Return the pan to the oven and bake just until the cheese melts, 1 to 2 minutes more.

Let cool slightly, cut into slices, and serve still warm or at room temperature, with salabat for sipping, if desired.

Salabat

GINGER TEA

Bibingka is often served with *salabat*, a simple ginger tea made from steeping fresh ginger root in hot water. It's also a go-to Filipino home remedy for soothing sore throats and high temperatures; you can make a similar tea with fresh turmeric root, too. **SERVES 4 TO 6**

1 (5-inch/12.5 cm) piece fresh ginger, peeled and coarsely chopped

¼ cup (55 g) packed brown sugar, plus more to taste

Juice of ½ lemon

In a medium saucepan, combine the ginger and 8 cups (2 L) water and bring to a boil over medium-high heat. Reduce the heat to low and simmer for 7 minutes.

Strain the tea through a fine-mesh sieve into a heatproof pitcher, discarding the ginger, and stir in the brown sugar until it has dissolved. Add the lemon juice and more sugar as desired, then serve hot. Store any leftover salabat in an airtight container in the refrigerator; reheat before serving.

BRAZO DE MERCEDES
Custard-Filled Meringue

BRAZO DE MERCEDES IS A LIGHT-AS-A-CLOUD, fluffy layer of meringue rolled around a custard filling. The name is Spanish for "arm of Our Lady of Mercies"—and the dessert, which looks like a Swiss cake roll, is likely based on Spain's cream-filled sweet roulades. The trick is to make a custard that isn't overwhelmingly yolky in flavor, the Achilles' heel of many a traditional brazo de Mercedes. Here the orange liqueur in the filling does the trick. **SERVES 4 TO 6**

Note: Make sure there is no egg yolk in your egg whites, which can prevent the egg whites from whipping into peaks or cause the meringue to deflate after baking.

Cooking spray, for greasing

15 large eggs, separated (see Note)

1 teaspoon cream of tartar

1 cup (200 g) granulated sugar

2½ cups (20 ounces/590 ml) condensed milk

2 ounces (60 ml) Grand Marnier or other orange liqueur

Confectioners' sugar, for dusting

Preheat the oven to 350°F (175°C) with a rack in the center position. Line a jelly-roll pan or rimmed baking sheet with waxed paper and spray it with cooking spray.

In the bowl of a stand mixer fitted with the whisk attachment, beat the egg whites and cream of tartar on medium speed (do not mix on high or your whites will collapse). Beat until the egg whites form soft peaks: when you pull up the beater, a peak will form, then collapse. (Alternatively, beat the egg whites in a large bowl using a handheld mixer.)

Slowly add the granulated sugar and beat until the egg whites form stiff peaks: when you pull up the beater, the peaks will form and then hold their shape.

Spread the egg whites in an even layer in the prepared pan. Bake for 18 to 25 minutes, rotating the pan twice throughout the cooking process, or just until the top of the meringue turns light golden in color. Remove from the oven and set aside to cool.

While the meringue is in the oven, fill the bottom of a double boiler or a medium saucepan with 1 inch (2.5 cm) of water and bring the water to a simmer over medium-high heat. Put the egg yolks, condensed milk, and orange liqueur in the top of the double boiler (or in a heatproof bowl that fits over the top of the saucepan without touching the water). Beat the egg yolk mixture until thick and custardy, 5 to 7 minutes. Carefully remove the top of the double boiler or the bowl from the heat and set aside to cool.

When the meringue has cooled, sprinkle it with confectioners' sugar and place a sheet of waxed paper over the top. Cover the waxed paper with another jelly-roll pan or a cutting board and gently flip the meringue out of the pan onto the waxed paper.

Spread the cooled custard mixture evenly over the meringue, leaving a 1-inch (2.5 cm) border. Gently roll the cake up from one long side so it forms a tube. Wrap it gently in the waxed paper, then refrigerate for 3 to 4 hours.

Slice the cake crosswise into 2-inch-wide (5 cm) pieces. It is best eaten the day it is made.

LECHE FLAN
Coconut Milk Flan

SMOOTH, CREAMY, AND CUSTARDY, CARAMEL-TOPPED FLAN is found around the world in Latin countries or those countries with a Latin influence, and the Philippines is no exception. But this flan is made with coconut milk, which tones down that often too-eggy flavor. Traditionally, Filipino flans are baked in an oblong pan called a *llanera* or in smaller individual molds, but you can use a pie pan or round baking dish and get the same result. Resist the temptation to eat it straight from the oven: the flavor and texture are best after a few hours of chilling. **SERVES 4 TO 6**

1 (14-ounce/415 ml) can
condensed milk

1½ cups (360 ml) coconut milk

5 large eggs

1 cup (200 g) sugar

Preheat the oven to 350°F (175°C).

In a medium bowl, beat together the condensed milk, coconut milk, and eggs until well incorporated. Set aside.

In a medium saucepan, melt the sugar over medium heat, stirring continuously with a spatula or wooden spoon until it begins to bubble and turn golden brown, about 5 minutes. Pour the caramelized sugar over the bottom of a 9-inch (23 cm) deep-dish pie pan or baking dish, making sure it coats the entire pan.

Pour the milk-egg mixture over the caramelized sugar. Set the pie pan into a large baking dish and fill the baking dish with water to come halfway up the sides of the pie pan, being careful not to get water in the pan. Carefully transfer the baking dish to the oven and bake for 45 minutes, or until the center of the flan is set and no longer liquid.

Remove the pan from the water bath and let the flan cool slightly, then refrigerate for 4 hours or up to overnight before serving. (The flan will keep in the refrigerator for up to 2 days.)

To serve, gently invert the flan onto a serving plate and cut it into wedges. Serve cold or at room temperature.

UBE ICE CREAM
Purple Yam Ice Cream

UBE, OR PURPLE YAM, is a Filipino ingredient that is increasingly becoming mainstream, most likely because of its brilliant color and taste of vanilla and pistachio. These true yams—not sweet potatoes—can grow to be enormous and are vividly purple, although white versions do exist. In the Philippines, you can find ube on the dessert table, where *ube halaya*—essentially sweetened mashed purple yams—is used in pastries and pies, eaten like jam, topped with *latik* (page 307), or folded into ice cream. **MAKES ABOUT 1 QUART (1 L)**

4 large egg yolks

⅔ cup (135 g) sugar

1½ cups (360 ml) whole milk

2 cups (600 g) Ube Halaya (recipe follows)

1½ cups (360 ml) heavy cream

Note: This recipe requires an ice cream machine and several hours of chilling and freezing, so plan ahead.

In a bowl, whisk together the eggs and sugar until the mixture turns pale yellow. Set aside.

In a medium saucepan, heat the milk over low heat until just warm. Watch it carefully, making sure it does not scald or burn.

While whisking continuously, add a little bit of the warm milk to the egg mixture to temper the eggs, then slowly pour the warmed egg mixture into the pot with the rest of the milk, stirring continuously. Cook over low or medium-low heat, stirring continuously, just until the mixture thickens. Stir in the ube halaya and the heavy cream until they are well incorporated. Remove the pan from the heat, transfer the custard to a storage container, cover, and refrigerate for 3 hours or up to overnight.

Transfer the custard to an ice cream machine and churn according to the manufacturer's instructions.

Transfer the ice cream to a storage container and freeze for at least 4 hours before serving.

> recipe continues →

**UBE
ICE CREAM**

Purple Yam
Ice Cream

continued →

Ube Halaya

UBE JAM

Though you can easily buy jarred *ube halaya* from most Filipino markets and some Asian markets (see Resources, page 342), like most foods, it is much better made from scratch. This buttery spread of mashed purple yams—*ube* in Tagalog—is richly flavored thanks to the brown sugar, condensed milk, and coconut milk and is often spread on bread like jam. It's also topped with *latik* (page 307) for a simple dessert, added to the crushed ice sundae *halo-halo* (page 294), or used as a filling for all kinds of sweets, pastries, pies, and doughnuts. **MAKES ABOUT 1 QUART (1 L)**

Notes: Fresh purple yams are hard to find outside of the West Coast, but most Filipino markets and some Asian markets typically sell them frozen whole. When you defrost them, keep the liquid that accumulates in the bowl or bag. For a deeper ube flavor, add 1 teaspoon ube extract to the mashed yams.

If you don't have a steamer pot, you can set a metal colander (or even a wire rack, if you have one that fits) into a large spaghetti or soup pot with a lid.

1 pound (455 g) fresh or thawed frozen purple yams (see Notes)

1 cup (240 ml) coconut milk

1 cup (240 ml) condensed milk

4 tablespoons (½ stick/55 g) unsalted butter

¼ cup (45 g) muscovado or brown sugar

If using fresh yams, scrub them well under running water and cut them into quarters. Fill a steamer pot with a couple of inches of water (make sure the water doesn't touch the steamer basket) and place the yams in the basket. Steam over medium-high heat until the yams are tender when pierced with a fork, about 30 minutes. Scoop the soft flesh from the skins, discarding the skins, and place the flesh in a large bowl. If using thawed frozen yams, place them in a bowl and skip to the next step.

Mash the yams with a fork or potato masher until very soft and smooth.

In a large saucepan, combine the coconut milk, condensed milk, and butter and heat over medium heat, stirring often, until the butter has just melted and everything is blended together. Add the mashed yams and stir continuously until the mixture becomes a thick paste, 20 to 30 minutes, being careful not to let the bottom scorch. Remove the pot from the heat and add the sugar a little at a time, tasting as you go until the ube halaya is sweetened to your liking.

Store the ube halaya in an airtight container in the refrigerator, where it will keep for at least a week.

UBE MILK SHAKE

THIS SUPERRICH, TROPICALLY FLAVORED MILK SHAKE gets a double shot of purple yam from both the *ube* ice cream and the *ube halaya*. For texture and a pop of color, sprinkle some crunchy rice cereal over the top, or, if you can find it, try the "original" Rice Krispies: the Filipino dessert topping called *pinipig*, toasted pounded young grains of glutinous rice. **SERVES 2**

½ cup (120 ml) coconut milk

2 tablespoons condensed milk

2 tablespoons evaporated milk

½ cup (30 g) Ube Ice Cream (page 289)

2 tablespoons Ube Halaya (see opposite page)

6 ice cubes

¼ cup (8 g) crispy rice cereal, such as Rice Krispies, for topping (optional)

In a blender, combine the three milks, ice cream, ube halaya, and ice cubes and blend until smooth.

Serve in tall glasses with straws, topped with a tablespoon or two of crispy rice cereal, if you'd like.

AVOCADO MILK SHAKE

THIS SHAKE IS A FAST, EASY, and delicious way to highlight the fact that avocados are technically a fruit. Their luscious natural fats and creamy texture are ideal pureed into a milk shake—no ice cream needed. **SERVES 2**

½ cup (120 ml) coconut milk

2 tablespoons condensed milk

2 tablespoons evaporated milk

½ Hass avocado, pitted and peeled

1 cup (125 g) ice cubes (about four 1-inch cubes)

In a blender, combine the three milks, the avocado, and the ice cubes and blend until smooth.

Serve in tall glasses with straws.

HALO-HALO
Shaved Ice Sundae

Notes: Pandan-flavored jelly, *nata de coco* (also called coconut gel), sweet red beans, young coconut meat, and red palm fruit are all found canned or jarred at Filipino markets (see Resources, page 342), as well as in some general Asian or Chinese markets, which may also stock ube ice cream, ube halaya, and leche flan. Don't worry if you can't find all the toppings. You can even try substituting other preserved fruits you find or like. Using only one or two toppings would be fine, too; the key is to have a mix of flavors and textures.

If you don't own an ice shaver, crush the ice by hand: Take the largest ice cubes you can find, wrap them in a clean plastic bag (such as a ziplock bag, left unzipped), and place it inside a dishtowel. Use a mallet or rolling pin to coarsely crush the ice.

HALO-HALO MEANS "MIX-MIX," which is an apt name for a dish that is both a combination of many ingredients and a combination of many cultures. It is a fusion of the Japanese shaved ice and condensed milk dessert *kakigori*, American ice cream sundaes, and Filipino ingredients and ingenuity. The base is a mix of crushed or shaved ice and condensed milk, evaporated milk, and coconut milk, which is layered with up to a dozen toppings of preserved fruits (all of which you simply buy canned or jarred from a Filipino market), plus ice cream and a small piece of *leche* flan. (Technically, the addition of flan makes it a "Halo-Halo Royale.") We think all the ingredients should be mixed together before you eat it, although some like to savor halo-halo layer by layer. Either way, the last spoonful is always the most amazing taste of flavored milk, rivaling any cereal milk. **SERVES 4**

2 cups (480 ml) coconut milk

1 cup (240 ml) evaporated milk

½ cup (120 ml) condensed milk

2 tablespoons pandan- or pandan-and-coconut-flavored jelly (see Notes)

2 tablespoons nata de coco (see Notes)

2 tablespoons sweet red beans (see Notes)

2 tablespoons young coconut meat (see Key Ingredients, page 37)

2 tablespoons red palm fruit (see Notes)

4 cups (450 g) shaved or crushed ice (see Notes)

4 small scoops Ube Ice Cream (page 289) or other ice cream

¼ cup (75 g) Ube Halaya (see page 292)

4 small squares Leche Flan (page 288; optional)

In a small bowl, whisk together the three milks. Set aside.

Place 1½ teaspoons each of the pandan-flavored jelly, nata de coco, sweet red beans, young coconut meat, and red palm fruit in the bottom of four dessert bowls or sundae glasses.

Place 1 cup (150 g) of the ice over the toppings in each bowl or glass. Add ¾ cup (180 ml) of the milk mixture.

Top each bowl with 1 small scoop of ice cream, 1 tablespoon of ube halaya, and a square of leche flan, if desired.

Serve immediately with long spoons.

Japanese influences are few and far between in Filipino cuisine, but one example is *halo-halo*. Other examples are Japanese words like *suki*, used to refer to a favored food vendor or customer, and the occasional use of miso, as in *sinigang na isda* (page 85). The Japanese lived in the Philippines before the arrival of the Spanish. The town of Agoo in the northern Luzon province of La Union was an early Japanese settlement.

PARADOSDOS

Sweet Coconut Soup

THIS POPULAR SWEET SOUP—A MIX OF tropical fruits, tapioca pearls, and rice flour dumplings in a thick, silky, coconutty sauce—is excellent eaten either as a *meryenda* or dessert. It's sometimes called *ginataang bilo bilo* (*bilo bilo* being the name of the rice flour dumplings) or even *ginataang halo-halo*, as *halo-halo* means "mix-mix." This sweet soup has a delicate flavor and floral aroma, thanks to the ripe bananas. You can serve it cold or warm, depending on your cravings or the weather. **SERVES 4 TO 6**

1 cup (160 g) glutinous rice flour (see Key Ingredients, page 40)

5 cups (1.2 L) coconut milk

1 cup (200 g) sugar

1 medium sweet potato, peeled and cut into ½-inch (1.5 cm) cubes

1 cup (120 g) seeded ripe jackfruit pods cut into strips (see Note, page 335)

3 ripe Saba bananas (see page 252) or 2 ripe regular bananas, peeled and cut into ½-inch-thick (1.5 cm) slices

1 cup (240 g) cooked tapioca pearls (see Note)

1 cup (145 g) fresh or thawed frozen sweet corn kernels

1 (14-ounce/415 ml) can condensed milk

1½ cups (360 ml) coconut cream (see Key Ingredients, page 37)

Note: To cook the tapioca pearls, place ½ cup (75 g) dried pearls in a pot and cover them with several inches of water. Bring to a boil over medium-high heat. Cover the pot, with the lid slightly ajar, reduce the heat to low, and cook until tender, 50 minutes to 1 hour. Drain in a colander and rinse under warm water. The tapioca pearls can be made a few hours in advance and held at room temperature.

Ginataang is used to refer both to cooking something in coconut milk and the resulting dish. A ginataang can be sweet, like this *paradosdos*, or savory, like the stewed greens called *ginataang tambo* (page 141).

In a bowl, mix together the rice flour and ½ cup (120 ml) water until it becomes a firm dough. Use your hands to shape the dough into balls measuring ½ inch (1 cm) in diameter and place them on a baking sheet or plate. Refrigerate for 30 minutes to 1 hour.

In a large saucepan, bring the coconut milk to a boil over high heat and stir in the sugar. Add the sweet potato, jackfruit, and rice flour balls and bring the liquid back to a boil, stirring often. Reduce the heat to medium and cook, stirring occasionally to make sure nothing is sticking to the bottom of the pot, for 5 to 7 minutes. Add the banana, tapioca, and corn. Simmer for 15 minutes more, or until the rice flour balls have cooked through (taste one to check).

Add the condensed milk and the coconut cream and stir until thoroughly combined. Simmer for 10 minutes more, then remove from the heat.

Serve this warm right away, or chill it for a few hours in the refrigerator and serve cold. It is best eaten the day it is made.

PANDESAL
Yeast Rolls

PANDESAL COMES FROM THE SPANISH *pan de sal,* literally "bread of salt," which is an interesting name considering that the rolls aren't salty. Some say this bread evolved from a crusty dinner roll similar to Portuguese bread, though it's more closely related to Chinese-style yeasted buns. These sweet, dense, moist dinner rolls are dusted with bread crumbs and are best eaten warm. They are great by themselves but even better with butter, jam, ham, or cheese. **MAKES 16 LARGE ROLLS**

Note: You can make these smaller or larger as needed. Just cut each rectangle of dough into more or fewer pieces.

2 tablespoons active dry yeast

2 cups (480 ml) warm water

¼ cup (50 g) sugar

2 teaspoons kosher salt

6 cups (720 g) all-purpose flour, plus more as needed

¼ cup (60 ml) vegetable oil or duck fat

Butter, vegetable oil, or cooking spray, for greasing

3 tablespoons plain white bread crumbs (optional)

In a small bowl, dissolve the yeast in ¼ cup (60 ml) of the warm water. Let stand for 10 minutes, until foamy, then stir until the yeast has totally dissolved.

In the bowl of a stand mixer fitted with the dough hook, mix the sugar, salt, and flour on low speed until combined. (If you do not have a stand mixer, do this in your largest bowl using a handheld mixer.)

Add the remaining water, the yeast mixture, and the vegetable oil or duck fat. Beat on low speed until the dough is smooth (or stir it in with a wooden spoon). Increase the speed to medium and beat for 4 minutes, or until the dough is elastic and smooth. Add a teaspoon or two of water if needed.

Transfer the dough to a floured work surface and knead it with your hands for 5 minutes. Form the dough into a smooth ball.

Grease a large bowl—large enough for the dough to double in size—and place the dough in the center. Loosely cover the bowl with plastic wrap or a clean kitchen towel and set it aside in a warm place to rise until doubled in size—this could take anywhere from 30 minutes to 2 hours, depending on whether your kitchen is very hot or very cold, but usually takes about 1 hour.

Preheat the oven to 400°F (200°C). Grease a small baking sheet.

Transfer the dough to a floured work surface and divide it into 4 equal pieces **(see page 300, photos 1, 2)**. Roll each piece into a log **(3)** and then cut the log into 4 equal pieces **(4, 5)**, so you have 16 pieces of dough total.

Use your hands to form each piece of dough into a slightly flattened round, as if you are making hamburger patties. Dip in bread crumbs, if using **(6)**. Place the pieces on the prepared baking sheet so they are almost touching (or fully touching, which is fine, too). Loosely cover the baking sheet or pan with plastic wrap or a clean kitchen towel and set aside in a warm place to rise until doubled in size, anywhere from 30 minutes to 1 hour. (Again, the time will vary based on the temperature of your kitchen.)

Bake for 10 to 15 minutes, until the tops are golden brown.

Serve the rolls right away while they are still warm, or gently reheat them before serving. They will keep in an airtight container at room temperature for 2 to 3 days.

> recipe continues →

HOW TO FORM PANDESAL

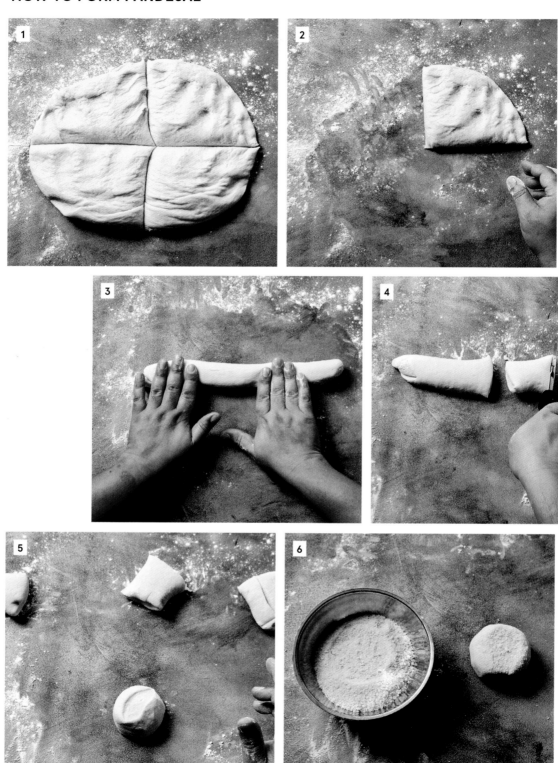

BAKED FRESH

In the Filipino countryside, *pandesal* vendors ride around on bicycles with nothing but a flashlight and a basket of freshly made bread to sell to farmers for a pre-breakfast meal. You won't find these vendors in the cities, but there are still bakeries, some more than a hundred years old, that make pandesal in ancient wood-fired ovens. Today, the bread is predominantly baked in commercial ovens, as the wood-fired ones are prohibited in some regions. Either way, it's a treat to pick up a bagful of warm pandesal to enjoy with a cup of *kapeng barako*, a varietal of coffee grown only in the Philippines. Pandesal dipped in a bit of coffee or hot chocolate or smeared with a slab of butter is an easy habit to adopt for breakfast. If you can find it, try pandesal with a bit of *quesong puti* (similar to a farmer's cheese or Iberian *queso blanco*) or a schmear of "cocojam," a spread made of caramelized coconut milk, eggs, and sugar.

ENSAYMADA
Cheese-Topped Yeast Buns

SALTY ELEMENTS are common in Filipino pastries, and these sweet coiled yeast buns—a cross between a soft dinner roll and a cupcake—are topped with melty sweetened butter and the grated Edam cheese Filipinos call *queso de bola*, or "ball cheese," after its traditional round shape. The word *ensaymada* derived, no doubt, from the *ensaimada* made on the Spanish island of Majorca, which gets its savory tang from dense pork lard instead of cheese. Ensaymada can be enjoyed any time during the day but are always best fresh from the oven. You can also pop one in the microwave to warm it a bit so you get the full effect of the melted sugar, butter, and cheese topping. **MAKES 10 LARGE OR 20 SMALL BUNS**

FOR THE FROSTING

½ cup (1 stick/115 g) unsalted butter, at room temperature

½ cup (100 g) sugar

FOR THE ROLLS

2 tablespoons active dry yeast

¾ cup (175 ml) warm milk

½ cup (100 g) sugar

3½ cups (420 g) all-purpose flour, plus more as needed

1 teaspoon kosher salt

3 large egg yolks, at room temperature

½ cup (100 g) vegetable shortening or lard

Butter, vegetable oil, or cooking spray, for greasing

½ cup (75 g) grated Edam cheese

Make the frosting: In the bowl of a stand mixer fitted with the paddle attachment (or in a large bowl using a handheld mixer), beat together the butter and the sugar on medium speed until the sugar has dissolved, about 4 minutes. Set aside.

Make the rolls: In a small bowl, dissolve the yeast in the warm milk with 2 tablespoons of the sugar. Let sit for 10 minutes, until foamy.

In the bowl of a stand mixer fitted with the dough hook, mix the remaining sugar, the flour, and the salt on low speed until combined.

Add the egg yolks, the shortening or lard, and the yeast mixture, a little at a time. Beat them together on low speed, scraping the bowl so everything is incorporated.

Transfer the dough to a clean work surface and knead it with your hands until it is smooth and elastic, about 5 minutes; the dough should be delicate and still slightly sticky. Form the dough into a ball.

> recipe continues →

Grease a large clean bowl—large enough to hold the dough when it's doubled in size—and place the dough in the bowl. Loosely cover the bowl with plastic wrap or a clean kitchen towel, and set it aside in a warm place to rise—this could take anywhere from 30 minutes to 2 hours, depending on whether your kitchen is very hot or very cold, but usually it takes about 1 hour.

Grease 10 fluted brioche molds, or 20 muffin cups (in two standard muffin tins).

Transfer the dough to a floured work surface, punch it down, and divide it into 10 equal pieces. Use a rolling pin to roll each piece into a flat rectangle about ¼ inch (6 mm) thick. Brush each rectangle with some of the frosting, then roll it up like a thin jelly roll and place it in the prepared molds or muffin tins.

Loosely cover the dough with plastic wrap or a clean kitchen towel, and set aside in a warm place to rise until they have doubled in size, 30 minutes to 1 hour. (Again, the time it takes will vary based on the temperature of your kitchen.)

Preheat the oven to 300°F (150°C).

Brush the tops of the buns with a little frosting and bake 18 to 22 minutes, until the tops are golden brown. Let the ensaymada cool completely in the pans on a wire rack.

When the ensaymada have cooled enough to handle but are still warm, spread the rest of the frosting over the tops and sprinkle with the cheese.

Serve right away. The buns are best the day they are made, but you can reheat leftovers gently in a toaster oven or microwave to get them warm before eating.

ENSAYMADA

Cheese-Topped Yeast Buns

← continued

TIBOK-TIBOK WITH LATIK

Coconut Custard with Caramelized Coconut Milk Curds

TIBOK-TIBOK ROUGHLY TRANSLATES TO "HEARTBEAT," and it's been said that you should give this coconut custard to someone you love or hope to love. This recipe, introduced to us by Atching Lillian (see page 137), a chef and culinary instructor who focuses on the traditional foodways of Pampanga, is similar to a dense Italian panna cotta and equally rich. The real star of the dish is the *latik*, sweet little crumbles of caramelized coconut milk curds that form when you slowly cook down coconut milk until it separates. **SERVES 8 TO 10**

6 cups (1.4 L) coconut milk

1 cup (200 g) sugar

⅓ cup (55 g) glutinous rice flour (see Key Ingredients, page 40)

½ cup (65 g) cornstarch

Zest of 2 limes

Cooking spray or vegetable oil, for greasing

1 banana leaf (see Key Ingredients, page 36)

⅓ cup (45 g) Latik (recipe follows)

In a large saucepan, stir together the coconut milk, sugar, glutinous rice flour, and cornstarch over low heat. Add the lime zest and cook, stirring continuously, until the mixture is smooth and thick, about 10 minutes.

Grease an 8-inch (20 cm) square baking pan and then cut a piece of banana leaf to fit the bottom of the pan. Grease the top of the leaf, then pour in the batter and spread it out evenly.

Let the mixture cool completely in the pan at room temperature, then sprinkle the latik over the top. Slice into squares and serve immediately. This is best eaten the day it is made.

Latik

COCONUT MILK CURDS

These sweet, caramelized coconut milk curds are traditionally used to top desserts, but we've also found they make a wonderful addition to savory salads. **MAKES ABOUT ⅓ CUP (45 G)**

3 cups (700 ml) coconut milk

1 tablespoon brown sugar

Pinch of kosher salt

Bring the coconut milk to a boil in a large saucepan over medium-high heat. Cook until the liquid begins to separate into oil and clumpy "curds," about 15 minutes (watch carefully and don't let the curds burn). Cook until the curds start to fry in the oil. Use a slotted spoon to transfer the curds to a baking sheet and let them cool. (Save the coconut oil for other uses, like cooking vegetables or even as a skin moisturizer.) When the curds have cooled, sprinkle them with the brown sugar and salt and toss until they are coated.

Store the latik in an airtight container in the refrigerator for up to 1 week.

KAMOTE CUE
Candied Sweet Potato

THESE CANDIED ROUNDS OF *KAMOTE*, or sweet potato, are often sold on skewers from street carts for hands-free eating. At home, you can place the soft circles on a platter. Either way, they are best eaten freshly fried, when their candied coating is still crispy and the insides are starchy and soft. The recipe includes only three ingredients, so don't let the frying dissuade you from making these treats. **SERVES 4 TO 6**

Note: Kamote cue is made with a white-fleshed sweet potato known as boniato in the United States. They are less sweet than regular sweet potatoes and are a bit fluffier when cooked; if you can't find them, substitute regular sweet potatoes or yams. For this recipe, you do not need to peel them.

2 cups (480 ml) vegetable oil

1 cup (220 g) packed brown sugar

2 boniato sweet potatoes, peeled (see Note) and cut crosswise into ½-inch-thick (1.5 cm) rounds

In a Dutch oven or large heavy-bottomed saucepan, heat the vegetable oil over medium-high heat until the oil begins to bubble or registers 300°F (150°C) on an instant-read thermometer. Line a plate or baking sheet with paper towels and set it nearby.

Carefully stir the brown sugar into the oil, watching for splatters. When it rises to the top of the oil after a minute or two, add all the sweet potato rounds, making sure they do not touch. Once the oil starts bubbling again, fry the potato rounds, moving them around occasionally, for 8 minutes.

Use a slotted spoon or tongs to remove the pieces from the oil one at a time and transfer to the paper towel–lined plate. Let cool for a minute or two, then serve hot or at room temperature. These are best eaten the day they are made, preferably right after you make them.

There's a similar Filipino snack made from sweet potatoes or Saba bananas that are roughly mashed or thinly sliced, layered like a fan, then battered, panfried, and sprinkled with sugar. These sweet fritters are usually known as *maruya*, for the banana version, or *kalingking*, for the sweet potatoes.

FOOD FOR THE GODS
Date Nut Bar

THIS QUIRKILY NAMED DATE-AND-WALNUT BAR is likely a cousin of the Spanish *pan de dátiles*, a date-and-walnut cake, though it's anyone's guess why it's called "Food for the Gods." Perhaps the name is an homage to how expensive the ingredients once were. Buttery and rich like a blondie, the dessert is far more decadent than the average *kakanin* and is usually put out for the Christmas holidays. **MAKES ABOUT 12 LARGE BARS**

Cooking spray or vegetable oil, for greasing

1 cup (2 sticks/225 g) unsalted butter, at room temperature

¾ cup packed (165 g) light brown sugar

¾ cup (150 g) granulated sugar

3 large eggs

¼ cup (60 ml) molasses

3 tablespoons brown rice syrup

1 teaspoon pure vanilla extract

1½ cups (190 g) all-purpose flour

½ teaspoon baking powder

1 cup (145 g) chopped pitted dried dates

1 cup (120 g) coarsely chopped unsalted walnuts

Preheat the oven to 350°F (175°C). Grease a 9 by 11-inch (23 by 27.5 cm) baking pan.

In the bowl of a stand mixer fitted with the paddle attachment, beat together the butter, brown sugar, and granulated sugar on medium-low speed until the mixture lightens in color, about 5 minutes, stopping to scrape down the sides of the bowl as needed. (If you don't have a stand mixer, beat the ingredients together in a large bowl using a handheld mixer.)

With the mixer running on medium-low speed, add the eggs one at a time, then the molasses, rice syrup, and vanilla.

Add the flour and baking powder and beat until the batter is well combined.

Fold in the dates and walnuts by hand using a rubber spatula or wooden spoon.

Pour the batter into the prepared pan and smooth the top with a spatula.

Bake for 15 minutes, then reduce the oven temperature to 300°F (150°C) and bake for 30 minutes more, or until a toothpick inserted into the center of the bars comes out clean.

Let the nut bars cool in the pan for 5 minutes, then invert them onto a wire rack and let cool completely before slicing and serving.

The bars will keep in an airtight container at room temperature for 3 to 4 days.

COMMODITIES

1 BASIC COMMODITIES
PROCESSED MILK
A. SWEETENED MILK
CARNATION ₱40.00
LIBERTY ₱37.00
ALASKA BLUE ₱37.00
B. EVAPORATED MILK 370 ml
CARNATION ₱30.00
ALASKA ₱24.00
C. POWDERED FILLED MILK 100 G
BEAR BRAND ₱25.00
ALASKA ₱23.00
POWDERED FULL CREAM 200 G
IDO ₱72.00
BIRCH TREE ₱80.00
ANCHOR ₱80.00
E. INFANT FORMULA 360g
S-26
PROMIL
BONNA
GAIN

2 COFFEE (REFILL)
A. NESCAFE   B. BLEND 45
25 G   25 G
50 G   50 G
          C. GREAT TASTE
          25

3 CANNED MARINE

A. SARDINES
LIGO   555
MASTER

5 SUGAR (PER KG)
REFINED ₱44.00
BROWN ₱37.00
6 BREAD (PANDESAL PC)
LOAF BREAD SMALL ₱20.00
7 SALT (PER KL)
IODIZED ₱22.00
ORDINARY ₱20.00
8 COOKING OIL (SPRING)
GIN SIZE ₱18.00
PRIME COMMODITIES
1 FLOUR (25 KG)
1ST CLASS
2ND CLASS
2 NOODLES (CHICKEN)
MAGGI
PAYLESS ₱6.50
LUCKY ME ₱7.50
3 TOILET SOAP (REGULAR)
SAFEGUARD
PALMOLIVE
TENDER CARE
4 LPG (PER 11 KG/TANK)

5 CEMENT (40 KG)
PORTLAND UNION
POZZOLAN NORTHERN
SHEETS (PER LINEAR FT)

10 mm
ORDINARY

9 HOLLOW BLOCKS (
4" ₱7.00 5" ₱9.00
10 CONST. NAIL (PER KL
CW NAIL 1" ₱70.0
CW NAIL 2" ₱70.0
CW NAIL 4" ₱70.0
11 TIE WIRE (PER KG)
#16 ₱70.00   #
12 FISH
BANGUS ₱130.00
TILAPIA ₱100.00
MUDFISH ₱130.00
GALUNG-GONG ₱1
13 MEAT
A. PORK   PURE MEAT
           REGULAR
           MIXED ₱17
           LEGS ₱13
           INTESTINES
           LIVER
B. BEEF   PURE MEAT
           REGULAR
           MIXED
           LEGS
           INTESTINE
           LIVER
C. CHICKEN
14 FERTILIZER (ORGAN
BIO-EARTH
BIO-SYNERGY
IN-ORGANIG FERTILIZ
1. 46-0-0

THOUGH SPANISH COLONIZATION of the Philippines lasted several centuries longer, the American influence on Philippine politics, culture, identity, and foodways somehow feels more pervasive. After three hundred years under Spain, the Philippines fought for and received momentary independence, only to be quickly handed off to the United States. Made an American colony by the Treaty of Paris, the Philippines was under American rule for almost fifty years, from 1898 to 1946, but the American military and culture have remained omnipresent ever since. So much so that up until 1992, Filipinos could join the U.S. Navy and receive citizenship in exchange for their service, leading to thousands of Filipino families (mine among them) moving to the United States, making the two countries forever intertwined.

America purposefully influenced the Filipino educational system (Filipino schools once taught American history and home economics), our democratic governmental processes, our language (English is the predominant language of Filipino commerce and culture), our music (hopelessly romantic American love songs are always playing somewhere), and our food. Unfortunately, U.S. culinary influence often took the form of bleached white flour, processed food, and shortcut cooking. Of course, we now know these American imports are problematic, not just for our diets but also because they meant a loss of many provincial and traditional recipes.

Yet the recipes in this chapter are about more than the influence of America and its culinary icons on Filipino food—though the Chori Burger (page 327) and the Fried Chicken and Ube Waffles (page 324) are delicious examples of that. Instead, these recipes reflect what happens when Filipinos and Filipino Americans transfer ideas, techniques, and flavors. We share recipes that may not be traditional or authentic but are delicious, from Banana Ketchup Ribs (page 316) to sausage-stuffed *lechon* (page 330).

Filipinos make rebuilding or remixing an art form. This is exactly what happened with jeepneys, the world-famous Filipino form of public transportation for the working class. Jeepneys began as a way to repurpose all the World War II jeeps left behind by American soldiers. Ever resourceful, Filipinos made them their own, decorating and designing them with brilliantly colored metal odes to everything from Catholic saints to a popular sneaker brand. In the present day, jeepneys are the de facto privatized, decentralized bus system for those who can't afford their own cars or taxis, available in every neighborhood and willing to stop almost anywhere along the route. Jeepneys have become such a part of our culture, they are now made from scratch with all-new materials.

BANANA KETCHUP RIBS

PORK RIBS ARE RUBBED with a spice mix that includes dried ginger and paprika and glazed with banana ketchup to make an homage to American Southern-style, slow-cooked ribs with Pinoy flavors. Banana ketchup is the go-to red condiment in the Philippines—like tomato ketchup, it is made with vinegar, spices, and sugar, but substitutes bananas for the tomatoes, and as a result it's a bit sweeter. The recipe is easy to make at home, since you cook the ribs in the oven. This is the recipe Miguel cooked on the Food Network show *Beat Bobby Flay* in 2015. Serve the ribs with *pinakurat*, a spicy vinegar, on the side for dipping. **SERVES 4 TO 6**

Notes: A common brand of banana ketchup is Jufran (though the label will read "banana sauce"), which you can occasionally find even in mainstream supermarkets, as well as in Asian supermarkets and from other sources on page 342.

After you bake the ribs, you can refrigerate them for up to 6 days before broiling them. You can also cut them into individual ribs before broiling—it's easy to do when they're still cold from the fridge—just be sure to rotate individual ribs once or twice while they're broiling so all sides are caramelized.

¼ cup (40 g) garlic powder

¼ cup (30 g) onion powder

½ cup (100 g) packed dark brown sugar

¼ cup (20 g) ground ginger

¼ cup (30 g) smoked paprika

2 tablespoons freshly ground black pepper

2 racks pork spareribs, membrane removed

2 cups (480 ml) banana ketchup (see Notes)

¼ cup (60 ml) soy sauce

¼ cup (35 g) minced garlic

¼ cup (60 ml) dry white wine

Pinakurat (page 34), for dipping

In a small bowl, whisk together the garlic powder, onion powder, ¼ cup of the brown sugar, the ginger, paprika, and pepper.

Place the ribs on a baking sheet or large plate and rub the spice mix generously over all sides. Let them rest, loosely covered with plastic wrap, in the refrigerator for 1 hour.

Preheat the oven to 350°F (175°C).

Wrap the ribs tightly in two layers of aluminum foil, set them on a baking sheet, and bake for 2½ to 3 hours, until the rib bones easily pop out when you twist them.

While the ribs cook, in a medium saucepan, combine the banana ketchup, soy sauce, remaining ¼ cup brown sugar, garlic, and wine and bring to a boil over high heat. Reduce the heat to medium-low and simmer for 30 minutes, then set the sauce aside.

When the ribs are done, remove them from the oven and switch the oven to broil.

Unwrap the ribs and return them to the baking sheet. Brush them generously on all sides with the sauce and broil them for 2 to 3 minutes per side, until the sauce begins to bubble and caramelize.

Cut the racks into individual ribs (if you have not done so already—see Notes) and serve immediately, with pinakurat on the side.

The story behind banana ketchup is that during World War II, bananas, not tomatoes, were in abundance in the Philippines, and so Filipina food technologist Maria Y. Orosa used them to create the condiment. (Without food coloring, its natural color is yellow-brown.) Today Orosa's banana sauce, more commonly referred to as banana ketchup, is ubiquitous in most Filipino households. It's great with fried foods like fried chicken, and especially yummy with a breakfast *silog* (page 183). One famous love-it-or-leave-it banana ketchup dish is Filipino spaghetti, which uses banana sauce as its base instead of marinara and often includes hot dogs.

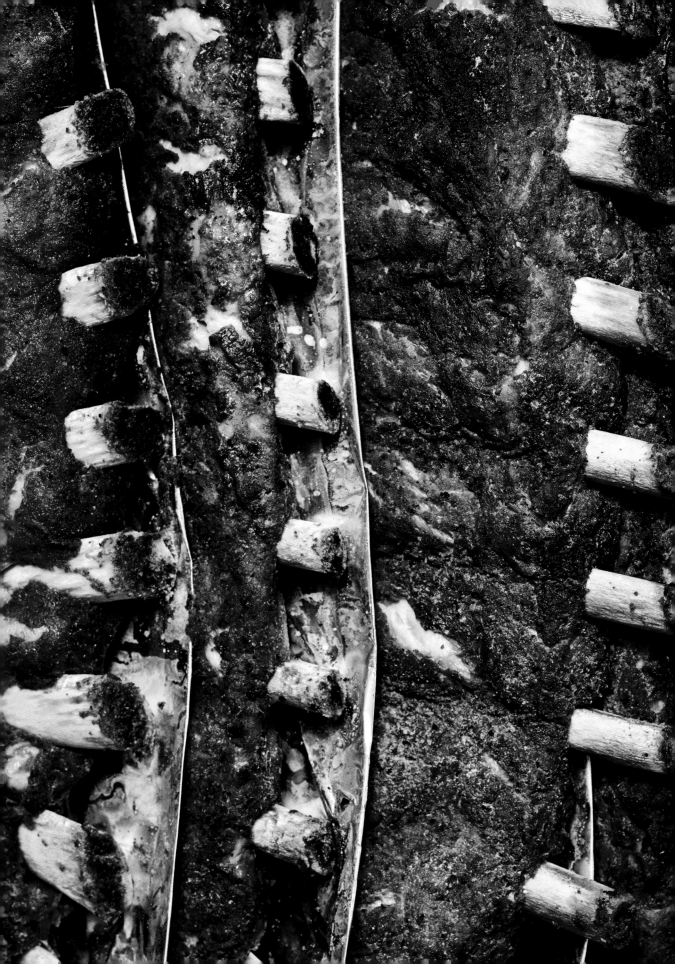

JEEPNEY EXPRESS

Smothered Pork Shoulder with Coconut, Sausage, and Chile Gravy

FOLKLORE SAYS THAT THE ORIGINAL VERSION of this dish—a celebrated stew called Bicol Express made with coconut and julienned chiles—is named after a World War II passenger train that was the fastest way to get from Manila to the region of Bicol. Bicol is one of only two regions in the Philippines known for using spicy chiles, though Bicolano cuisine doesn't get anywhere close to the level of heat used in many other parts of Southeast Asia. The original dish, which can vary from mild to expressly spicy, is made with just a little pork or shrimp as flavoring, while this recipe is a riff on an American-style smothered ham steak. It's a showstopping slab of whole roasted boneless pork shoulder served in a spicy, meaty, coconutty sauce that tastes amazing. (Try the leftovers with the poached eggs on page 170, too.)

Something to know about Philippine cuisine: there's a little leniency with ingredients. One slight ingredient swap changes a dish into something new with an altogether different name. So out of respect to that Filipino culinary tradition, we changed the name of this dish from Bicol Express to Jeepney Express. **SERVES 8 TO 10**

Notes: You can ask a butcher to butterfly the pork butt for you, but if you want to do it yourself, slice the meat *almost* all the way through on its long side so that you can open it like a book.

You will need butcher's twine for this recipe.

Coconut milk powder can be found in small packets in most Asian or natural foods stores or stores that stock baking supplies; King Arthur sells it from their baking supply website as well.

FOR THE PORK SHOULDER

½ cup (75 g) garlic cloves

2½ tablespoons coarsely chopped long red chiles (see Key Ingredients, page 37)

2½ tablespoons coarsely chopped shallot

1 (8-pound/3.6kg) butterflied boneless pork butt (see Notes)

Kosher salt

FOR THE SAUCE

1½ pounds (680 g) Vigan longanisa (see Key Ingredients, page 39), casings removed

1 cup (135 g) minced garlic

1 cup (170 g) minced shallots

1 cup (100 g) minced fresh ginger

⅓ cup (80 ml) bagoong guisado (page 36)

5⅓ cups (1.3 L) coconut milk

2 teaspoons coconut milk powder (see Notes)

2½ tablespoons sliced bird's-eye chiles (see Key Ingredients, page 37)

2½ tablespoons sliced long red chiles (see Key Ingredients, page 37)

4 teaspoons fish sauce

FOR SERVING

8 to 10 cups (1.6 to 2 kg) cooked white rice (see page 40)

Pickled Chiles (recipe follows)

> recipe continues →

JEEPNEY EXPRESS

Smothered Pork
Shoulder with
Coconut, Sausage,
and Chile Gravy

continued →

Preheat the oven to 350°F (175°C).

Prepare the pork shoulder: In a blender, combine the garlic, long red chiles, and shallot and puree to make a paste; set aside.

Spread open the butterflied pork on a clean work surface so that the inside is facing up. With a sharp knife, score the inside of the butt lengthwise two or three times. (The cuts should be about 1 inch/2.5 cm apart and no more than ⅛ inch/3 mm deep.) Sprinkle the surface with salt.

Use your hands to spread all but about 2 tablespoons of the paste all over the inside of the pork butt, making sure it gets into the scores. Roll up the pork like a jelly roll, starting from one short side. Tie it together with butcher's twine in three places—in the center and near each end—so the roll holds together. Sprinkle the outside of the pork lightly with salt and spread it with the remaining seasoning paste.

Place the shoulder in a roasting pan and roast until it is tender, 2 to 3½ hours, basting it several times with the collected juices as it cooks. When the pork is done, transfer it to a serving platter and let it rest for at least 20 minutes.

While the pork is resting, make the sauce: In a large skillet, cook the longanisa over medium heat, breaking it up with a wooden spoon as it cooks, until the fat has rendered, about 7 minutes. Drain and discard the fat. Stir in the garlic, shallots, ginger, and bagoong and cook, stirring occasionally, until the garlic and shallots are soft, about 3 minutes.

Stir in the coconut milk and coconut milk powder and cook over medium heat until the sauce is thick like a gravy, 5 to 7 minutes. Stir in the chiles and the fish sauce, and cook for a minute or two, just until the chiles start to soften. Keep the sauce warm while you slice the pork.

To serve, slice the pork into ¾-inch-thick (2 cm) slices (about the thickness of a pork chop) and pour a generous amount of the warm sauce over the top. Serve immediately, with rice and pickled chiles.

PICKLED CHILES

The flavor of these quick-pickled chiles is best after they sit for 24 hours, and they will continue to improve over time. They'll keep for several months in your refrigerator. You can use them to top stews, sandwiches, and salads or include them as part of sawsawan for any meal. **MAKES ABOUT 1 QUART (1 L)**

2 cups (480 ml) white wine vinegar (at least 5% acidity)

¾ cup (150 g) sugar

1 pound (455 g) hot chiles (see Note), washed, dried, and cut into ⅛-inch-thick (3 mm) slices

3 garlic cloves, halved

2 small bay leaves

¼ teaspoon whole black peppercorns

Note: You can use any chiles you want for this, or even a mix: red, green, yellow, hot, mild, or in between. If they're small, like habaneros, you can leave them whole and slice them as you use them.

In a medium saucepan, combine the vinegar, sugar, and ½ cup (120 ml) water and bring to a boil, stirring until the sugar has dissolved. Turn off the heat.

Place the chiles, garlic, bay leaves, and black peppercorns in a clean 1-quart (1 L) glass jar or plastic container with a lid. Pour the hot brine over the peppers and let the mixture cool to room temperature. Use right away or cover and refrigerate for up to 3 months.

FRIED CHICKEN AND UBE WAFFLES

THE CHICKEN IN THIS DISH is an ode to a long-standing Filipino restaurant known for its fried chicken. The chicken is not breaded but instead marinated—overnight, if possible—in egg whites, which creates a seal around the chicken to keep it crispy and moist. Pair the chicken with waffles made with the technicolor purple yam known as *ube*, found in desserts throughout the Philippines. **SERVES 4**

Notes: This recipe requires a waffle iron and at least 1 hour of marinating.

Ube powder, or dehydrated purple yam powder, is found at Filipino stores as well as via the online sources on page 342.

Many spice companies produce an ube flavor extract that's sold in the same small bottles as vanilla and almond extracts. It's available from Filipino stores, too (see Resources, page 342).

FOR THE CHICKEN

10 egg whites

1 tablespoon garlic powder

2 tablespoons ground ginger

1 tablespoon Spanish paprika

1 tablespoon onion powder

1 tablespoon kosher salt

1 tablespoon freshly ground black pepper

8 pieces bone-in chicken parts, such as thighs, legs, or breasts

Vegetable oil, for frying

FOR THE UBE PASTE

2 tablespoons ube powder (see Notes)

⅓ cup (42 g) confectioners' sugar

¾ teaspoons pure ube extract (see Notes)

½ cup (120 ml) coconut milk

¼ cup (4 tablespoons/60 g) cold unsalted butter, cubed

FOR THE WAFFLES

1 cup (125 g) all-purpose flour

2 tablespoons and 2 teaspoons granulated sugar

1 teaspoon baking powder

1 teaspoon kosher salt

1 large egg

2 tablespoons (40 ml) vegetable oil

½ teaspoon ube extract (see Notes)

Cooking spray

Maple syrup or pancake syrup, for serving

Marinate the chicken: In a large bowl, combine the egg whites, garlic powder, ginger, paprika, onion powder, salt, and pepper.

Add the chicken and toss to coat in the spices. Cover the bowl and let the chicken marinate in the refrigerator for at least 1 hour, and preferably overnight.

Make the ube paste: When you are ready to make the dish, in a medium saucepan, whisk together the ube powder, confectioners' sugar, ube extract, and coconut milk until well incorporated. Heat the mixture over medium heat.

While stirring, add the butter, cube by cube, until it is fully incorporated. Cook, stirring, for about 5 minutes, until the mixture develops a paste-like consistency; do not let it burn. Turn off the heat and set aside, but keep warm.

Fry the chicken: Preheat the oven to its lowest setting. Set a wire rack over a rimmed baking sheet.

Fill a Dutch oven about halfway with vegetable oil and heat the oil over medium-high heat until it registers 325°F (160°C) on an instant-read thermometer. Working in batches, fry the chicken a few pieces at a time for 12 to 15 minutes, or until an instant-read thermometer inserted into the thickest part of a piece registers 165°F (75°C). Transfer the chicken to the rack on the baking sheet and place it in the oven to stay warm. Repeat with the remaining chicken pieces.

Make the waffles: Preheat a waffle iron.

In a medium bowl, whisk together the flour, sugar, baking powder, and salt.

In a large bowl, whisk together the egg, vegetable oil, ube extract, and 1 cup (210 ml) water.

Stir the dry ingredients into the wet ingredients, just until the mixture becomes a smooth batter, then gently fold in the ube paste until it is just mixed through.

Spray the preheated waffle iron with cooking spray. Pour in just enough batter to coat the bottom of the waffle iron, leaving about ½ inch (1.5 cm) of space around the edges. Close and cook until the waffle is golden brown, 2 to 3 minutes. Transfer the waffle to a plate and cover with a clean kitchen towel to keep warm, or place on a baking sheet in the warm oven with the chicken. Repeat until you have used all the batter.

Serve the waffles topped with the warm fried chicken, with syrup on the side.

KINUNOT CHOWDER
Fish and Coconut Milk Chowder

TRADITIONAL *KINUNOT* IS A COLD SALAD eaten in Del Carmen that features coconut milk and flaked stingray, a fish found in abundance off the coastline of the Philippines. Here we turn those same flavors—coconut, black pepper, garlic, sugarcane vinegar, and mild sweet fish—into an American-style chowder. The soup is nearly as easy to make as the salad, and with the addition of slightly bitter, nutrient-packed *mulunggay* leaves, it's also a hearty cold-weather meal. **SERVES 4 TO 6**

5 cups (1.2 L) coconut milk

1 medium white onion, quartered

6 garlic cloves, smashed with the side of a knife

3 bay leaves

1½ pounds (680 g) swordfish or other firm white-fleshed fish, cut into 2-inch (5 cm) chunks

1 cup (180 g) thawed frozen mulunggay leaves (see Notes, page 106)

2 tablespoons white sugarcane vinegar (see Key Ingredients, page 42)

Kosher salt and freshly ground black pepper

In a large saucepan, combine the coconut milk, onion, garlic, and bay leaves and bring to a boil over high heat. Reduce the heat to medium-low and simmer for 10 minutes.

Add the fish and simmer just until it begins to turn opaque, 3 to 5 minutes. Add the mulunggay leaves and cook for 4 minutes more.

Add the vinegar, season with salt and pepper, and serve immediately. The chowder will keep in an airtight container in the refrigerator for 1 to 2 days, and should be gently reheated on the stovetop so as not to destroy the texture of the fish.

THE CHORI BURGER
Chorizo Burger

ON THE ISLAND OF BORACAY, a boardwalk-lined beach destination in the southwest-central Philippines, a street vendor sells tiny "chori burgers," sliders made with slightly spicy Filipino-style chorizo sausages known as *longanisa*. The Filipino chori burger is just the perfect bite: a little griddled fatty meat engulfed in a soft yeast roll called *pandesal* (page 298). Our version of the chori burger is a hefty double-sided burger—with beef and *longanisa hamonado*, a sweet, garlicky Filipino sausage—topped with the sweet pickled vegetables called *atsara*, Maggi-Kewpie mayo (see below), and banana ketchup on a challah bun. The burger is our pride and joy: it won first place in an annual New York City "Battle of the Burger" in 2014, beating out many beloved favorites in the city. When they called our name for first place, we couldn't believe it: a Filipino burger winning an all-American contest! **MAKES 4 BURGERS**

1½ pounds (680 g) ground Angus beef (see Notes)

½ pound (225 g) longanisa hamonado (see Key Ingredients, page 39), casings removed

½ cup (120 ml) mayonnaise

2 tablespoons Maggi seasoning sauce (see Note, page 246)

1 tablespoon Kewpie mayonnaise (see Notes)

Vegetable oil

Kosher salt and freshly ground black pepper

4 challah buns, potato sandwich rolls, or soft hamburger buns, such as Martin's

Spicy or regular banana ketchup (see page 316)

¼ red onion, very thinly sliced

1 cup (120 g) Atsara (page 118)

4 green lettuce leaves

Notes: For best results, use ground beef with a ratio of 80 percent lean to 20 percent fat.

We use a 3½-inch (8.75 cm) ring mold to build a double-sided burger, but a tuna can is about the same size. Just remove the top and bottom of the can and voilà: DIY ring mold. Just be sure to wash it really well before and after using it. You can also simply form the meat into a double patty with your hands.

Kewpie mayonnaise is a Japanese brand of mayo that's silky and smooth, boosted with a little extra umami, spice, and sugar. It's now widely found in regular supermarkets or specialty food stores in addition to most Asian grocers.

Line your work surface and a plate or baking sheet with waxed paper.

Set a 3½-inch (8.75 cm) ring mold (see Notes) on the lined work surface, then press one-quarter of the ground beef (about 6 ounces/170 g) into the bottom of the mold. Make sure the surface of the beef is flat and firmly pressed down into the mold.

Top the beef with one-quarter of the longanisa (about 2 ounces/56 g). Gently but firmly press the sausage down onto the beef in a single layer so the surface is flat and the sausage is firmly pressed down into the mold against the beef.

> recipe continues →

Gently remove the patty from the mold and set it on the lined plate. Repeat to make 3 more burgers. Refrigerate the burgers while you make the Maggi-Kewpie mayonnaise and prepare the griddle.

In a small bowl, stir together the mayonnaise, Maggi, and Kewpie mayonnaise until totally incorporated. Set aside.

Grease a griddle or large skillet with vegetable oil. (The pan should be large enough to comfortably hold all four burgers without touching, but you can also cook them in batches, if necessary.) Heat the griddle over medium to medium-high heat, until it is very hot and a drop of water sizzles on contact.

Remove the burgers from the refrigerator, season them on all sides with salt and pepper, and place them on the griddle with the longanisa side down. Cook for about 3 minutes, or until the longanisa side develops a black-brown crust. Flip the burgers and cook for about 4 minutes more for medium-rare, or until the inside registers 135°F (55°C) on an instant-read thermometer. Transfer the burgers to a cutting board or plate to rest.

Reduce the heat under the griddle slightly and place the buns cut-side down in the fat. Cook until golden brown, about 2 minutes. (You will probably have to do this in batches.)

Once all the buns are toasted, spread both sides of each bun with a little of the Maggi-Kewpie mayonnaise. Put the burgers beef-side down on the bottom buns, then top the patties with a dollop of spicy banana ketchup, a few slices of onion, a quarter of the atsara, and a lettuce leaf. Add the top bun and serve immediately.

THE CHORI BURGER

Chorizo Burger

← continued

> Otherwise known as the Navy Exchange, the PX is where Filipino American families would purchase tax-free fruits, meats, and other convenience-style foods, which is perhaps the biggest way America has influenced Filipino cuisine. U.S. military bases in the Philippines also introduced enlisted Filipinos to ingredients like Spam, ketchup, pasta, hamburgers, and more. Today, the impact is still seen in dishes like *Spamsilog* (see page 183) and *sopas*, a chicken noodle soup made with macaroni.

NUEVA YORK LECHON
New York–Style Roasted Suckling Pig

Notes: This recipe requires at least 1 day of prep time for air-drying the pig. Suckling pigs generally weigh between 10 and 24 pounds (4.5 and 11 kg), but 15 pounds (9 kg) is about the largest that will fit into a regular home oven, and those on the smaller side are also easier to refrigerate and to cook so that the skin gets nice and crispy. (You can order suckling pigs from most butchers or from online sources; see Resources, page 342.)

This recipe provides enough stuffing for a 10- to 12-pound (4.5 to 5.5 kg) pig. If yours is larger, just increase the filling by half or double it. You will get a crispier skin if you cook the pig on a baking sheet or in a low-sided baking dish rather than in a roasting pan, but you will have to watch both carefully to drain the fat that accumulates in the bottom so it doesn't spill out of the pan and burn.

THE CEBU REGION IS FAMOUS for its *lechon,* or whole roast pig, which has been the inspiration for poems and has been described as the best pork in the world. It's stuffed with a bouquet of aromatics like lemongrass, and slow-roasted over an open pit while being painstakingly rotated (often by hand) so as to cook and crisp—but never burn—the skin on all sides. You can re-create that crackling skin and juicy flavorful meat with a suckling pig roasted in a home oven: the secret is to let it dry in the refrigerator for at least one day and preferably two. The less moisture in the skin, the crispier it will be. Then it's brushed with soy sauce and stuffed with sweet, garlicky sausage in addition to a seasoning paste of lemongrass, scallions, garlic, and onions. It's our slightly Spanish (thanks to the sausage stuffing) New York spin on a Cebuano classic. Lechon is meant to be the center of a feast: serve it with rice and *sawsawan,* of course, but also with at least one fresh salad, such as Classic Ensalada (page 122), as well as appetizers like *lumpia* (page 152) or *ukoy* (page 249) and a noodle dish or stew. **SERVES 10 TO 12**

1 (10- to 12-pound/4.5 to 5.5 kg) suckling pig (see Notes)

1 bunch scallions, coarsely chopped

2 stalks lemongrass, smashed with the side of a knife and coarsely chopped

½ cup (70 g) minced garlic

1½ tablespoons kosher salt

1½ teaspoons freshly ground black pepper

1 pound (455 g) longanisa hamonado (see Key Ingredients, page 39), casings removed

2 small white onions, quartered

½ cup (120 ml) soy sauce

10 to 12 cups (2 to 2.4 kg) cooked white rice (see page 40), for serving

Sawsawan (see page 34), for serving

Clear out one shelf in your refrigerator. Place the suckling pig in a large baking dish or on a baking sheet (see Notes) and refrigerate it, uncovered, for at least 24 hours and up to 48 hours. This will help remove moisture from the skin so it will crisp up nicely.

When you're ready to roast the pig, preheat the oven to 400°F (205°C).

In a blender or food processor, combine the scallions, lemongrass, garlic, salt, and pepper and puree until well combined. Remove the pig from the refrigerator and use your hands to rub the mixture all over the inside cavity of the pig.

Stuff the pig with the longanisa and quartered onion, making sure to fill in its rear so that it looks nice and fat, which also helps the skin to crisp. Brush the skin with the soy sauce, cover the ears and tail with foil to protect them from burning, and roast the pig for 30 minutes.

Reduce the oven temperature to 275°F (135°C) and cook for 4 hours more, or until the internal temperature of the thickest part of the leg reaches 145°F (65°C) on an instant-read thermometer. Every hour or so, be sure to spoon off or use a baster to remove some of the fat that has accumulated in the pan and transfer it to a saucepan.

When the pig is done, transfer it to a cutting board and let it rest for 30 minutes.

While the pig rests, remove any collected juices and fat from the pan and add them to the saucepan. Bring the juices just to a boil over high heat, then pour them into a gravy boat or serving container.

To serve the pig, use a sharp knife or cleaver to cut through the crispy skin and cut it into manageable pieces. Use tongs or a serving fork to pull off pieces of the tender pork beneath, and use a spoon to remove and serve the stuffing. Give each plate a little skin, sliced pork, and stuffing, and serve the rice, drippings, and sawsawan on the side.

AVOCADO ICE CREAM

FILIPINOS ARE WELL AWARE THAT AVOCADOS are technically a fruit: when my mother was growing up, she used to cut open a ripe avocado, sprinkle it with sugar and drizzle it with a bit of condensed milk, and eat it right out of the skin. (Eating avocados as a savory snack was a foreign concept for me until years later, when I discovered guacamole.) The fat content and butteriness of an avocado make for a wonderful ice cream, which is a special flavor commonly found in the Philippines and just one step removed from my mother's quick snack. This recipe is adapted from one created by our friend Ian Carandang, a *sorbetero* (ice cream maker) based in Manila. **SERVES 4 TO 6**

Note: This recipe requires an ice cream machine and several hours of chilling and freezing, so be sure to plan ahead.

4 large egg yolks

½ cup (100 g) sugar

1½ cups (360 ml) whole milk

1½ cups (360 ml) heavy cream

¼ cup (60 ml) condensed milk

2 ripe Hass avocados

In a bowl, whisk together the eggs and sugar until the mixture turns pale yellow, 3 to 5 minutes. Set aside.

In a medium saucepan, combine the whole milk, cream, and condensed milk and heat over low heat until just warm. Watch it carefully, making sure it does not scald or burn.

While whisking continuously, add a little bit of the warm milk mixture to the eggs to temper the eggs, then slowly pour the warmed egg mixture into the pot with the rest of the milk mixture, stirring continuously.

Cook over low or medium-low heat, stirring continuously, just until the mixture thickens. Remove the pan from the heat, transfer the ice cream base to a storage container, cover, and refrigerate for 3 hours or up to overnight.

When you're ready to churn the ice cream, pit and peel the avocados and place their flesh in a blender. Add the cooled ice cream base. Blend until smooth, then transfer to an ice cream machine and churn according to the manufacturer's instructions.

Transfer the ice cream to a storage container and freeze for at least 4 hours before serving.

LANGKA ICE CREAM
Jackfruit Ice Cream

LANGKA, OR JACKFRUIT, has a flavor that tastes like the tropical trifecta of papaya, banana, and mango all mixed together. While we often stew or braise the sturdy unripe fruit, using it more like a starch, here you want the bright yellow pods inside the jackfruit to be soft and sweet. Its flavor concentrates as you cook it down into a jam, which is blended with the custard base just before you churn the ice cream. Jackfruit is not a traditional flavor of ice cream in the Philippines, though modern dessert makers are embracing it. **SERVES 4 TO 6**

Note: This recipe requires an ice cream machine and several hours of chilling and freezing, so be sure to plan ahead.

4 large egg yolks

⅔ cup (135 g) sugar

1½ cups (360 ml) whole milk

1½ cups (360 ml) heavy cream

1½ cups (360 ml) Langka Jam (recipe follows)

In a bowl, whisk together the eggs and sugar until the mixture turns pale yellow, about 3 minutes. Set aside.

In a medium saucepan, heat the milk over low heat until just warm. Watch it carefully, making sure it does not scald or burn.

While whisking continuously, add a little bit of the warm milk mixture to the eggs to temper the eggs, then slowly pour the warmed egg mixture into the pot with the rest of the milk, stirring continuously.

Add the heavy cream and Langka Jam. Cook over low or medium-low heat, stirring continuously, just until the mixture thickens. Remove the pan from the heat and let the ice cream base cool completely in the refrigerator for 3 hours or overnight.

Transfer the cooled ice cream base to a blender and blend until smooth. Transfer the mixture to an ice cream machine and churn according to the manufacturer's instructions.

Transfer the ice cream to a storage container and freeze for at least 4 hours before serving.

Langka Jam

JACKFRUIT JAM

This jam is also a great spread on *pandesal* (page 298) or on biscuits, or served on top of vanilla ice cream; use it anywhere else you'd have jelly or jam. **MAKES ABOUT 2 CUPS (480 ML)**

5 cups (755 g) seeded ripe jackfruit
pods (see Note)

½ cup (100 g) sugar

Slice or tear the jackfruit pods into 2 or 3 pieces each. In a large saucepan, combine the jackfruit, sugar, and 1 cup (240 ml) water and bring to a boil over medium-high heat, stirring occasionally.

Reduce the heat to medium-low and simmer, stirring occasionally, until the jam thickens and reduces to the consistency of marmalade, about 30 minutes.

Let cool before using or storing. Store the cooled jam in a glass or plastic container in the refrigerator for up to 2 weeks.

Note: If using fresh jackfruit, look for ripe, soft, aromatic fruit, which will have a sweet, banana-like flavor. Remove the bright yellow fleshy pods from the fibrous core, then tear or cut the pods open to reveal the large seeds in the middle. You can discard both the fibrous core and the seeds, though the seeds can be eaten once cooked. You could substitute canned ripe jackfruit (but not young or green jackfruit), which is usually sold packed in syrup.

TIKI COCKTAILS

YEARS AGO, when we were developing our restaurants, I was pleasantly surprised to learn from Marlo Gamora, the self-described tiki-phile who helped create the drinks at Jeepney, that tiki bar culture and Filipinos are inextricably linked. Marlo taught us about the role of Filipino bartenders in the tiki era of the 1930s, starting with Don the Beachcomber, the first Polynesian bar in Los Angeles. It gave soldiers returning home from the war in the Pacific a form of escapism. The drinks featured lots of rum, additional sweet liqueurs, and fruits like oranges, guavas, coconuts, and pineapples, and were deliberately constructed to help the drinker forget the troubles of daily life in a place that looked and tasted like paradise. The Beachcomber had a hand in creating some of the most iconic of these drinks, including the Mai Tai and the Painkiller. That legacy lives on with bartenders like Marlo. Despite the tropical flourishes found on the next few drinks, all are easy to construct once you gather the ingredients and garnishes.

JUICE MARY AND JOSEPH

MAKES 1 DRINK

1½ ounces (45 ml/3 tablespoons) very cold mango puree

1 ounce (30 ml/2 tablespoons) very cold coconut cream, preferably Coco López

¾ ounce (22 ml/1½ tablespoons) honey-flavored syrup (see Note)

¾ ounce (22 ml/1½ tablespoons) blue Curaçao liqueur

½ ounce (15 ml/1 tablespoon) fresh lemon juice

2 ounces (60 ml/¼ cup) Japanese shochu, preferably Mizu

1 fresh pineapple wedge, for garnish (optional)

1 fresh orange wedge, for garnish (optional)

1 fresh pineapple leaf, for garnish (optional)

Note: Honey syrup is a flavored sugar syrup typically found in specialty food and cocktail supply shops, and is used in cocktails or flavored coffees. You can make your own by heating equal parts mild honey and water over medium-low heat in a small saucepan, stirring, until the honey completely dissolves into the water. It will keep in an airtight container in the refrigerator for several weeks.

In a blender, combine the mango, coconut cream, honey syrup, Curaçao, lemon juice, and shochu and blend just until smooth.

Transfer the drink to a hurricane-style (tall and curved) cocktail glass or a tall iced tea glass, garnish with the pineapple and orange wedges and the pineapple leaf, if desired, and serve immediately, with a straw.

PINAY COLADA

SERVES 2

3 ounces (90 ml/⅓ cup) coconut cream, preferably Coco López

5 fresh pineapple rings, cored

2 ounces (60 ml/¼ cup) dark rum, preferably Tanduay Asian Rum

¾ ounce (22 ml/1½ tablespoons) banana liqueur

1 teaspoon Angostura bitters

2 pinches of kosher salt

12 ounces (360 g) ice, or 12 (1-inch/2.5 cm) square ice cubes

1 hollowed-out fresh pineapple (optional)

2 tablespoons coconut flakes, toasted

2 maraschino cherries, each skewered on a toothpick

Garnishes of your choice (see opposite)

In a blender, combine the coconut cream, 3 of the pineapple rings, the rum, banana liqueur, bitters, salt, and ice and blend just until smooth.

Transfer the drink to the hollowed-out pineapple (if using) or divide it evenly between two hurricane-style (tall and curved) cocktail glasses or tall iced tea glasses.

To garnish the drink(s), sprinkle the toasted coconut over the top of the drink(s), then stick a skewered cherry into each of the remaining pineapple rings and lay them on top of the toasted coconut. Continue to garnish as desired, using the photo opposite for inspiration, and serve immediately, with two straws.

FILIPINO FLASH

MAKES 1 DRINK

Ice cubes, for shaking and serving

2 ounces (60 ml/¼ cup) dark rum, preferably Tanduay Asian Rum

¾ ounce (22 ml/1½ tablespoons) ginger syrup (see Notes)

¾ ounce (22 ml/1½ tablespoons) pineapple juice

¾ ounce (22 ml/1½ tablespoons) fresh lemon juice

Fill a cocktail shaker with ice, then add the rum, ginger syrup, pineapple juice, and lemon juice. Shake for about 15 seconds, or until the outside of the shaker feels ice-cold to the touch.

Fill a rocks glass with clean ice and strain the drink into the glass. Serve immediately.

It is hard to deny the Filipino influence on tiki cocktails, given that Filipinos were part of the birth of the culture. Although Don had the final say on what made it onto his menus at the Beachcomber, many of the bar's original cocktails were actually created by the Filipino bartenders Don employed, and a handful carried on the tiki cocktail tradition at their own places. From the 1930s to the 1950s, the Filipino bartending community in Southern California was a small and tight-knit group, and Hollywood stars and celebrities like Ava Gardner and Frank Sinatra followed these bartenders from bar to bar because of the discretion and hospitality they bestowed on their patrons. They were also sought-after because they had secret, coded recipe books only they could translate, ensuring that they were the only bartenders who knew how to create these popular drinks.

Notes: You will need a cocktail shaker and a strainer to make this drink.

Ginger syrup is a flavored sugar syrup that is usually available at cocktail supply shops and some natural food markets. You can also make your own by combining ½ cup (100 g) sugar, ½ cup (120 ml) water, and a 5-inch (13 cm) piece of peeled fresh ginger in a small saucepan and simmering it over medium-high heat for 30 minutes. Let cool, then strain out and discard the ginger. Store the syrup in an airtight container in the refrigerator for up to several weeks.

Resources

If your city doesn't have a Filipino grocery store (you'd be surprised how many do, when you actually take the time to look), try large pan-Asian supermarkets; most will carry basic Filipino pantry ingredients like *bagoong, patis,* sugarcane vinegar, and frozen calamansi juice. You can also usually find fish sauce, salted duck eggs, and other staples at Chinese, Thai, Vietnamese, Korean, and other specialty markets.

If you can't get these shelf-stable items in person, thankfully, you can now easily order them online: for those in the United States, two great online vendors are Filstop (Filstop .com) and Yollie's Oriental Market and Gift Shop (YollieOrientalOnline.com).

Some other special ingredients, like tropical fruits and vegetables (including the chayote on pages 90, 110, and 130 and the tamarind pods on pages 82 and 101), are expensive and more difficult to source online. If you don't have a Filipino or Asian market nearby, check Hispanic, Latino, Caribbean, and Indian markets for these fruits and vegetables, as they are cultivated in those parts of the world as well.

For information on travel and culinary education in the Philippines, you can visit tourism.gov.ph and tpb.gov.ph.

In the Philippines, the corner store or bodega is the *sari-sari* store, a compact convenience store that sells easy-on-the-pocketbook sample-like sizes of everything from shampoo to snacks, all neatly displayed in their packages, often hanging from every possible nook and cranny. They're found throughout the Philippines in neighborhoods of all social statuses.

Acknowledgments

I want to thank the people who opened doors—figuratively and literally—for us. Asking for or needing help often happened at the eleventh hour, and the universe revealed once again its ability to provide exactly what we needed at exactly the right time. Angels come in many forms, and for us they were chefs, family, friends, writers, journalists, foodies, activists, and the peculiar herb salesman during curfew in Sagada or motorcycle mechanic at midnight in Mindanao.

I encourage everyone to travel to the Republic of the Philippines—beyond areas with the modern pleasures of AirCon and shopping, if only for an hour or two. The experiences and flavors you'll discover are unlike any others, and it might also teach you a little about humanity and humility, like it did for me. We are indebted to chef Claude Tayag, chef Atching Lillian Borromeo, chef Cocoy Ventura, hoteliers and restaurateurs Milo Naval, Glenda Barretto, and Ian Carandang, and adventurer Clang Garcia for opening a world of joy, kindness, generosity, beauty, and spirit that is only in the Philippines.

When we pitched the idea to do a book, some publishers said no and some said yes; one publisher convinced us that they would honor our voice and champion it. *Maraming salamat* to our Artisan publishing team and representation: publisher Lia Ronnen, executive editor Judy Pray, creative director Michelle Ishay-Cohen, and agent Laura Nolan, who all kept up goodwill even through my personal way of interpreting deadlines. Thanks to our publicity and marketing team: Theresa Collier, Allison McGeehon, and Amy Kattan. (That's an all-women crew, for those keeping score.) Also, thanks to Sibylle Kazeroid, Zach Greenwald, Jane Treuhaft, Toni Tajima, Nancy Murray, and Hanh Le. Thank you to Justin Walker, Victoria Granoff, Martha Bernabe, Claudia Saimbert, and Kaitlyn Du Ross Walker, for the good lighting, props, and imagery. A special round of applause goes to Junot Diaz, Melissa Sipin, Elda Rotor, Jose Vargas, Jessica Hagedorn, sisters Liz Casasola and Lyn Casasola, Nancy Bulalacao, Lara Stapleton, and Lulu Phongmany for encouraging me to write and for always putting things (i.e., narratives, opportunities, good times) into perspective.

To Mom and Dad, our little family: just us three. From the streets of Philadelphia to the sunny skies of San Diego, thank you for being so fearless and curious with food and fashion. Our trips gallivanting around cities fed me. My independence comes from you. I hope that you are sufficiently proud of me, even though I did not become a nurse. I hope you know you are responsible for this. Thank you. I love you both, separately and equally.

To Miguel, had I known what I know now, I would have thanked you more over the last ten years. From the top of my head to the bottom of my pogo stick, thank you. You filled in the blanks that only you could and taught me about family. You said yes when everyone else said no. I'm forever grateful to you for adding much-needed color and spice to my life. *Mahal kita.*

—N. P.

I want to thank all the people who made this book happen: the team at Artisan, especially Judy Pray and Michelle Ishay-Cohen; our agent, Lauren Nolan; and writer and recipe tester Rachel Wharton, who I am sure wanted to choke me at times but held her composure every step of the way. You all showed me a world I had no clue about.

Claude Tayag, *kuya*, friend, inspirer. Thank you for your kindness and friendship, and for always responding to emails. Aniel Ponseca, your recipes were the building blocks for the style of Filipino food I cook. Your patience and understanding (of what Nicole likes) made my life easier. To Clang Garcia, Cocoy Ventura, Mike and Vanessa Santos, Liquid Maestro, Bong, Chloe, Ige, Ian, Ate Melody, and Kuya Mario, Quark, and the Lim Family: thank you for opening your homes and hearts to us. You all mean the world to me.

To my family—Mom, Nancy, Cesar, Diana, Ali, Chancy, Red, Dannie, KC, Jennifer, Nyle, Harold, Humberto, Norman, Nat Nat, and my nieces and nephews—thank you for always supporting and telling me that if anyone could do it, it would be me.

To Luis and Diomedes, you make me better. With both of you leading the kitchen, I can sleep. *Los amo.*

To all the Maharlikans and Jeepneyites, thank you for your support.

Finally, to Nicole Ponseca! I thank you. For having this dream to make Filipino food more mainstream and trusting me to help you make it a reality. We did it, and it couldn't have happened without your ambition and strive for perfection, your generosity and way of receiving people, your love for the food, and that brain of yours. I am humbled by your trust in me.

I love you all.

—M. T.

Chasing down a dream always seems like a good idea at the time. Thank you to everyone who ran with us:

Adeena Sussman, Adette Contreras, Alexandra & Rey Cuerdo, Alexis Loinaz, Anthony and Yvonne Castro, Ariel Torres Layug, Barbra Streisand, Bobbie Yanoupeth, Brie Allio, Bryan Lozano, Carissa Villacorte, Carmen Oloresisimo, Cela Rose Garcia, Cecilia Pagkalinawan, chef Alec Francis Santos, chef Anna Beatrice Trinidad, chef Bong Sagmit, chef Carla Hall, chef Claude Tayag, chef Cris Comerford, chef Cristina Racelis, chef Diomedes Rincon, chef Gene Gonzales, chef Glenda Baretta, chef Ian Carandang, chef Ige Ramos, chef Jo Chan, chef Kalel Chan, chef Luis Carchi, chef Nichole Pantanilla, chef Rafael Jr Jardeleza, chef Renato Jao, chef Sergio Garcia, chef Sonny Lua, chef Soulayphet Schwader, chef Sunny Yuki de Ocampo, Diane Paragas, Doreen Fernandez, Dr. Elizabeth Fraga, Enzo Lim, Erik Lopez, Erin Bellsey, Erwin B. Valencia, Freddy Anzurez, G. Tongi, Geena Rocero, Giuseppe Gonzales, Ian Ruiz, Jamie Steinberg, Jason Benjamin Alinea Tengo, Jeff Castaneda, Jo Koy, Joanne Boston, John Deshields, John Floresco, John Leguizamo, John Moss, Jonsen Vitug, Jose Llana, Josh Ozersky, Justin Schwartz, Justin Law and Maiysha Kai, Kalel Ervin Demetrio, Kat Popiel, Kerry Diamond, Kyle Ancheta, Lance Dornagon, Lawrence Weibman, Leejay Razalan, Ligaya Mishan, Liza Hernandez-Morales, Lucille Javier, Lynn Trono, Marisa Pizarro, Maurice Saatchi, Matt Libatique, Melissa Sipin, Meredith Talusan, Michael Balaoing, Miguel De Leon, Milo Naval, Monette Rivera, Monica Alvarez, Mrs. Loida Lewis, Mr. Ramirez, Ms. Conway, Nancy and Ken Bulalacao Leung, Nastasha Ablan, Natalia Roxas, Nathalie Nera, Neil Armstrong, Nelson George, Nick Ayala, Noah Fecks, Noel Cruz, PJ Quesada, Quark Henares, Rachelle Ocampo, Randy Reyes,

Rechelle Balanzat, Rich Rama, Robert Aloia, Ryan Gleason, Ryan Letada, Sarah Meier, Stephanie Crispin, Susan Burdian, the Susan Davenport, the Afable Family, the Arias Family, the Kantrow Family, the Libas Family, the Lim Family, the Mercaders, the Nadal Family, the Santos Family, the Orellana Family, the Santos Family, the Shepheard Family, the Ventura Family, Tita Oprah, #Thesilkmafia, Tomas and Kara De Los Reyes, Vicky Zawisny

Mario Lopez de Leon Jr., former Consul General, Philippine Consulate General in New York

Ma. Theresa B. Dizon-de Vega, former Consul General, Philippine Consulate General in New York

Khrystina P. Corpuz Popov, Vice Consul, Philippine Consulate General in New York

Jose Lampe Cuisia, Jr., former Ambassador of the Republic of the Philippines to the United States of America

Don Conrado A. Escudero, President, Villa Escudero Plantations and Resort

Cocoy Ventura, CEC, F&B Director, Villa Escudero Plantations and Resort

Hon. Maria Imelda Josefa R. Marcos, Governor, Provincial Government of Ilocos Norte

Ms. Marie Venus Q. Tan, Regional Director, Cordillera Administrative Region Department of Tourism

Hon. José María Clemente "Joey" Salceda, Representative of Albay's 2nd District in the Philippine House of Representatives

Hon. Robert Lee Rodrigueza, Governor, Province of Sorsogon

Hon. Atty. John G. Bongat, Mayor, City Government of Naga

Hon. Ayesha Vanessa Hajar M. Dilangalen, Secretary, Department of Tourism, Autonomous Region in Muslim Mindanao

The OG Jeepney and Maharlika family and team of managers, servers, bartenders, expos, dishwashers, cooks, and hosts

Alaskeros, Anghelica's Desserts, Ayala Foundation, Broadway Barkada, Center for Culinary Arts, Manila Filipino Journalists, F.I.N.D., Fylpro Family, Holy Angel University Pampanga, Institute for Culinary Education, The Katipunan, Kundiman (the Asian American Writer's Conference), Delano Manongs, Manila Men, the Filipino Food Movement, the Philippine Consulate General in New York, the Philippine Board of Tourism, the University of San Francisco

Index